Black Star

Black Star

African American Activism in the International Political Economy

RAMLA M. BANDELE

UNIVERSITY OF ILLINOIS PRESS
Urbana and Chicago

Manufactured in the United States of America
c 5 4 3 2 1

∞ This book is printed on acid-free paper.

Library of Congress Cataloging-in-Publication Data
Bandele, Ramla M., 1949–
Black star : African American activism in the international political economy / Ramla M. Bandele.
p. cm.
Includes bibliographical references and index.
ISBN-13 978-0-252-03339-1 (cloth : alk. paper)
ISBN-10 0-252-03339-6 (cloth : alk. paper)
1. Universal Negro Improvement Association—History.
2. African American businesspeople—History.
3. African diaspora—History.
4. Pan-Africanism—History.
5. African American political activists—History.
I. Title.
E185.8.B18 2008
320.5'4—dc22 2008006401

This work is dedicated to my mother,
Evelyn Marie, and my daughter, Zakiya Marie.
Both of these women have encouraged and loved me,
thus giving me the perseverance to pursue scholarship.

Contents

Preface

How can a denigrated racial group with minimal resources participate in international politics and make even minimal progress toward their goals? I am fascinated that black activists over the course of two centuries have tried to work with similarly situated African-descended populations outside of Africa, as well as tried to link with the perceived African homeland, which is, broadly speaking, West Africa. I have sought to find an empirical methodology to objectively study how these somewhat disparate communities form coalitions and commit scarce resources to transnational political activism. One might argue that historical studies such as those of the Du Boisian pan-African conferences explain such activism. But conferences are not the same as activism, and therefore do not explain coalitions that implement projects or strategies to attain a specific political or economic improvement.

My research uncovered a useful conceptualization that could facilitate my empirical research of this subject. I found that the amorphous concept *African diaspora* afforded me the basic building block of a model that could clearly diagram the politically active "sister" communities within the diaspora and their counterparts in Africa. This concept was enhanced by insightful information about the African diaspora in particular. These findings were the foundation for my own definition and model for exploring the why and how of African diaspora politics. My model was further calibrated by conjoining diaspora theory to an institutionalist political economy approach, which insured a focus on political activity and economic activity relevant to diaspora activism. A full discussion of my model is in the first chapter, as is my definition of the diaspora concept and the African diaspora in particular.

The goal of this study is to test the robustness of my model in the study of African American transnational politics. To accomplish this, it was necessary to find a case wherein the transnational character of the political activities was clearly present. And the case had to be completed, that is to say, the political project had been initiated and played out to a definitive end point. Finally, the episode had to be reasonably documented by scholarly historiography, memoirs, government documents, and other archival materials.

The Universal Negro Improvement Association's (UNIA) 1919 merchant marine project, known as the Black Star Line, fit all these criteria. Why? Because it was a historic episode that is reasonably well documented. The Black Star Line (BSL) began in 1919 and was officially ended in March 1922, when its stock was removed from the market.

It was launched in a dynamic political period for African Americans, in the interwar period in an American economy that was in the midst of metamorphosis from reliance on agrarian exports to industrial domination. It unfolded in a politically competitive and diverse activist era, where ideological loyalty by black activists usually followed intense commitment to black survival. As a result, there is data on the Black Star Line from every conceivable ideological view. And that wealth of information made it ideal to study the interaction of black activists and ordinary people across national borders as they tried to make the Black Star Line operable, a cornerstone to the UNIA's twin goals to develop a black enclave economy and ultimately a black nation-state in West Africa.

So it is important to recognize that although UNIA research has focused on Marcus Garvey, the founder and president of the organization, this study focuses on the Black Star Line, the UNIA's most popular and successful program. This study does not look at the UNIA in its entirety nor is it a comparative study of the UNIA with other black organizations throughout the interwar era. Rather, this work seeks to study the life of the BSL and learn how black people supported, operated, and funded it and how these activists were perceived and countered by contemporary black organizations and "host" nation-states, especially the U.S. and Britain.

Theorizing that the diaspora concept would be useful in framing the study, I pulled together relevant political research on it. This helped me to develop a model of the African diaspora in which the BSL operated. I applied my model to analyze the BSL effort, which existed from August 1919 until March 1922. I found that my model was robust and the study uncovered significant findings about transnational black activism. One of the most important findings was the probable reason for ongoing diaspora politics, including efforts to link with the perceived homeland, West Africa. I argue that such activism may be traceable to existential concerns regarding the ability of the black race to survive derogation and economic marginalization in the international political economy. Some activists go even further, working for racial independence to the point of building an autarkic nation-state.

Another important finding was that the African diaspora is not a monolith, either politically or economically. There are "sister" communities of diaspora in different types of nation-states. Those settled in industrialized, democratic nations have more freedom to form political groups and have more "disposable" income to apply toward transnational activism, as compared to those in colonized or underdeveloped areas with weak economies. There are also intracommunity differences, whereby strong ideological positions and assimilative effects attenuate efforts to act in unison.

However, I found that when a cause or project enables the minimization of these problems, diaspora projects can be effective, even successful for a time. The UNIA's merchant marine project seemed to galvanize activists throughout the diaspora, and for a brief time even ideologically opposed groups regarded it as a useful project. The UNIA developed strategies and reconfigured some Western institutions that facilitated the development of an effective political and economic network that allowed the linkage of diaspora communities and the latter with West Africa. Prudently, the UNIA relied on small contributions, which enabled people to afford to risk investing a fraction of their scarce resources in the venture. The accumulation of small investments across the diaspora resulted in the consolidation of over $800,000. This was an impressive collaboration for a project launched in 1919, before the advent of commercial radio and when there were relatively few black industrial workers in the United States.

The UNIA was centralized through its constitution, which standardized the behavior and work of the membership throughout the diaspora. Having a standard set of rules, responsibilities, reprimands, and leadership structure enabled effective communication and management of resources and personnel. However, this centralization was augmented by authoritarianism, which muted criticism, suggestions, and therefore adaptation in the political arena and to turbulent economic forces. This intolerance for dissenting opinions and democracy contributed toward the demise of the Black Star Line and depleted the strength of the UNIA.

Of course other variables contributed to the downfall as well. Most interesting of these were assimilative effects. The member communities of the diaspora were under the control of different nation-states and cultures, and these differences contributed to the internecine issues that attenuated UNIA unity and strained relations with continental African activists. Of course, government intervention is the obvious variable contributing to the downfall; if governments find that subcommunities disrupt economic systems such as production and labor relations, they will move to intercept and subdue those activities.

So this is not another book on whether Garvey was an organizational genius or impetuous autocrat. The UNIA's Black Star Line effort is the subject of this study, the vehicle that I have used to learn about African diaspora political activism, or, if you wish, transnational activism.

Acknowledgments

I could not have completed this work without the loving support of my family and extended family. They have always encouraged my dreams and supported my work. However, I must also acknowledge other people who played important roles in bringing this work to fruition.

First, I must acknowledge my colleagues at Northwestern University. My adviser, Dr. Benjamin I. Page, kept me on the right track, asking probing questions and encouraging me to stay the course. He made sure that I kept the political economy approach integral to the work. Dr. Michael Hanchard was insistent and meticulous in his assessment of my work. He insisted that I read everything on the African diaspora whether I thought it relevant or not. I also worked with Hanchard on an innovative diaspora project that mapped the politics of the African diaspora throughout the twentieth century on an interactive Web site. This did much to increase and enrich my knowledge on diaspora politics.

I also owe a debt of gratitude to Dr. Meredith Woo-Cumings, my professor for the study of political economy. It was her work, *Race to the Swift,* which gave me the idea to study African American transnational politics from a political economy perspective. Her timely work on South Korea's economic development and entrance into the international political economy not only helps us to remember that small non-European states are a part of international politics and economics but have an impact on their efforts to achieve their modernization agenda. Thank you, Dr. Jung En Woo.

Kathleen Bethel, the African American studies librarian at Northwestern University library, was key in helping me find the most arcane materials and enhancing my skills in the field of archival research. Dr. Sandra Richards also broadened my knowledge by selecting me to work on a fascinating diaspora project in the program of African Studies at Northwestern University. I also need to acknowledge the help and encouragement of the late Dr. Jacob Carruthers, who provided prudent advice. Thanks also to Dr. Allison Jones Harmon and Dr. Carol D. Lee.

The Frederick Douglass African and African American Studies Institute at Rochester University supported this project. In particular, political scientists at Rochester University were very helpful; Frederick Harris and Valeria Sinclair Chapman provided suggestions and listened to my reasoning about the relevance of diaspora theory to our discipline and about my views of the UNIA and the Black Star Line. My research at the National Archives in Washington, D.C., was made more efficient by the congenial help of Kibibi Tyehimba and Wautella Graham; they helped me to get around the city and introduced me to elder UNIA members, who still debate and work for UNIA goals and shared with me their interpretation of UNIA goals in the 1920s.

The Schomburg Center for Research in Black Culture in Harlem, New York, is a small gem that holds a wealth of information about African Americans and African people. I thank the center for all the help I received during my research tour there. It is at the Schomburg that I found rare visual interviews with actual participants in the BSL.

I am grateful to Heather Easton, James Randolph Newbrough, Lorie Shuck, and Sharmin McGown—all instructional technologists at Indiana University-Purdue University at Indianapolis's Office of Professional Development for all their help with technical assistance on the manuscript. I must also thank my colleague Dr. Bill Blomquist for his encouragement and insight into the publishing world. And of course I am indebted to Dr. Darlene Clark Hine for including this work in the Diaspora series published by University of Illinois Press and all the people at the press who brought this work to life.

Thanks to Jerral West, Kemati Porter, and Mshai Mwangola for just listening. And saving the best for last, thank you Zakiya Marie for hanging in there with your mother; you are my pride and joy.

Black Star

1

A New Take on an Old Term: Operationalizing the Diaspora Concept

For many students of African American politics, the African diaspora is a paradox.[1] On the one hand, a careful researcher can find many instances of political activity between African-descended populations situated outside of Africa. But on the other hand, there is no single African country with which to associate the diaspora. There is no specific language, religion, or culture to assign the African diaspora—attributes which normally signify a diaspora. In order to clearly focus on this phenomenon, one must move away from the rigid and passé definitions of diaspora. The diaspora concept has cogent possibilities as a model that maps a basic triadic relationship between communities of an ethnic group distributed throughout the international political economy; this is particularly true when the term is kept free of any additional fixed criteria.[2]

It may be helpful to employ an analogy to clarify this point. A useful analogy is the flexibility inherent in the term *human being;* it refers to a specific type of mammal, a primate, but other physiological criteria are not necessary for a clear designation for one termed a human being. Height, color, gender, or weight does not put a person in another category than human. The same type of reasoning can be made applicable for the term *diaspora.* Each diaspora has a triadic link to sister communities and to a place of ethnic origin, but beyond that each has its own psychological basis and its own physical attributes. With this rational yet open-minded understanding, one comes to realize that there must be many diasporas, including an African one. And studying political and economic activism within these formations helps us to parse international political activity of non-state actors, units as small as underresourced ethnic groups.

The genesis of a diaspora is the fallout from political and/or economic instability in a nation-state or region—usually states which have been weakened by colonialism, homegrown despotism, corruption, or resource depletion. However, the émigrés attempt to take their nation with them, including the group's culture, political institutions, and structures, intrinsically believing that these intangible assets might survive the upheaval by existing outside the homeland in small, distinct but dependant communities in states with viable economies. Within these communities are political activists who link to their counterparts in sister communities and also to their homeland. The states in which they settle have an interest in the behavior and activities of such communities and may monitor or intervene in the émigrés' political activities. Thus there are three political actors involved in the transnational activism of diaspora activists: the activists themselves, the nation-states in which émigrés have settled, and the homeland, which may depend on diaspora remittances or lobbying assistance. Diaspora communities may acquire long-term life spans, until such time that the homeland might be reinvigorated or rebuilt. This "permanence" characteristic, pointed out by Elliot Skinner, differentiates diaspora communities from refugee communities.[3]

Nevertheless, the amorphous nature of the African "homeland" has fueled debate over whether the "scattering" of African peoples could be deemed a diaspora. In addition, it was born out of slavery: the migration was forced and destinations could not be selected. But are not all diaspora formations forced by harsh circumstances? And does not ethnic or religious designation lead to marginalization? The answers to such questions suggest that there are enough similarities to use the designation for the African-derived sister communities around the Atlantic.

Cultural and historic investigations about the elusive African diaspora captured the footprints and other fragmentary evidence to document the links between descended populations and actual African locations. Useful political historiography grew out of this work, as did political macro-analytic monographs. This scholarship suggested that ongoing political relationships were based on the struggle against racial derogation and exploitation, but ideological contention and resource scarcity may have obstructed the establishment of stable political linkages. Then the debate centered on whether blacks, who are dispersed throughout the Western world, can still be considered Africans.[4] The quest to answer this seems to be stymied by a debate as to whether diasporans have retained cultural memories or some cultural attachment to Africa. Whether or not they do is only part of the puzzle. There are diverse cultures even in continental Africa within any given state (artificial states born out of colonialism). Unity of political action is further complicated by differing colonial experiences: one ethnic group may be divided between so-called Anglophone and Francophone states. Does this mean they are not African or no longer form one nation? As Drake so astutely observed, "The solidarity, in the final analysis, has to be based on common interests not common values, for diversity in tribe, class, religion and cultures abound."[5] Cultural diversity does not negate the fact that the black race (regardless of nationality) is derogated in the international political system and its economy. So the fact that African-descended peoples scattered throughout the Western hemisphere do not have identical cultural imperatives or retain a complete package of African rituals, language, and religion does not diminish their consanguineous ties or the derogatory categorization assigned to their places of origin on the African continent.

Rather it is the European political outlook (and its imperialism) that affects African and diaspora politics. In addition to Europeans conquering militarily weaker nations and colonizing them, they also categorized these groups by phenotype. For whatever reasons, European states and cultures by and large derogate black people, erroneously stereotyping the entire African race and any descendants—creolized or not—as less intelligent and less capable than others. Imperialists carried this belief into their economic relations. Since Europe and by extension the United States dominate the international political economy, they have circumscribed the ability of black people—whether continental Africans, West Indians, or U.S. African Americans—to acquire resources, employment, and political power well into the late twentieth century. For over one hundred years, subsequent generations of black activists have concluded that an effective way to combat these problems was through what Drake calls phenotypical pan-Africanism—in my view, another term for African diaspora-based politics.

There is another reason that such efforts continue to be pursued. This reason is as strong as religion or culture are for other historic diasporas such as those of the Jews and the Armenians. This is the consanguineous links that are nurtured by *existential* issues. The preservation of the phenotypical group is of paramount concern because to eliminate, enslave, or exclude by racial classification is to endanger members of that group wherever they are. Unity around safety to exist is a powerful cohesive. By this I mean that when one studies the literature on black nationalism, pan-African politics, and other political efforts, activists and speakers often warn that the marginalization of black people is intended to be permanent, that the intention of global leaders is to retain the control of African land and mineral resources and keep the race as surplus labor and in servitude. Not only political activists but black ministers, journalists, and academics have fought the derogatory classification through what have been termed vindicationist sermons, lectures, and both nonfiction and fictional writings.[6] In short, activists of various ideological positions believe that at a minimum, derogation will keep black people in subordinate political status. Some (considered extremists by the mainstream) go further and have argued that the race will be destroyed.

This view is augmented by diasporans' need and desire to pursue their origins. That is to say, in addition to concerns about permanent servitude, African diasporan activists are concerned about learning about their origins, both the ethnic groups and other genealogical attributes. These concerns are similar to those of adoptees: whether or not adoptees accept their present lives, they often long to know their birth families. Adoptees have a compelling need to know their own "creation" story and, as Andersen points out, "to heal the wound caused by separation and thereby to provide a more authentic base for living their lives."[7] Such propositions can be extrapolated to explain in part African diasporan activism and attachment to Africa despite temporal and physical distance from the actual traumatic separation. To know and align with Africa is to address existential needs.[8] So above and beyond the desire to ameliorate political and economic status, African diasporan activists seek to explore their origins and vindicate their branch of humanity from charges of inferiority and other eugenic myths. These are issues related to the basic human right to exist and exercise free will, as do other ethnic groups and races. As such, these are deeply felt issues that create the motivation within politically active diasporans to address them.

Given these points, I do not need to be convinced of the existence of an African diaspora; it does exist, and as the above argument suggests, there is a political dimension. And within that diaspora are different types of actors: those interested in vindication of the race, those interested in religious and education proselytism to "uplift" the race, those who safeguard and expand cultural ties, and those who participate in transnational political efforts focused upon the amelioration of the political and economic status of black people globally.

In fact, a primary purpose of a diaspora, at its root, is necessarily political: ethnic groups are trying to survive and prosper as distinct historical groupings, regenerate their societies and thus their own well-being—these are political goals. I do not argue that diaspora politics is the only way in which black people participate in transnational politics; black people should not be stereotyped politically and ideologically. History notes their participation in religious, humanitarian, labor, and communist world movements (even here, however, some activists oscillate between or attempt to merge the movements with racial concerns). Rather, I argue that diaspora politics is one alternative selected by black activists and that these political activities are well documented in the historical record; this is clearly substantiated in the literature review.

With substantial evidence supporting the existence of an African diaspora and the presence of political activism within it, I felt in a position to develop an empirical study of the phenomenon. I designed a model with which to study the political actors in the African diaspora. I reasoned that I might be able to isolate the political activities and observe how external stimuli influence or cause political activity to operate within an obscured triadic network. I wanted to discern what seems to motivate intense organized political activity at certain junctures, while at other times political linkages are moderate. I also wanted to explore how these activists accumulated and employed scarce resources to reach their transnational political and economic goals. What activities implemented by activists causes the other two actors to react or respond?

Thus, for the purposes of this political study, the term *diaspora* is associated with a model that encases the political action between three principle actors in the international political economy. The "stars" of this triad are the African American activists who through available means attempt to link to and work for the homeland, identified as the second actor. This familial relationship may be interrupted or modified by the third actor, the host country—that is to say, one of the countries that has allowed diaspora communities to settle within its territories. The host countries will intervene in diaspora political or economic activism if it is deemed to be in the hosts' best interests to do so.

Like many contemporary diasporas, the African one is fragile and resource poor. In this way contemporary diasporas differ from what we call classic diasporas—those growing out of great ancient empires. Classic diasporas were composed of skilled émigrés who migrated from collapsing empires to areas of Europe that were just ascending into organized bureaucratic states. As such, members of classical diasporas had skills that could be useful to the states. The resulting relationships included some political incorporation for the diaspora communities, and they came to know well the states that they had helped to build. Over centuries, such well-positioned diasporas, while suffering setbacks, have acquired resources and a political strength that has allowed them to augment their communities and supply consistent help to their homelands. Examples of such diasporas include the Jewish diaspora and the Chinese diaspora in Southeast Asia.[9]

Contemporary diasporas, established after modern nation-states had matured, had no chance to experience such incorporation or beneficial political agreements to insure economic access and resource accumulation. They are in the process of surviving, finding ways in which they can augment their own economic position while simultaneously contributing toward the betterment of the homelands. As they practice transnational activism, they simultaneously are learning how the international political economy works, and many have been invaluable to their homelands as well as steadily moving into the middle class. These modern diasporas include the Indian diaspora in southeast Africa, Great Britain, and the United States, and the Irish diaspora, which has settled in the United States, Canada, and Australia.

Contemporary diaspora activists do not have the luxury to thoroughly test workable strategies before implementing them. Thus they are still on a steep learning curve as it relates to politics. For this reason, I refer to contemporary, marginalized diasporas as *liminal:* they are a transitional stage in a process. That is to say that the diaspora is growing experientially toward maturity in its political and economic dimensions. Therefore liminal diaspora activism may be ephemeral or attenuated, making it difficult to locate political activism in the midst of so much activity by the dominant nation-states and groups in the international political economy. The challenge for this study was to identify a transnational political venture in the African diaspora that endured long enough to allow sufficient observation of the actors and the outcomes.

Methodology

Transnational political activism must take place within the international political economy because virtually all land mass is controlled by some nation-state. African diaspora activists had to find ways to manipulate and maneuver within and around international political institutions set in place to protect the interests of the hegemonic states. Thus some part of their strategies must have been geared toward these constraints imposed by powerful nations, and my methodology must embrace an approach to analyze the political and economic institutions of the era under study as well as the institutions developed by diaspora activists to circumvent constraints and operationalize their own in pursuit of their goals. To achieve this, I have chosen an *institutionalist* political economy approach and conjoined it to my diaspora model.

Institutionalists (in the field of political economy) are interested in power and how it is expressed within economic and political institutions to achieve organizational or societal goals (in this case, diaspora goals). In order to better understand the functioning of modern society, institutionalists look at how people attempt to implement programs, policies, and plans through institutions of varying power assets and legitimacy.[10] From this point of view, I can follow what happens as diasporic people attempt political activism and look at the institutions they design for this purpose; define them; discern if they are novel, modified, or imitative of one or more of the host countries; and try to determine why these particular activities were chosen. Discerning the reactions of the host countries to the global economic relations disturbed by diaspora activity, I can determine what concerns nation-states have about such political efforts. I can observe what institutions of the nation-states become operable to respond to diaspora activism and why they do so. This reveals at least a few reasons why nation-states may become actors in diaspora politics.

The institutionalist approach is also attractive because it can embrace a critical analysis of power relations between political organizations such as the Universal Negro Improvement Association (UNIA) and government agencies. It highlights the role of government in economic affairs. Further, it has the flexibility to follow power relations from political to economic institutions and supports the principle that social values influence the building and administration of institutions of not only government but of citizen-based political organizations.

Using a political-economy approach insures that the study remains political and does not drift off into cultural, historical, anthropological, and sociological realms, as past studies seem to have done. This is not to say that these approaches are not useful; indeed, social movement theory has proven invaluable in improving our understanding of domestic black political movements. Resource mobilization theory, in particular, seems most plausible because it focuses upon the very obstacle that seems to plague diaspora activism: the accumulation and distribution of resources to implement programs. However, integral components of diaspora theory are neutralized by resource mobilization theory. The political, cultural, and psychological goals are key elements in understanding the motivation of African diaspora activists, and resource mobilization theory seeks to exclude "emotional" and ideological variables. Aldon Morris points this out: "Grievances, psychic strain and other psychological states of participants are not central to the analysis."[11] Beyond this constraint, resource mobilization theory posits that activists tightly in tune with their communities and with access to its resources are best situated to launch independently funded movements. And if they organize effectively, they are more likely to be successful in protest activity. Similar results come from an institutionalist analysis. A key proposition of political economy is that if the researcher follows the money trail, the source of power will be discovered. Institutional political economy directs the researcher to examine the institutions along that path, and, in doing so, activism may be traced to its institutional power base.

Social movement theory often has been applied to domestic protest movements—to attempts by groups to reform the status quo or to facilitate democratization of political institutions.[12] I am trying to study an aspect of the transnational politics practiced by African Americans in the black Atlantic region. I want to understand how black activists permeate borders, combine slim political and economic resources in attempts to improve the condition of their communities and, where possible, the homeland. It does not seem to me that they are attempting to change government policies so much as they are trying to build their own infrastructure, emphasizing independent action. Diaspora political groups do seek to improve conditions in host countries: they want citizenship benefits and equal treatment. However, simultaneously, diaspora activists are trying to retain their ethnic dignity and character. This is why Ronald Walters concluded that the immigrant model does not fit diasporans.[13] They want to continue their ethnic existence rather than simply meld into the mainstream. While social movement theory probably can address or be modified to address these differences, I can achieve equally effective outcomes with the application of institutionalism.

Next I applied my model (conjoined institutionalist approach and the diaspora concept) to a specific instance of political activity within the African diaspora. This type of microanalysis helps us to see the political mechanics of this attenuated diaspora. I reasoned that to study one key political project from beginning to end would facilitate our understanding of the techniques by which marginalized ethnic groups can organize, link, and impact transnational politics. I selected as a case study a well-documented project rooted and completed in the past. This permitted me to extract the political steps and strategies followed by the diaspora activists to implement the program, identify political patterns as well as outcomes, and then conduct an analysis of the variables introduced by Sheffer but firmly rooted in the institutionalist political economy approach.

The Universal Negro Improvement Association's bold launch of a transnational shipping venture for the benefit of the African diaspora and homeland affords me a particularly useful case. The UNIA inaugurated the Black Star Line in 1919. Thus, I had to employ historical methods, particularly archival research. In addition to primary data, I studied biographies of Marcus Garvey, president of the UNIA, focusing upon his involvement with the Black Star Line. Further, I studied materials on the history of the era as well as the economic relations in force at the time.

Hypotheses

A key reason why diasporas form is politics: such groups are working to survive as distinct historical groupings, to protect their societies and therefore themselves. I argue that political activity in liminal diasporas, such as the African diaspora, often is imperceptible due to their limited resources.[14] And unlike historical or classic diasporas, the African diaspora's cohesion is not cultural but existential, and its politics is focused upon the elimination of its derogated position in the international political economy. Sheffer's conceptualization affords us a useful descriptive categorization of the term diaspora, which led him and colleagues to build a useful diaspora theory applicable to political studies. Augmenting Sheffer's conceptualization of a diaspora with Walters's concept of sister community activism, and my theoretical insights into the African diaspora, and then marrying these to a political economy approach, suggests the following hypotheses:

(1) Liminal diasporic political activity may be ephemeral but can impact the international economy and political relations, albeit in subtle and possibly refractory ways.
(2) Hegemonic powers will intervene in diaspora political activity if they perceive that their political or economic interests are negatively impacted.

Two other caveats must be put forth. My work should not be considered a study on immigration, whereby one primarily looks at the labor supply needs and concerns of the developed world. Rather, I seek to look at the other side of the coin: how ethnic workers classified as immigrants resist the control and assimilation of the developed world and strategize to rejuvenate their homelands as well as the well-being of their diaspora communities. At the same time, this study does not address what has been called "ethnopolitics."[15] Joseph Rothschild, for example, explores the rise of politics based on ethnicity and how this plays out in multiethnic societies. He particularly looks at ethnic groups resisting the colonization of hegemonic states or their attempts to secede from such states and form a state based on their ethnic characteristics. Rothschild's work looks primarily at domestic politics in several multiethnic states; he does not concentrate on the transnational political relations of the ethnic groups he studies. My study, again, focuses on the diaspora's contribution to such efforts or diasporan attempts to help overcome the economic and political problems facing their homelands—whether outside colonialism is involved or not.

So the focus here is not on the developed world and its concerns about "guest" workers who are from other ethnic groups, raising cultural tension and political problems for the host state. Nor is it the efforts of undeveloped nations to develop or resist colonial relations. Instead, the question here is how diasporas *resist* developed nations' attempts to marginalize them and *help* their homelands develop into independent prosperous states. Thus the émigrés themselves are the focal point of this study. Émigrés make up another actor in the international political economy in their own right, and they work through their own collage of institutions and strategies, based in their communities. And when these geographically disparate communities are referred to together, the term for them is *diaspora.*

As stated earlier, an institutionalist political economy approach is employed to insure that the study is contextualized and institutions made visible for analysis. It is through institutions that diasporas work and it is host government institutions that constrain them.

The Organization of This Study

Chapter 2 is a detailed literature review of the three areas relevant to this study: the diaspora concept in general, focusing on political aspects in particular; historical and political writings on the African diaspora, very useful in identifying the attributes and goals of black transnational activism; and finally, literature on the Black Star Line and its parent, the Universal Negro Improvement Association. Here again, I highlight the political organization and goals of the UNIA and its intended goals for the shipping line.

In chapters 3 and 4, I argue that one has to understand the international political economy because it is not possible to work transnationally without venturing into the territory or economic relations of nation-states. Thus, nation-states will take an interest in diaspora activity, and those interests will be influenced by the issues and problems embedded in the international economy. For this reason, the primary nation-states and their political agendas, challenges, and economic positions are presented for the era under study, which is immediately following World War I, 1919 to 1925 (1923 is the year the Black Star Line directors faced trial). These chapters provide an informative background on the international arena that the Black Star Line (BSL) entered and help to clarify the obstacles and challenges the effort faced from the operating political economy.

The purpose of chapter 5 is to contextualize the study in the African American politics of the era. This will be useful in assessing why the BSL formed as it did and how the UNIA related to other black organizations during the years of BSL's existence. Because the UNIA was the parent of the BSL, its ideological position and programs need to be understood in the context of other ideological positions circulating in black politics.

The narrative history of the BSL is presented in chapter 6. The BSL serves as a case study that shows an instance when the African diaspora attempted to link communities and carry out a transnational political and economic project. Because the BSL is well documented, a close look at this case helps make visible the processes by which relatively marginalized communities can manage to link and work for political amelioration.

Chapter 7 focuses on government intervention in the operations and organization of the BSL. There is evidence that nation-states were concerned about this African diaspora project, to the point that they surveilled the shipping line. While the financial operations of the BSL were a primary reason for its demise, surveillance and sabotage cannot be dismissed as contributors to the line's ultimate collapse.

Chapter 8 is devoted to the thorough analysis of the effort, why the Black Star Line was successfully launched and also why it ultimately failed. The analysis is placed within a diasporic framework, looking at the attributes first applied by Sheffer and colleagues: ideology, political structures, financial bases, mobilization strategies, education/skill levels, and so forth. That is to say, in addition to the analysis of the rise and fall, I look at the contributions, participation, mistakes, and so on of the participating communities. Why did they support it? What did they contribute? What were their expectations? Each community brought different resources and skill levels to the project.

Chapter 9 concentrates on what the case study has taught us about the politics of the African diaspora and—by extension—of liminal diasporas generally.[16] Casting the net still further, we can ask what may be applicable to diaspora theory as a whole. How does the African diaspora compare to those presented in Sheffer's work? Is the level of resources the primary difference in performance? Is lack of ideological unity a culprit in the ultimate failure of BSL and the real reason for the African diaspora's ephemeral political performance? Does diaspora theory enhance the political economy approach by altering the perspective by which political scientists can look at states in the international political economy? Can a diaspora be a legitimate political actor in the international political economy?

These questions are answered in chapter 10. Diaspora theory does provide insight into how the African diaspora has practiced transnational politics. At the same time, it helps us understand the diaspora phenomenon generally, which is much stronger in more resource-rich networks. Further, ethnic networks can be legitimate actors in international politics and economics, and can impact the international economy. Political economists, in particular, should integrate diaspora analysis into their research on nation-states, particularly deciphering the financial impact such networks may have on a particular state and its ability to affect resources flowing to the state under study.

I am convinced that the activists in any given diaspora do not always function as a unit; that is to say, the total assemblage of communities composing the diaspora do not have to be working in unison on one project in order for political activity to occur within that diaspora. There may be dormant communities and active communities in a diaspora simultaneously. Various communities may work together, or they may work separately, even if on the same issue or goal.

The pivotal exercise for the political economist may be to look at the cumulative impact of diaspora activity on the homeland and/or the host nations. The evidence of BSL suggests that centralization boosts the ability of the African diaspora (and other liminal diasporas) to be politically effective. This is because collaboration, especially pooling resources, strengthens the capability to fund programming and employ its human resources in its political interests. The result is that the marginality of diasporic peoples is palliated and non-state political activism has a better chance to be sustained.

2

An Exploration of the Relevant Literature

There is a plethora of studies on the diaspora concept from different perspectives. Most of those that influenced my study are of historic origin, but there are a few from the political science discipline. Because my emphasis is on political activism, the voluminous literature on cultural aspects of diasporas is not elaborated on in this work.[1] This chapter also explores the literature on the Black Star Line and its parent company, the Universal Negro Improvement Association (UNIA).

One of the best studies that looked at the diaspora concept as a research model was conducted by historian Kim Butler. Her epistemological study looks at diaspora as a heuristic tool for conducting comparative studies of various black communities around the black Atlantic. Butler sees the concept as a useful way to discern how these communities have evolved and also protected their interests. She goes further to propose that there are variations in the diaspora that influence how communities should be studied. Her goal differs from mine in that she would compare the historical development and experiences of communities, not limiting the investigations to political activism as I do. Her research facilitates the reworking of the classical diaspora concept and improves research possibilities because she considers the nuances inherent in the formation of each community. Her approach proves useful in evaluating resource acquisition by the various communities as well as their ability to adapt to various economic systems and cultural environments.[2] Research into political attributes of the generic diaspora concept has been relatively sporadic. J. A. Armstrong and Gabriel Sheffer found that the concept has been ignored in political research and has not been explored much when examining related topics such as nationalism, immigration, and ethnic politics.[3]

Armstrong conducted one of the earlier political studies of diasporas. His work categorized two broad types of diaspora, which he further refined. The broad categories were *mobilized* and *proletariat.* His work intentionally emphasized the mobilized diaspora, which he viewed as a nonterritorial quasi-society situated in a larger, usually dominant polity. There are two types of mobilized diasporas: *archetypal* and *situational.* Mobilized diasporas seem to be formed from classical, culturally respected ancient societies that have eroded over time or have been absorbed by militarily stronger empires. These classic or archetypal diasporas included Jews that established communities in various European polities, and because it is the oldest, it is considered the model of categorization. The situational mobilized diaspora refers to highly skilled émigré groups formed after the classical period and include the Germanic peoples in Eastern Europe and Russia. Armstrong's study details how groups of skilled laborers penetrated and assisted in the modernization of European nations and the political alliances formed between the elites of the diaspora communities and the elites of the host nations. While he discusses how developing imperialist powers shared and competed for such groups, Armstrong does not look at the relationship between diaspora communities and their homelands, nor does he clearly articulate intradiaspora political linkages. Armstrong does discuss the triadic relationship by pointing out that rising imperialist powers were more tolerant of a diaspora/homeland nexus when it fell within the perimeter or the influence of the growing host state. Mobilized diasporas grew and sustained themselves by serving as middlemen in the international political economy for their host nations, using their superior language and administrative skills. However, when the indigenous populations of the host countries became able to handle such tasks, mobilized diasporas often became displaced.

Armstrong's discussion of the proletarian diaspora is terse and only serves to contrast the mobilized diaspora with the more modern "undifferentiated mass of unskilled labor" that lacked the skills and communications network to develop and acquire social mobilization experienced by the more classic variety. Armstrong's condescending view of the proletarian diaspora is akin to that of many immigration studies, which are conducted from the standpoint of the labor supply needs of the developed world. In only considering this angle, such studies ignore political organization and capability of marginalized diasporas and neglect the vast array of diaspora political strategies and activities.

Nevertheless, Armstrong's work provides evidence of diversity within diasporas. This diversity appears not only in their skills array but also in the institutionalized experience that protects a diaspora and perhaps even ingratiates it to a host country or hegemonic power. Armstrong helps us to understand why the composition and abilities of modern diasporas seem distinctly different from classic ones.

Classic diasporas migrated from politically unstable regions or dying powerful states and relocated in inchoate modern states—inexperienced states with resources but that were still grappling with modernity and industrialization. Contemporary liminal diasporas come from a different type of instability: unstable economies, developing states emerging from colonization. Western host countries, long since comfortable with modernity, do not need instructors or what we might call conveyors of modernization and industrialization. Rather, they need labor and technicians—what Armstrong calls proletarian diasporas. But the desire to escape from poverty and possible despotism is not confined to unskilled labor. Workers and professionals relocate and try to extend support to family networks and redevelopment of their homelands. They do not fit Armstrong's categorization of the diaspora as consisting of an "undifferentiated mass of unskilled labor."

Although Joseph Rothschild does not elaborate on diaspora relations, he provides insight into the cogency of ethnicity as an operative force behind political organizations in multiracial states.[4] His study of ethnic politics is useful to the understanding of the internal mechanics of ethnic political operations. He also elaborates on how the state "type" determines the political cogency and flexibility of an ethnic group. For example, if the state is stringently hierarchal, the ethnic group may be stymied in its ability to effect political change. But an industrialized or developing society may also be more democratic, and an ethnic group will have inroads into the political arena. The host states in this study are considered democratic (at least for their privileged groups), and as Rothschild theorized we will observe in this study ideological flexibility and some interaction with state as well as economic institutions. From his work, we are better prepared to take the step into diaspora politics or, for our purposes, transnational ethnic political activity. Other researchers help accomplish this transport of ethnic politics into the international arena. Abdul Said highlights the presence of ethnic group politics in the international arena when he argues, "The human need for a sense of community is gradually dissolving the bonds of geography that united diverse groups within states."[5] Said presents evidence that ethnic groups realizing their powerlessness within state structures have ventured outside their nation-state of residence in search of political empowerment.

J. Bertelsen concurs and further highlights ethnicity in international politics with her characterization of the "non-state" nation. She defines a non-state nation (NSN) as "any entity that operates in a manner normally associated with a nation-state but is not a generally recognized nation-state." Of course this categorization is not exclusive to diasporas, but one of her findings may help explain the oscillation detected in the effectiveness of diaspora politics: Bertelson argues that nonstate actors may want both audibility—a voice in politics—and also durability. She notes that acrimonious audibility can negatively impact its durability. "[The] NSN desires to remain both durable and audible . . . the NSN wishes to continue to exist and wishes to be perceived. But these two goals can be in conflict: sometimes a high degree of audibility (if seen as a threat to a nation-state) may lead to the loss of durability."[6]

Gabriel Sheffer and his colleagues conducted a broad study to explore the diaspora phenomenon and discern how such networks practiced politics. They set out to find the role and influence of ethnic diasporas on international politics.[7] Their studies led to a definition that is more than descriptive; it operationalizes the structure of my case study. In part, the definition is as follows: "Ethnic diasporas are created either by voluntary migration or as a result of expulsion from the homeland and settlement in one or more host countries . . . In their host countries diasporas preserve their ethnic, or ethnic-religious identity and communal solidarity. This solidarity serves as the basis for maintaining and promoting constant contacts among the diasporas' activist elements." So a diaspora is a functional trans-state network that involves three main political actors that may conduct political activity, each actor functioning primarily for its own interests. The three actors are the home country/region, the migrant population, and the host nation.

Sheffer's group studied several ethnic immigrant groups that have been considered participants in triadic or diaspora politics. Each political scientist on the team studied various political aspects of several groups, including Jews, Chinese in Southeast Asia, and East Indians. The researchers looked at the ideologies of the diasporas, political structures, financial bases, mobilization strategies, education/skill levels, and channels of influence. They found that the presence and effectiveness of each of these attributes differs for each diaspora; the constant is that the triadic network between the three actors is present and political activity is practiced. They concluded that these diasporas do in fact have an impact on international politics for several reasons.

One important reason is that many diasporas provide remittances to their homelands that augment the latter's balance of payments and—if significant enough—facilitate capital accumulation for economic development.

Diasporas were also found to be effective lobbyists, helping homelands compete for additional resources or gain political voice or standing. On the other hand, diasporas can challenge homeland governments and fund guerilla groups and other revolutionary efforts seeking to replace the homeland government. Sheffer found this to be true with the Sikhs of the Indian diaspora and also of the Irish diaspora. The Chinese of Southeast Asia played a principal role in the overthrow of the Chinese Nationalist Party government and the installation of the People's Republic of China.

Sheffer also clarified the forms that these triadic networks take. For example, the homeland is not always discernable in modern geopolitics: it may exist only in the historical memory or folklore of the group. The Jewish state was destroyed for over a millennium; now the Palestinian state is fragmented and obscured. Yet whether the homeland is actually material or is housed in more than one nation-state, group patriotism and commitment to the homeland can remain strong and unshakable. Walker Conner argues, "The emotionally pregnant concept of 'my roots' implies soil. The psychological associations thus made between homeland and one's people are more—not the less—intense for being emotional and resisting exposition in rational terms."[8] So recognition by nation-states may be irrelevant to the political commitment of diasporas.

Yet even given the elegant approach of Sheffer and his colleagues, their studies seem highly influenced by the older classic diasporas, particularly the Jewish diaspora. Their grasp of relatively "younger" diasporas, such as those of the Irish and Africans, while insightful, seem less robust than their discussion of classical diasporas. Like the classic diasporas, the younger diasporas include a cross-section of the workforce of the societies that they represent. Thus, they have professional workers and artisans, but because most of their countries of origin are underdeveloped, the population might include fewer workers prepared for modern technological positions or other complex occupations in a highly industrialized economy. The skill complement of their workers may be incompatible with the technology and financial sectors of their host countries. Thus their resource levels are often less than those of classical diasporas, which are better established in their host countries.

Systematizing the study by introducing variables for evaluation, the Sheffer volume suggests that diasporas are organic: they grow with nourishment, learn to protect themselves and seek out better conditions. However, I would argue that a diaspora can be malnourished too and lie dormant as the result. The introduction of resources that induce growth and development will allow dormant diasporas to function, perhaps intermittently. Continued educational and occupational development can strengthen a diaspora to the point of being a political actor with the capability of influencing international politics, as has often occurred with the Jewish diaspora and Irish diaspora.

Thus émigré groups settled in various countries form diasporas that can influence international politics, and their interests have instigated the formation of a politicized triadic network. But as Iliya Harik points out, "The greater the limits on political freedom in the host societies, the less effective is the diaspora organization."[9] When this insight is coupled with the varying resource levels of diasporas, it becomes clear why some diasporas may at times be ineffectual.

African Diaspora Literature

The Sheffer volume included Locksley Edmondson's political exploration of the African diaspora. Edmondson's article is provocative in three ways. First, he convincingly argues how the African diaspora activists participate in transnational politics:

(1) attempting to influence American foreign policy as it relates to issues affecting black people.
(2) working directly with continental African activists on what he calls "non-government activities." This comprises pan-Africanism, including efforts such as BSL.
(3) intervention on "international systemic levels"—trying to work with and through international organizations such as the United Nations and International Monetary Fund.

These strategies suggest sophistication in the political understanding of black activists and in-depth involvement in international politics. The second critical insight offered by Edmondson is his capturing of twentieth-century pan-Africanism as not only diasporic activism but an alternative to traditional lobbying techniques, which were obstructed due to racism, and therefore excluded the issues from American foreign policy formation: "for a long time, the search for transnational linkages especially under the rubric of pan-Africanism became a necessary substitute for Black inability to gain access to, let alone seek effectively to influence, the United States decision making system."[10] He goes on to argue that it was the African diaspora that "provided place and resources which assisted in the development of African political leadership outside the framework of colonization." This is an excellent point, and because he analyzed the three activist strategies separately, he shows that the African diaspora has been much more effective in nongovernmental efforts than in trying to influence American foreign policy.

While Edmondson states that he uses the term "mobilizing" differently than Armstrong, he does use the term to argue that as black Americans increase their skills and earnings, they will be better able to access the foreign policy regime and therefore influence international issues of concern to black people. However, it is clear that indigenous and diaspora Africans interacted politically well before the era studied by Edmondson.

Clarence Contee provides a useful historical account of the building of one of the premier political coalitions that would marshal in an era of diaspora activism, a coalition that eventually assisted in the independence movements of African nations.[11] Contee provides a detailed analysis of the 1919 Pan-African Congress and how it was funded, organized, and implemented. He found that funding had to be acquired outside the diasporan resource base. Convinced by W. E. B. Du Bois of the importance of lobbying the Paris peace conference on behalf of black people, including Africans, the NAACP funded Du Bois's Pan-African Congress after the U.S. government forbade black American participation in the peace conference. But in order to gain European permission to hold the Pan-African Congress, Du Bois had to ally with a francophone African politician, Blaise Diagne, the only black politician with access to the European conveners of the Paris Peace Conference. The Pan-African Congress enabled a meeting of black activists from around the world to discuss black political and economic marginalization and develop strategies and demands to alleviate these. Part of their strategy involved the presentation of a petition to the peace conference; however, only representatives of nation-states were able to address the conference. Pan-African Congress leaders gained limited access to present its proposals to peace conference attendees through the efforts of one of the two free black nations there, Haiti. In other words, activists from three different black populations contributed toward an effort to publicize the grievances of black people. Contee illustrated the political point of why blacks saw benefit in diaspora activism.

However, in most instances, the literature on the African diaspora is justificatory: it focuses upon providing evidence that there is in fact an African diaspora. Usually one of two aspects of the diaspora is studied. First, the diaspora is presented in historical perspective. Thus George Shepperson and Vincent Thompson describe various African communities outside Africa and the communication and working relationships between these communities. Shepperson (along with Joseph Harris) is often cited as one of the first researchers to refer to dispersed African communities as a diaspora, arguing that Africans experienced a "scattering" very similar to that of the Jews.[12] He argues that without using the term *diaspora,* many scholars and political activists such as Blyden and Du Bois wrote about and participated in it. Since the early 1960s, Shepperson has encouraged historians and other social scientists to use diaspora theory as a way to better understand African history and slavery. Further, he advocated the study of the diaspora not only as an effective comparative approach to the study of slavery but to the study of a people, tracing their history and development both on the continent and throughout the world.

Vincent Thompson documented the origin and development of the diaspora before and during the African slave trade.[13] His exhaustive study provides a detailed history of the African diaspora in North and South America as well as in Central America and the Caribbean. He covers the diaspora's development from the fifteenth century through the nineteenth century. This epoch study provides the necessary background to any political study of the African diaspora.

Another source of significant evidence about the political and social attributes of the African diaspora is the work of Julius Scott.[14] Scott argues that as early as the 1700s, African diaspora communities were able to communicate and network, despite the slavery system. His scholarship uncovers a developing network as early as the eighteenth century in the Caribbean and along the eastern seaboard of the United States. Blacks created pivotal institutions, which evolved out of the international economic relations. Interaction between sailors and workers at ports and in marketplaces facilitated the weaving of the black Atlantic's communication system. Interestingly, most interactions (between the black shipmates and those in ports) were linked to the shipping industry, and were natural outcomes of the economic relations of the era.

One of the ways that the network began was the assignment of slaves to work on ships in various capacities. Slave owners often "leased" enslaved people to other business enterprises, including to shipowners and farmers. Compared to agricultural work and other businesses, work on ships offered relative freedom and less intense work. Freedmen (and escaped slaves) who found work at sea more preferable to working under the close scrutiny of whites joined them. These black seamen carried news and reading material between Western Europe, the United States, and the Caribbean. Sailors, slaves, and freedmen formed informal market systems at port cities. Sailors traded items such as salted meat and linens for the fresh produce grown by slaves and freedmen on their modest subsistence plots. They often assisted others to escape and entered modest commercial trading with black communities throughout the Caribbean and along the American coastline.

Taken together, Thompson and Scott lay the foundation upon which I build my model for studying the political activity in the African diaspora. Thompson provides the map illustrating where most African diaspora communities are located. And Scott documents the birth and mechanics of the institutions that were developed and used over centuries to cement these communities together in a network—a network that was key to the pan-African political activism of late-nineteenth-century and early-twentieth-century black transnational political activists.

Historian Joseph Harris has applied a comparative approach successfully in his studies of the diaspora. Like Shepperson, his work focuses on historical diaspora studies, but he includes a considerable amount of political analysis. Harris is one of the first researchers I found who substantiates my impression of an underlying dynamism in the African diaspora; in his view this dynamism encompasses four stages:

> one should take into account the stages in the migratory process: primary, secondary, tertiary and circulatory. The primary stage is the original dispersion out of Africa; the secondary stage occurs with migration from the initial settlement abroad to a second area abroad; the tertiary stage is movement to a third area abroad; and the circulatory stage involves movements among the several areas abroad and may include Africa. This perspective encourages an analysis of the dispersion as a continuous and dynamic process involving various spatial dimensions and time frames.[15]

J. Ayodele Langley adds significantly to the understanding of diaspora political evolution by highlighting the role of African American and Caribbean nationalist organizations to the development of continental African nationalism and liberation movements. His work informs us how—with limited resources—these diaspora organizations penetrated colonial barriers in West Africa to work with African activists, such as Caseley Hayford and Kobena Sekyi, on political liberation between 1900 and 1945.[16] Further, he documents the relationships and correspondence between activists such as Hayford and John Edward Bruce, a popular journalist and activist in the United States. He provides evidence that continental African activists held political views about the diaspora and had suggestions as to how such communities could best work with African activists.

In a comparative analysis of the African diaspora to the Jewish and other diasporas, Elliott Skinner provides insight into the impact of ideological diversity upon these political efforts. He finds that diasporas are usually permanent settlements that seek to not only improve their political and economic status but those of *sister* communities and the homeland. Thus we learn that the "return to the homeland" mantra often assigned as a primary goal of diasporas is not valid in all cases. Accurately reading the political position of their homelands, diasporan political activists may realize their "expatriate" communities will be long-standing and that their role is to provide support for the homeland and sustain the life of the ethnicity and its civilization.

Ronald Walters adds to Harris's vision of the dynamic character of the African diaspora by diagramming the political relationships that may exist within the African diaspora and with the homeland region.[17] A political scientist, Walters explores ideological divisiveness within the African diaspora further, which he terms the "two-line" struggle. From his view, this ideological struggle impeded progress in pan-African politics in the last quarter of the twentieth century. He also provides insight into the consultative relationship that developed between U.S. African American political groups with newer black communities in Western European metropolitan areas. His case studies are particularly insightful about the relations between sister diaspora communities and the obstacles posed for diasporan activists involved in (African) continental political affairs.

Michael Hanchard also explores transnational political relations ongoing in the African diaspora.[18] Like Walters, he recognizes the consultative dialogue between transnational black activists, but he also provides instructive insight into the African diaspora intelligentsia's manipulation and reconfiguration of Western technologies and institutions to achieve political goals. For example, the appropriation of newspaper technology greatly facilitated the diaspora's ability to educate interested supporters in an efficient manner. Hanchard has made a major contribution to the study of African diaspora politics by producing an interactive visual depiction of the political activism within the diaspora during the twentieth century.[19] Using maps, one can study the political activities of various eras or regions of the world and see temporal characteristics as well as diaspora political connections, which often suggest wider social movements than are usually articulated in African American political literature.

These political studies, with the exception of Contee, are macro studies, looking at diaspora communities' interactions with each other or with regions of Africa. They look at the outcomes of aggregate work actually done through organizations, coalitions, and individual activists across time. They generally do not explore the essential steps and institutions developed to achieve the connections between political groups/organizations necessary for the planning, funding, and implementation of transnational political projects.

More often than not, African diaspora organizations are working outside (host) government institutions and therefore must develop themselves in such a way as to pursue political activity and then find resources and effective ways of linking politically with sister communities of African groups (who during the era under study lived in colonized states). To get a grasp of these processes, microanalysis is necessary. To study one project from beginning to end can facilitate our understanding of the methods by which ethnic groups can organize, link, and impact transnational politics. Therefore, this book is a microanalysis, a case study that will permit exploration of black transnational politics through the lens of diaspora theory magnified by an institutionalist political economy approach, discussed later in this chapter.

It must be emphasized that this study would not have been plausible without the groundbreaking evidence discussed in this literature review. These researchers provide insight into important characteristics of the post-slavery diaspora. Especially important are the observations that diasporas have varying attributes, are dynamic, and exhibit ideological diversity. Armed with these insights, I was able to select an appropriate case study that would facilitate a deeper exploration into the diaspora phenomenon. The hidden liaisons masked by larger, more complex political relations between nation-states are made visible by an in-depth study of the Black Star Line.

Literature on the Black Star Line

I uncovered few studies that dealt exclusively with the Black Star Line. However, I was able to assemble substantial information on the BSL from primary materials: especially the trial transcript *Marcus Garvey v. United States*, memoirs of key participants, contemporary news reports—particularly in the black press—and two videos of UNIA members that were found in the Schomburg archives.[20] In addition, there do exist comprehensive histories on the UNIA, which was the parent organization of the shipping company.

The primary sources available on the UNIA are found in several places. But unfortunately these are fragmentary because the federal government confiscated the UNIA's administrative and financial records as part of its investigation of alleged fraud in the BSL's financial operations. Two of the foremost scholars of Marcus Garvey and the UNIA, Professors Robert Hill and Tony Martin, confirm that office records were lost as the result of the federal investigation. Other researchers decry this loss in bibliographical essays included in their works on the UNIA and/or Garvey.[21] The UNIA had a newspaper, the *Negro World,* but unfortunately practically all of the 1919 and a substantial number of the 1920 issues have vanished. This is a significant loss because the prime life of the BSL was November 1919 through the summer of 1921. Research libraries have microfilmed issues covering 1923 to 1940, but this is after the demise of the BSL. Some 1919–20 issues are filed away with various federal agencies involved in surveillance of the UNIA; these include the Bureau of Investigation, the Military Intelligence Division, and the U.S. Post Office. A special microfilm collection of the *Negro World* for 1919 to 1926, housed in UCLA's Afro-American Studies research library, included a few damaged copies from 1919, incomplete but sparse issues from 1920, and a good representation from 1921.[22]

This glimpse of the *Negro World*'s coverage of the BSL in its zenith was pivotal to my grasping the UNIA's approach in convincing its readers of the fundamental practicality of the BSL. It also illustrates the UNIA's ability to withstand biting criticism in two ways. First, *Negro World* retaliated against other black organizations' criticism by pointing out their own problems. This was especially effective because these counterattacks and evaluations of rival organizations were done by Dr. William Ferris, a highly educated contemporary of the NAACP's W. E. B. Du Bois, and by John E. Bruce, a popular journalist and satirist in the black press. What follows is one critique by Ferris during the period that the BSL was under attack by not only the NAACP and its newspaper, the *Crisis,* but the organization Friends of Negro Freedom:

> who gives Dr. DuBois authority to say what people should do with their money and what other organizations should do? Did Dr. DuBois ever call a mass meeting and invite churches, fraternal organizations and racial organizations to send delegates and elect officers . . . as Marcus Garvey did? No. Both in forming the Niagara Movement and in forming the NAACP, Dr. DuBois and those he associated with him sent out invitations to choice and selected individuals of the race, the same as he and they would send out invitations to a pink tea affair, a banquet . . . He has the legal and moral right to do this. But he has not the right to assume that any group or organization so constituted and so organized represents the colored people of the country as a whole.
>
> It only represents Dr. DuBois and those he and his wealthy white and prominent colored friends and associates have been able to mobilize and corral. The difference between Dr. DuBois and Marcus Garvey is that while Dr. DuBois

> was appointed by a few white and colored friends of wealth and prominence to his present position, Marcus Garvey was elected by a widely advertised convention at which all other leaders and representatives were invited to attend. Thus Dr. DuBois is partly his own and partly Mr. Oswald Garrison Villard's appointee as referee and umpire of the affairs of the Negro race.[23]

Secondly, the *Negro World* shrewdly covered mishaps of other shipping lines, especially the British, to demonstrate the unavoidable difficulties encountered by even the best in shipping transportation. UCLA's collection of the *Negro World* also shares a great deal about how the UNIA's organizational business was conveyed through the newspaper. The BSL management even communicated program changes and corrections with investors through the paper. For example, there were notices to various stockholders requesting additional information, such as "William Smith, Buffalo New York, send your full address." And given the eventual charges of mail fraud, it was interesting to find ads from November 1920 announcing that some shares were cancelled due to fraud on the part of spurious sales agents. The advertisements requested that investors contact BSL offices to have them replaced.

These issues (1919–26) also extended my information on the various methods of purchasing BSL shares. In particular, a letter appearing in the April 9, 1921, issue revealed that BSL shares could be bought collectively: "Sir: - Enclosed please find thirty-five dollars ($35). This money is the effort of worthy members of the UNIA who are desirous of helping the cause by purchasing shares in the B.S.L. The method adopted for raising this money was that each member put in 50 cents per week and in ten weeks they were able to purchase one share."[24] This may explain why so many shares could be sold to a relatively liminal and suppressed diaspora, with the substantial part of its population forced into menial labor and peonage.

The *Negro World* provided space for UNIA division reports, and in that way the organization's international membership could keep abreast of organizational business, changes, and activities. Knowledge of the international reach of the UNIA more than likely contributed to the enthusiasm and commitment on the part of its core membership. Division reports came from a wide range of regions: in the Caribbean from Jamaica, Panama, Cuba, Spanish Honduras, Guatemala, and Nicaragua. In North America, reports came from British Columbia, Nova Scotia, and Montreal. In the United States, rural areas such as Mississippi, South Carolina, Alabama, and Texas were represented.

I was struck by the social emphasis conveyed by these reports as opposed to political and business updates. However, any inference as to the capability or political astuteness of the divisions would be premature because no official division reports to UNIA headquarters were available to substantiate any such conclusion. The division reports in the *Negro World* do reveal that leading UNIA leaders often visited divisions to speak and participated in the reorganization of several. Collections are also mentioned for membership dues, BSL, and other funds.

Most importantly, the *Negro World* confirms the political understanding of the UNIA leadership at its New York headquarters. There were not only news articles on current events but specifically on international politics and economics and the Paris Peace conference and other meetings of European leaders. This suggests that the leadership was well read on current events. Editorials and columns by Garvey, Ferris, Hubert Harrison, and Duse Mohammed Ali often addressed controversial political issues and grounded their analysis in their ideological positions. Thus, the *Negro World* went far in contextualizing my understanding of the UNIA diaspora activists who attempted to establish a shipping line.

Contemporaneous black print media provided other ideological views as well as critiques of the BSL effort. These newspapers demonstrate that other activists also had an astute understanding of international political and economic matters. Four are highlighted here because they were located in New York and provided coverage of the BSL effort on a continual basis. The first three are organizational newspapers: the *Messenger, Crusader,* and the *Crisis.* The fourth is a standard black weekly newspaper, the *New York Amsterdam News.*

The *Messenger* was considered a socialist newspaper, not only because the American Socialist party financed it in part, but also because its editors, A. Philip Randolph and Chandler Owen, were among the most prominent black Socialists of the era. News and chronic problems facing the black urban population, workers in particular, were analyzed from a socialist perspective. Initially Randolph and Owen had associated with the UNIA, but the *Messenger* was among the first publications to question the BSL effort. Though Randolph and Owen did not seem to understand the shipping industry, they did provide a critical analysis of why a large corporate venture was beyond the resources of the black world. Therefore the *Messenger* provided the larger black population, particularly in New York, with a different take on the plausibility of a black-owned shipping concern and sounded the alarm on the UNIA's financial disparities.

The *Crusader* was the news organ of the African Blood Brotherhood (ABB), and eventually it evolved from a purely nationalist ideology to a communist organ. It received financial and political support from the U.S. Communist Party, which was interested in incorporating black labor into the international movement. Because the ABB wanted to convert the UNIA's political beliefs, it did not criticize it consistently in 1919–1920. Yet the *Crusader* became the most virulent critic of the BSL. Established by Cyril Briggs and other pro-Soviet activists, the *Crusader* arguments were similar to those of the *Messenger.*[25] However, the vituperative tone and ongoing feud between Briggs and Garvey diffused the power of the arguments made because they suggested that the purpose was to vilify the UNIA rather than inform the public. Nevertheless, the *Crusader*'s attacks weren't entirely personal: supporters of the ABB were involved in the UNIA and therefore provided Briggs with insider information. Upon resigning from the UNIA, several former officials published in the *Crusader,* in particular W. A. Domingo. Domingo was a member of the UNIA and editor of the *Negro World* until his increasingly socialist stance led to his departure. He wrote extensively about the UNIA and wrote a particularly comprehensive critique of the UNIA's financial management.[26] However, like the *Messenger,* the *Crusader* did not have writers familiar with shipping industry operations. Thus the *Crusader* inadvertently passed along misinformation. For example, the financial agreement between the BSL and North American Shipping Company for the first BSL ship was convoluted in order to evade the stipulations of Canada's shipping department, which attempted to block the purchase until the BSL's financial position could be clarified. While buyer and seller had agreed to the purchase, an interim lease had to be employed to complete the sale. The *Negro World* carried the story of the purchase before the mitigating stipulations occurred, and even after referred to the ship as BSL owned. This was rational because BSL had arranged to pay in installments, as an individual might purchase an automobile or home. The *Crusader* and other black media, without complete knowledge of the financial agreement and the surrounding circumstances, concluded that the BSL had misled investors and the larger community. The reporting in the *Messenger* and the *Crusader* give us insight into contemporaneous black viewpoints of the BSL, but these opinions are colored by inexperience with shipping operations, ideological contention, and the personal animosity between Briggs and Garvey.

The NAACP's *Crisis* is most often quoted in secondary monographs as the major critic of the UNIA and the Black Star Line in particular. This may be because the *Crisis* was one of the largest black publications and its editor, Dr. Du Bois, was considered a scholar and a highly respected activist. Initially, the *Crisis* analysis of the BSL was most comprehensive. Its early objectivity illustrated that the BSL concept in and of itself was seen as plausible, and the *Crisis* cautiously predicted that the wider black community might be open to use its services should it be competently established. Like the *Messenger* and *Crusader*, however, the *Crisis* became more critical over time. These newspapers document the initial guarded approval of an independent black shipping service, initial fascination with the fund-raising acumen of the BSL organizers, growing skepticism borne out of ideological differences but also out of observation of UNIA managerial mistakes, and finally disdain based on general BSL operations, particularly of its financial management.

Not all black press was so partisan that the focus was on proselytizing a particular ideological position. The *New York Amsterdam News* covered Harlem and often interjected a voice of reason into the ongoing acrimony between black organizations. In particular, the *Amsterdam News* chastised both the NAACP and the UNIA on their ongoing feud. In an editorial by Floyd J. Calvin, he points out that both programs seek to improve the well-being and political and economic plight of the people and that their programs and concerns did not really contradict each other. He argued that personalities were getting in the way of progress:

> The very foundations of each [organization] denote a continuous struggle in their respective fields . . . if the public finds that the cardinal principles are suddenly forgotten and the controversy drops to the level of personalities then both sides should be let severely alone. If members of two organizations cannot go about their business carrying out their respective programs—which are basically not programs of destruction—without being disgraced by the personal fights between their respective leaders, then both leaders should be repudiated.[27]

The *Amsterdam News* gave the most objective coverage of the trial. And though it came to the conclusion that Garvey had "blundered," it urged the UNIA to continue its program without Garvey.

Comparative analysis (made possible by Hill's collection) of the New York–based black newspapers with those of the Caribbean and Europe suggests that the further removed from UNIA headquarters, the more frequent the inaccuracies about BSL.[28] These papers are not without value, however: the foreign papers, particularly the "Negro" press, show the ongoing debate on BSL and the ideological road that blacks as a people should select. This debate is reflected in both the Caribbean and Africa. The European press was surprisingly sensationalist, particularly in Belgium. The European press routinely confused the UNIA with the NAACP. Although the black population in

Europe during this time period was relatively small, there were black media there, especially in London where the black population was reasonably well informed. Afro-Caribbeans received better information on BSL because it was supplemented through correspondence from family in the United States.

Letters and circulars also provided evidence that black people debated BSL globally. This speaks to a far-reaching web of communications links throughout the diaspora and Africa. Letters and circulars in the *UNIA Papers* provide documentation of diverse ideological positions within the diaspora, but with the unified concern about the derogation of the black race and its economic marginalization.

The *UNIA Papers* also document the evolution of the UNIA and its attempts to establish BSL. In particular, the speeches of Garvey and Ferris document the economic position and goals of the UNIA. These economic arguments were used to underscore the need for an independent shipping line, and the speeches provide insight into the UNIA's response to the criticism of its competitors. The organizational documents included in the *UNIA Papers* provide limited insight into how the UNIA assembled the BSL. For example, the incorporation documents are included; transcripts of meetings convey how the effort was explained to the membership and how subscriptions and collections were organized. Diverse memoranda and letters provide information on not only internal UNIA communications but parallel developments that were unfolding in competitive black organizations. For instance, Du Bois wrote letters to the UNIA and U.S. Shipping Board (USSB) requesting information about the BSL for his *Crisis* article. Du Bois also received letters from black citizens asking whether they should invest.

Government surveillance reports almost serve as an ongoing narration of the effort. The U.S. Justice Department's Bureau of Investigation's weekly reports detail conversations informants had (or overheard) with UNIA members and also between the UNIA and other organizations. These reports describe mass meetings and confirm the large attendance figures and the wide range and unlikely special guests from organizations such as Sinn Fein, noted feminist and socialist Rose Parker Stokes, the grandson of Frederick Douglass, Ida B. Wells, white politicians from New York, and African entrepreneurs. Even though UNIA leaders disavowed political liaison with some movements (especially communist groups), such organizations were allowed to present at mass meetings. These groups helped the UNIA convey the anti-imperialist political struggle unfolding globally and that the time was right for black people to surge toward independence as other groups were.

Statements taken by government agents during their investigation of BSL are rare gems that allow us to hear directly from the leadership of the BSL. Keeping in mind the UNIA/BSL participants' probable concern with self-incrimination, these statements explain their administrative roles in daily operations and financial processing and their growing frustrations with top management. Bureau of Investigation (BI) agent Mortimer Davis also reported on information gathered from BSL's vendors, which substantiate the continuous expensive repairs required.

The reports of BI forensic auditor Thomas P. Merrilees built an extensive picture of the UNIA and BSL finances over the two-and-one-half years of BSL operations. Unfortunately the raw data that the BI gathered is not available. Nonetheless, these summary reports are the main account available of overall financial operations. For instance, Merrilees assembled a table outlining numbers of shares sold per month, which gives an idea of interest in the line and a helpful working estimate of monthly income available for BSL operations—and, it seems, for the UNIA's use. Merrilees also breaks out financials for each ship, accounting for the purchase price and repairs for each. Comparing this report to the report of shares sold gives us a reasonable idea of the percent of funding which may have gone to the BSL effort.

Yet this data must be qualified. First, Merrilees reported that there were missing stock books and that the bank records may have been incomplete. Secondly, it must be remembered that the raw data wasn't available for scrutiny, and Merrilees' job was to help the Justice Department build a case against the BSL directors. Therefore the data was probably organized to augment the strength of the government's case. Finally, BI reports suggest that UNIA and BSL officials, who had been forewarned of the impending BI raid and arrests, may have removed some records. The types of records removed are not identified. While it is reasonable to surmise that some financial information was removed, other records, including those for the UNIA militia and other alliances and plans, could have been removed as well.[29]

The British surveillance reports included in the *UNIA Papers* are more comprehensive. Many of these reports were written for the colonial office, and copies were sent to various U.S. agencies. While these reports do provide some information on the BSL, their reports suggest that they were more concerned about how the BSL could disrupt labor relations in the colonies by offering laborers economic alternatives. They are also concerned with connections with West African activists for similar reasons, including the likelihood that production and shipment of raw resources could be disrupted.

Hill contextualizes the *UNIA Papers* by providing brief biographies of people and organizations active in the era. Mostly contained in footnotes, these biographical sketches provide invaluable information on activists and organizations not duplicated in other sources used in this study.

Another very useful and concise assemblage of UNIA and BSL materials is edited by Professor John Henrik Clarke.[30] Clarke presents an admixture of primary materials and informative essays by noted scholars of Garveyism, including Hill, Martin, and Stein. The primary materials include representative articles from newspapers, a few already noted, and autobiographical excerpts as well as retrospective assessments of the UNIA by contemporaries of the era. The section devoted to the era of BSL is titled the "Years of Triumph and Tragedy." It includes an interesting article by Garvey explaining why he believed the BSL failed. The article was written in 1930 and corroborates the view that he held several BSL financial officers responsible for the financial malfeasance. Garvey also believed that ideological differences between him and principal UNIA administrators who pushed for communism collaborated with other critics to derail the nationalistic movement. His argument is plausible and reflects some of the political dynamics of the era. For example, he traveled extensively and could not therefore provide daily supervision of financial operations. However, a professionally organized financial system would have minimized the misappropriation of investment funds. Nor does Garvey's essay explain why allegedly unscrupulous officers continuously were selected by UNIA leadership or why shipping protocol was ignored. Nevertheless, the article is a useful proxy (albeit limited) for providing Garvey's personal assessment of the BSL effort. Throughout the volume, Clarke provides contextualization, which made it a useful text to clarify information from other sources. Combined with Hill, Clarke helps us to see through the primary data the extent of understanding that black diaspora and political activists had of the politics and international economy of the era.

The primary documents available suggest that UNIA activists had mastered the newspaper industry and law. The contributions of black lawyers to the UNIA have been ignored, as has the extent of the international communications network. Hill and Clarke have enabled us to see the strengths of the UNIA as it worked its way into the international economy via shipping. And government surveillance reports (both U.S. and British) provide valuable insight into the reasons these governments obstructed the BSL effort. Still, incomplete minutes and financial reports and the lack of personal papers for Garvey and other UNIA leaders leave us with a fragmentary picture of BSL administration.

The transcript of the mail fraud trial gives partial but direct, objective access to key actors in the BSL project. Because of its function—an unbiased recording of testimony and evidence played out in the courtroom—it could not be organized to convey any particular viewpoint. The testimony of BSL directors, spokespersons, and office staff created a picture of the headquarters and daily administrative operations and provided access to the reasoning and views of officers. For example, clerks and financial officers explained the processing of funds. The supervisor of stock sales agents described their procedures and problems. Additional details of the circumstances under which ships were purchased were in the transcript.

The transcript also corroborated details about BSL gathered from other primary sources. In discussing operations, witnesses confirmed that officers and staff for the UNIA and its corporations and leagues were virtually indistinguishable. UNIA officials and BSL directors were paid from the same funds. These funds included UNIA dues, newspaper subscriptions, and purchases. UNIA salaries were also paid from investment funds for BSL and the National Factories Corporation the largest source at one point being BSL funds. Dissension, accusations, and mistrust detailed in surveillance reports and rival black newspapers were substantiated.

Conversely, the trial transcript underscores the earnestness with which some of the UNIA and BSL officers pursued their goals, especially with the BSL. They did intend to run a race-based shipping company and develop settlements in Liberia. Because of the trial, we become privy to the daily struggle to acquire the *Phyllis Wheatley*, the missteps taken, government stalling, and the UNIA's efforts to retain public support and investment in the line (a side note: the UNIA used the spelling *Phyllis* in the ship's name, but the poet's name was spelled *Phillis*).

The trial transcript did have limitations; the most significant being caused by Garvey's decision to represent himself. I believe that much more information might have been revealed, but Garvey did not have the legal training to introduce evidence germane to his case and ironically to my study. These circumstances made for interesting reading but also suggested that the BSL effort was more complicated than the historiography on it indicates.

Memoirs were useful also. Amy Jacques Garvey's memoir, *Garvey and Garveyism*, allowed me to glimpse the uppermost management of the UNIA and the administrative obstacles that hampered the effort. Amy was Marcus Garvey's second wife and office manager to the UNIA's office, although it seems sexism prevented her from actually carrying out such responsibilities. From her, we know that the line initially was meant to be a cooperative, and the programming grew out of the concerns voiced by seamen and businesspeople connected to the UNIA. African Americans from the Caribbean as well as the

United States were knowledgeable about the role of shipping in commercial trade.[31] In addition to increased trade opportunities, these seamen knew that a black merchant marine would increase job opportunities for stevedores and, if the effort was successful, nautical officers and administrators.

We also know that the BSL's popularity with black people caused the New York office to be swamped with requests for information and for shares. The small staff was inundated and ill prepared to undertake the immense increase in financial administration. Amy Garvey also corroborates the wide travel undertaken by Garvey to increase membership and funding. Because UNIA governance was authoritarian, his frequent absences exacerbated the tension developing within the overworked staff. She also provides a chronological account of the growth of the BSL, defending Marcus Garvey's performance, commitment, and abilities. Her biographer, Ula Taylor, elaborates on this point and also corroborates Amy Jacques Garvey's integral role in the UNIA.[32] Garvey's memoir is the best account on the daily operations of the line and the stress that the UNIA/BSL staff was under trying to cope with administering so many different programs simultaneously: the BSL, weekly mass meetings, annual conventions, the Liberian settlement, Negro Factories Corporation, not to mention the divisions and finances of the organizations.[33]

Another informative memoir is that of Captain Hugh Mulzac.[34] Mulzac was one of a few BSL officials who had fundamental knowledge of the shipping industry, particularly in the areas of operations and regulations. He had been a licensed "master" in the British fleet until he relocated to the United States. Mulzac became the first black man licensed in the United States in the twentieth century. His evaluation of the ships and the shipping competence of BSL officers and ship crews are invaluable. However, Mulzac did not get involved in the concern until after the purchase of the first ship and also after its first voyage. His assessment of the BSL's initiation is based on his discussions with Captain Joshua Cockbourne. The latter served as the first captain of BSL, and he seems to have played a duplicitous role in the purchase of the *Yarmouth*. Mulzac provides a firsthand account of mistakes made in the administration of the line's operations, including contracting cargo, maintenance problems, and managing seafaring personnel and finances. Because he served as first officer aboard the *Yarmouth* on two voyages and was to be captain of the *Phyllis Wheatley*, Mulzac's account of the BSL's operations is an excellent source for insight into how money was absorbed by expenses such as passenger upkeep during delays, increased fuel consumption, and payroll increases due to malfunctioning equipment and forced diversions from schedules. For a time, Mulzac believed that BSL could be made a profitable concern. His practical reasoning was based upon his experience as a marine officer familiar with international cargo traffic and British shipping. He understood that a market existed with the underserved black population and smaller islands.

It is clear that Mulzac had a basic understanding of shipping economics. However, his memoir suggests that he did not understand the postwar economic variables, which temporarily escalated shipping costs as documented by economists assessing the interwar economy.[35] Therefore his estimate as to the cost of the *Yarmouth* in particular must be tempered by our understanding that the tight market inflated ship prices beyond their physical value until the war-devastated shipping industry could be rebuilt. But Mulzac's credentials and experience do confirm the mediocre quality of the ships purchased by BSL as well as its mismanagement, and eventually he resigned from the BSL. One incident in particular highlights the BSL directors' disregard of the shipping knowledge of the few experienced black captains, and this is why he finally resigned from the BSL:

> After two such profitless trips, I found myself losing confidence in Mr. Garvey and his business acumen. I decided to make a firm effort to put the line's operations, at least, on a sound commercial basis, and drew up a cargo plan containing detailed proposals for accepting and handling freight by weight and cubic measure, and many other provisions, which would assure a profitable cargo-handling operation. I submitted this plan to Mr. O. M. Thompson, general manager of the company. He could not have been less interested . . . As it turned out, I was too late anyway—the Yarmouth had made her last voyage.[36]

The scholarship most cited relating to the BSL are works by three researchers, all noted historians.[37] To these I would add the excellent work of several other excellent researchers.[38] However, most of these works focus on Marcus Garvey and to a lesser extent on the UNIA. Attention had to be paid to the BSL in these works because it was the largest, most successful program the UNIA developed. The BSL attracted more investment, membership, and talent than any of the other programs, including the Liberian settlement and the Negro Factories Corporation. As a result, these Garvey biographies devote at least a chapter to the BSL; other major topics are the Liberian settlement, the development of a distinct UNIA liturgy, the *Negro World,* and contention between the UNIA and the NAACP.

The first general biography of Marcus Garvey was written by Len S. Nembhard immediately following Garvey's death in 1940.[39] It is considered an eulogium and does not give a detailed account of the BSL. E. David Cronon is considered the first academic biographer of Garvey. His is a basic historic account of Garvey and the development of the UNIA. Cronon includes a descriptive, chronological narrative of the BSL effort that focuses on the journeys made, the cessation of operations, and the trial. While he does discuss the specific purchases of ships, he does not delve into the organization of the shipping industry or the economic issues surrounding shipping in the era. He concluded that BSL paid exorbitant amounts for the ships and mismanaged the line. His coverage of the rivalry within the black media is instructive. Cronon did not have access to the numerous UNIA materials made available to Hill. Nevertheless, when compared to later studies, Cronon's work can be judged to be a liberal account and basically correct.

Theodore Vincent increases our information on the motivation and strategy of the BSL organization by presenting the UNIA's history from their ideological perspective. Vincent probes the economic circumstances of blacks in the era and provides details as to how the UNIA decided to launch the BSL. Interviewing people who remembered the effort and the generation of UNIA members who followed that era, Vincent gives us a view of the dissension within the movement and thus enriches our knowledge of the internal ideological struggles that led to cleavage between nationalists and socialists, with the latter joining the ABB and/or becoming critics of the UNIA. A second major cleavage he uncovers occurred over financial management, a disagreement that eventually led to a split between nationalist factions who called for new leadership and those who supported Garvey. Vincent clarifies the composition of the UNIA and BSL. His interviews with members dispels the long-held conclusion that the UNIA was composed of only low-income West Indian immigrants, and he includes biographical sketches of educated and middle-class leaders in the movement. He calls these leaders (members) "young renegades" from both the U.S. black American and West Indian middle classes.

Unlike other researchers of the UNIA and BSL, Vincent does not chronicle the BSL voyages nor does he detail the chronic financial problems of the effort. But he does shed light on the market BSL hoped to serve, and he shares membership views about the reasons ships were so expensive. Vincent is highly critical of Cronon's conclusion that BSL managers were benighted as it related to the cost of ships. His interviewees pointed out that most companies would not sell to the line, so BSL directors knew that this limited the supply of ships available to them and led to higher prices. This attests a basic understanding of microeconomics on the part of UNIA leadership. And it may be a plausible explanation for their actions; however, it also evinced that the researcher and interviewees were unfamiliar with the economic circumstances surrounding the shipping industry of that era.

While acknowledging that the BSL was incorporated, Vincent concluded that the BSL (and other UNIA corporations) functioned more as cooperatives than corporations. This suggests why BSL operations, particularly financial management, did not meet corporate norms. While this may have facilitated program implementation from the UNIA leadership's perspective, it provided the government with legal inroads to dismantle what it considered a subversive organization.

Tony Martin often is categorized as an apologist for the UNIA because, like Vincent, he seeks to incorporate the nationalistic view into the literature on the UNIA. However, Martin's purpose is made clear in his preface: "This book is based on the simple premise that no one could have organized and built up the largest black mass movement in Afro-American history, in the face of continuous onslaughts from communists . . . black reactionaries . . . and the most powerful governments . . . and yet be a buffoon or a clown, or even an overwhelmingly impractical visionary . . . This study attempts to treat Garvey and the UNIA with seriousness and respect they deserve."

Thus the book is organized in such a way as to present a cogent defense of his thesis. Accuracy is not sacrificed, however, and Martin does not evade the financial problems in the Black Star Line's management. He does explore and document more fully the governmental intervention (such as constant British surveillance and BI efforts to thwart the effort) and the internal "general business incompetence" as well as the UNIA's internecine struggles. His narrative supplements the *UNIA Papers* nicely by weaving the UNIA story around the chronologically arranged documents in the *UNIA Papers*.

Nevertheless, his presentation of the BSL does not add very much to the information on its organization or operations in the Caribbean. He does corroborate that the BSL traffic agents were in Jamaica and provides a better count on the passengers using the line. For instance, Martin documents that the *Yarmouth* accommodated over 500 passengers, and in its three voyages carried well over 700 passengers. This suggests that the UNIA leadership's belief that there was a passenger market was reasonable. Martin provides some documentation of white engineers sabotaging boilers but presents no evidence of government sabotage of ships.

Another historian, Judith Stein, employs a socialist analysis of Garveyism that considers the political economy of the era. Thus her discussion of the BSL provides more insight into the international economy, including the importance of the shipping industry and labor relations. In terms of the international economy, Stein probes the economic position of blacks in the United States and Caribbean and the reasons why they believed shipping was a reasonable component to their uplift. Stein shows why a shipping venture was seen as not only politically astute but economically lucrative. Smaller Caribbean islands with irregular exports were cut off by the larger shipping lines that were trying to enhance efficiency. Itinerant laborers in search of work needed transportation around the Caribbean and along the U.S. eastern seaboard. Monopolies by Elder Dempster Shipping in West Africa and United Fruit Company in Cuba meant growers wanted transport alternatives for their produce. An ethnically based enclave economy could have proven profitable, particularly if organized to meet the idiosyncrasies of the black market.

Although Stein emphasizes the importance of shipping to the rebuilding of markets and state economies, she does not go far enough. She rightly discusses the scarcity of shipping space and how that allowed smaller shippers to enter the international market, but she does not discuss the corollary inflation, which led to inflated prices for even secondhand vessels in the short boom period following World War I. Nevertheless, she provides the best discussion of the costs associated with the effort. Also, by emphasizing economic issues, Stein helps expose the keen competition between the hegemonic powers to acquire (or rebuild) market share. In addition to fear of communism, nations had another important reason to capsize the efforts of small competitors that could obstruct their plans in any way.

Thus, Stein adds two important pieces of information. First, there was a market to be served in the Black Atlantic. Second, black labor was vital to BSL's limited success: laborers in the industrial centers of the northern United States and those engaged as stevedores and so forth in Panama and sugar production in the Caribbean may have made up the significant portion of investors.

The conflation of Stein and Martin—considered ideologically opposed in academe—brings out two important aspects of the UNIA's success in diaspora politics. Stein highlights the integral role of black workers not only as BSL stevedores and seamen but as investors. Martin underscores the invaluable contributions of diaspora activists to the interlacing of black political organization on three continents to back the BSL effort. In fact, respected diaspora activists and independent political activists were instrumental in convincing workers to trust and invest in BSL. Martin's work illustrates why the United

States and Britain were concerned that an international network of black activists could cause problems. First, labor unrest and insurrection would disrupt production and possibly call for military containment, both bringing additional costs that Britain in particular could ill afford. And secondly, each state reasoned that the black political network could be used by competitors and/or enemies to disrupt market development and labor relations.

As stated earlier, the editor of the UNIA papers has not completed the volume devoted to the UNIA in the Caribbean. Most researchers of Garvey and/or the UNIA concentrate on the organizational headquarters in New York and contention with rival black organizations and critics, yet BSL investors were found all over the black Atlantic, as well as in other regions. A few writers give us glimpses of the UNIA outside New York and allowed me to extend my analysis of the BSL into the Caribbean.

While Rupert Lewis is another biographer of Garvey, he also facilitated insight into how the UNIA operated in the Caribbean, especially in Cuba, Panama, and Costa Rica.[40] His work provides details of Garvey's 1921 tour of the Caribbean and how and why the political leadership of some islands embraced him. He also sheds light on how the United Fruit Company gingerly managed its black workforce during the BSL era and worked with the U.S. State Department to contain UNIA development in the Caribbean region.

James C. Boyd provides a rare look at UNIA membership in the Lesser Antilles, focusing upon Tobago and its connection to the Trinidad Workingmen's Association, an organization with significant UNIA membership.[41] The TWA was a workers union, which led effective strikes for wages throughout Trinidad. Boyd documents strong African cultural retention in Tobago and the islanders' support of UNIA's Liberian settlement program. He also gives insight into migration patterns within the Caribbean and how islanders were politicized as they left the smaller islands in search of work and liberty. Several became UNIA leaders in the Caribbean and some eventually in the United States. Boyd also provides the best treatment on the UNIA's National Factories Corporation, detailing its brief success providing uniforms for UNIA and its branch businesses.

Emory Tolbert provides the only study that concentrates on one division (Los Angeles) specifically. It therefore provides the perspective of an "outpost" of UNIA programming and the organizational structure that could function outside the New York fold.[42] Tolbert documents that L.A.'s UNIA/BSL supporters were not confined to working-class communities but rather included experienced, respected activists of varying political views. His study is all the more important because it was the Los Angeles contingent, led by Noah Thompson, that forced debate at the 1921 UNIA convention on the financial management of the BSL. As a result of Thompson's critical rebuke of management, BSL financial records were presented at the 1921 convention and read into the record. These are a few of the surviving primary financial documents available on the BSL.

Taken together, the research on "outpost" divisions points up the diversity in the reasons for the UNIA's large membership even as members shared the desire to eradicate racism, particularly economic exclusion. This work suggests that membership in underdeveloped areas such as Tobago and Mississippi was most repressed, and members in these areas were more receptive to African immigration and BSL as a means to that end. More economically integrated areas such as Trinidad, Jamaica, and the Gold Coast were more politically attuned and wanted commercial shipping and passenger service from the BSL. A few in more industrialized, cosmopolitan areas like New York, Chicago, and London wanted profitable investment opportunities and other diaspora-based employment and African development possibilities.

These writers document the UNIA's fixation upon international economic and political programming, especially the establishment of BSL and the UNIA Liberian settlement. But some branches may have wanted local development and political representation as suggested by Tolbert. Further, they point out the organization's resistance to the viewpoints and suggestions of the general membership and the expansion of local programming in the chapters.

Finally, I contextualize the study by looking at African American urban history. This comparatively new field has produced studies that query earlier research about how African Americans engaged prejudice, segregation, and terrorism. Researchers such as Goings and Smith point out that "blacks used kin and friendship networks, pooled resources, shared information and played pivotal roles in organizing their own movement into expanding cities of the North and South."[43] And just as they migrated North, African Americans also moved further west, usually settling in urban areas and building strong communities, but they also developed many black towns in the western United States.[44] Earlier works suggest that black people were compliant in local political arenas nationwide. But studies by Joseph Trotter, Darlene Clark Hine, and others provide evidence of political resistance and amelioration of racial injustice in cities throughout America. These studies present a pattern of specific resistance and community building, relying on traditional mutual aid societies, legal activism (where possible), and self-defense.

Moreover, in several cities, black leaders negotiated with white politicians regarding both political and economic issues. These negotiations were often possible after African Americans demonstrated determination to defend against racially based attacks.[45] Kaskow takes a closer look at many of the riots during the "Red Summer" of 1919 and describes several of these racial clashes as "fight-back" riots.[46] His evidence shows conclusively that in racial clashes in Washington, D.C., and Chicago, African Americans did not acquiesce to the displaced anger and ignorance of their attackers. When it was clear that they would not be protected by the police, African Americans went on the offensive and retaliated, wounding and sometimes killing their attackers. In the South, activists accosted terrorists that would have lynched black citizens with impunity without organized resistance.

This represents the political component of the New Negro, demonstrating that a focus on the arts renaissance does not fully convey how black people had grown and developed their political skills. For example, they demonstrated their knowledge of the industrial economy by strategically challenging economic situations in effective ways. In some instances they gained location in the industrial economy through striking.[47] At other times, they made inroads by being strikebreakers. Where possible they went to court to defend constitutional rights and protect growing business development. They did not rely exclusively upon representation by NAACP, UNIA, or other national organizations; rather, they represented themselves, negotiating with city officials and business leaders. National organizations relied on these local activists to support national lobbying and political activism. It was from grassroots activists that national organizations received their funding, support, and even personnel. National organizations were valuable resources when locals needed more support: after the Elaine, Arkansas, racial riot, the NAACP stepped in and defended sharecroppers and farmers who had tried to work through the courts.

Still other researchers go further and present anecdotal evidence of people resisting specific acts in civil society. Manufacturing workers, such as those in the textile industry, have been documented as using sabotage. Individuals resisted racist verbal and physical violence on public transit and other venues. And of course there were always infrapolitics, wherein blacks would quietly and subtly obstruct racist institutions.

African American urban history researchers set the tone of this study, bringing clarity as to where the courage and political experience came from. Political activism and determination percolated up to national organizations just as much as it trickled down to the local communities where the majority of people lived, worked, and battled. This information explains much about the success of national political movements: the people were behind these organizations, not beholden to them.

3

Still Waters: Understanding the Political Economy of the 1920s

To understand the creation and development of the Black Star Line, it is necessary to look at the international political economy[1] of the era in which it functioned. Doing so contextualizes the study and assists in our understanding of some critical choices made by the BSL board of directors and its parent organization, the Universal Negro Improvement Association, and its principal leader in the era, Marcus Garvey.

The shipping line functioned from 1919 to 1921, and it was discontinued in early 1922. During this era, three nation-states, the United States, Great Britain, and Russia, ultimately shaped the global economy, and they each had particular concerns about the activism of marginalized populations trapped in their empires, including African diaspora movements. As an international shipping concern, of course the international environment was a factor for BSL operations. Great Britain, in particular, was influential because many of the diaspora communities in the Caribbean were within the British colonial empire. The second power, Russia, threatened the structure of the international economy and planned to incorporate African Americans within its revolutionary agenda. This assumption did not take into consideration that African Americans had their own political agenda and expected a partnership with Russia rather than a paternalistic arrangement. Looking at the concerns and actions of these states as it relates to the BSL clarifies much, because the latter had to maneuver around these powers and manipulate international agreements in order to sail.

The predominant position at this time of Great Britain and the United

States is obvious. Russia must be discussed because it posed a significant challenge to the economic system of the West that would dominate the global economy. Russia also provided state power and legitimization to labor and ethnic movements in Western Europe and the United States. This undercut the Western states' ability to control political dissent. This discussion will proceed from the general economic environment to the specific dynamics of BSL trying to come alive in the American political economy.

The BSL was established in 1919 after World War I. It was a time of unprecedented human loss and great political and economic upheaval. Over 10 million lives had been lost in World War I, historic political empires such as the Habsburg and Ottoman had disintegrated, and the economic infrastructure of the major European powers had been decimated. The war had not only destroyed the German imperial system; the financial resources of the remaining European powers, Great Britain and France, had been significantly depleted.[2] The global economy was destabilized as a result. The major economic powers had shifted, with the United States replacing Great Britain, which had served as the undisputed hegemon for over seventy years.

The exhaustion of the European powers' resources and the disorganization of their bureaucracies afforded revolutionaries opportunities to gain voice in colonial empires. The colonized in Africa, Asia, the Caribbean, and Central America all wanted freedom from Western Europe and the United States. Moreover, socialists and labor organizations *within* the European states challenged traditional economic arrangements that favored manufacturers and the wealthy. The United States also experienced significant labor unrest, the growth of socialist and communist political organizations, and resistance by African Americans. Though without significant military or monetary resources, these revolutionaries and disgruntled workers on both sides of the Atlantic were taken seriously because their protests and strikes could disrupt the rebuilding of the economic order by threatening to at least attenuate the remaining power and resources of the established political regimes.

There was also concern that the Bolshevist revolutionary movement could become the leader of the European and American radicals. The Bolsheviki sought to replace the destabilized global economy with a communist regime, redistributing the wealth and power, and threatened the capitalist order in Western Europe. Thus Western European and U.S. governmental and business leaders had to rebuild Europe while simultaneously safeguarding capital and global markets from revolutionaries and other discontented groups. Lenin was politically astute and was intricately connected with socialist movements throughout Europe and America. He called for the overthrow of the colonial empires upon which Western Europe depended for agricultural and mineral resources, including gold bullion, which was the foundation of the financial system that the West planned to reinstate.

For Britain and the United States, a communist world order was considered much more dangerous than appeasing or incorporating worker demands into political and economic rebuilding plans. This new set of circumstances meant that two new blocs confronted each other for the power to organize the international political economy similar to the earlier struggle between imperialist factions, which had culminated in the war.[3] The major difference was that this time the struggle was composed of imperialist/capitalist states on one hand and labor unions, communist/socialist organizations, and black and other minority groups (some directly tied to Russia) on the other. Each of their strategies for control affected the political economy of the era.

Rebuilding the International Political Economy

For Western Europe in particular, the rehabilitation of the global economy was critical. Having lost much of its wealth, infrastructure, and most importantly millions of people, including from the educated elite classes who made up its bureaucracy and landed aristocracy, it was in no position to simultaneously rebuild, oppose Russia, and control colonial empires. The military, economic, or human resources just were not available. In this compromised position, Western Europe had no choice but to grant considerable leverage to the United States for the rebuilding of the global economy. This was the only safe way that these weakened states could regain economic footing and rebuild their nations.

Understanding the struggles between and within these two powerful blocs is key. If we evaluate the formal agreements reached to begin the arduous rebuilding of the international political economy (IPE), including the Treaty of Versailles, as well as the economic challenges of each state, we can better follow the strategies and relationships that formed the IPE environment in which the BSL operated.

The Treaty of Versailles outlined the rebuilding of Europe and distribution of Germany's colonies. Drawing up the treaty focused attention upon the colonial possessions of Europe and brought subjugated peoples to Paris to argue for autonomy. In many instances, these delegations were ignored, including African and diaspora attendees.[4] Yet these marginalized groups achieved important political cohesion. They interacted with each other and came to better understand the underlying institutions of their oppression because the Versailles conference was well covered by the media. While some meetings were private, public meetings and proclamations provided these attendees with a better understanding of the global issues, the political competition within Europe, the purposes and terminology of imperialism, and the opportunity to meet among themselves and form stronger bonds. Though these delegations had no voice in the proceedings, they were encouraged by the discussions about a League of Nations, an organization that possibly could be convinced to address their subjugation at some future time.

The United States' position in retaining the capitalist world order was perhaps to be expected because America was in many ways an extension of Western Europe. Most American leaders and ethnic groups shared British, German, and French ancestry. Many of the American political and economic institutions were modeled from the ideals of historic European thinkers such as Locke, Rousseau, J. S. Mill, and Weber. Thus alliance with the United States was not such a radical change from European political and economic traditions; the unfolding structure of the rehabilitated international political economy still would be undergirded by European culture, traditions, and institutions. The emerging global system was to remain under the control of the West and capitalism.

There was an element of competition as well. Clearly, Europeans were reluctant to cede economic hegemony and therefore wealth, power, and prestige to the United States until the economy could be rebuilt. European leaders were cognizant of the fact that President Wilson was not simply being altruistic in pushing the enactment of his League of Nations. While Wilson was an ardent supporter of the liberal-capitalist international system, his priority was to expand American markets and influence and secure dominance of the Caribbean and Pacific. The United States had accumulated over $14 billion in debt as the result of the war;[5] after Europe rebuilt, the demand for American goods would decline—American farmers, manufacturers, and other producers would earn less money—after five years of impressive gains. This situation added urgency to Wilson's goal of expanding American markets by building a competitive merchant marine and protecting the waterways for free trade. Yet to become a presence at sea would put the United States in direct competition with its major ally, Great Britain. In addition to being allies, the United States and Britain were also competitors.

A Closer Look at Russia and Great Britain

Given the seriousness of the Russian challenge, one might assume that the United States and Britain would minimize competition in order to safeguard the capitalist economy, and to the extent possible, they did so. However, more immediately important than the consideration of the global economy was the economy of each state. Each of these nations was primarily concerned with its own preservation. Britain and the United States needed to balance their alliance agenda with that of the growth and recuperation of their individual nations. Already protests within each state warned that their capitalist-oriented governments could be voted out and replaced by socialist regimes; even worse, communism or anarchy were considered distinct possibilities. Each state had experienced crippling strikes in principal industries and state bureaucracies as well as riots after the war.[6] These concerns informed the redevelopment strategies of both states in terms of prioritizing the capture of market share and raw resources necessary to stabilize the home political climate and rebuild a strong reliable economy.[7]

Russia

At first glance, one can understand why Western Europe and America feared Russia. Russia could impede the rebuilding of Western Europe by disrupting labor relations and the administrative work of the political superstructure. The Bolshevists had cancelled all tsarist debts and thus could apply their resources to building a strong industrial base and increasing market share. Such expansion would likely mean that Western Europe in particular would lose more market share (much already lost to ascending economic nations such as the United States and Japan).[8] Secondly, unlike Western Europe, the old Russian empire had access to natural resources in nearby territories, such as Ukraine and Georgia. The "Russification" of these populations under the rule of the old Russian empire ensured that business and political ties could be rejuvenated and the resources used to fuel industrialization of the new revolutionary state. Third, Russia's revolution was perceived as highly contagious in that its radical economic philosophical base and egalitarian ideology was anathema to capitalists and white supremacists.[9] Any socialistic economic system would eliminate their control over the industrial sector and therefore over wealth and power. And here was a free state (that is, a state outside of Western control) initiating such revolutionary economic change: there was the possibility that socialism—or even worse from their perspective, communism—could infect Western Europe with unknown and uncontrollable consequences. Further, political dissidents and activists could hide within the Soviet Union and launch guerilla warfare.

From the perspectives of the colonized and marginalized of the world, such as the communities of the African diaspora, Lenin's thesis of the national and colonial question presented opportunities to gain resources and allies for their struggle against imperialist powers and improve their political status vis-à-vis these racist colonial powers. And because the Bolsheviki were interested in "darker peoples" of Asia and Africa, some African American activists considered the value of a coalition with the new Russian state.

It turned out, however, that the new state was not in a position to compete with Western Europe economically, and in fact needed capital badly for its new economic order. Several factors impeded Russia's ability to implement socialistic policies, including the challenges of implementing a unique political state in the face of internal dissension, a decimated agrarian base, and a declining industrial sector.[10]

BUILDING A UNIQUE STATE

Unlike Britain, Russia was not trying to revive a nation-state but attempting to *create* a new one based on an entirely untested economic system.[11] As Michael C. Morgan puts it, "Here was the first socialist state, alone in a feudal and capitalist world." And because it was first, it had no model to follow, only the theories of Marx and other revolutionary scholars. To complicate the situation further, Marxist theory applied to advanced industrialized states, not a feudal economic system like that operating in Russia at the time. To theorize about the need to replace a repressive state is far different from actually building one.[12] The Bolsheviks had to implement socialism by building new economic, political, and cultural institutions. According to Morgan, by 1919, the Communist Party had only 313,000 members out of a population of 175 million. The people, overwhelmingly poor, former peasants, and belonging to several ethnic groups, were unfamiliar with modern industrial and international economic systems, and their cultural and political roots were in the Russian Orthodox Church and tsarism. The war had cost Russia over 5 million lives and destroyed industrial and transport infrastructure. The Bolshevists had to repair war damages and resuscitate the economy while simultaneously guiding the people through the tumultuous political and economic transition to a new socialist state.

INTERNATIONAL RELATIONS

Even with serious internal problems, the new state was active in forging new international relationships. In 1919, the Comintern superseded the Second International and made its goal the implementation of worldwide proletarian revolution. There were efforts to work with socialists and communists in various countries. Lenin publicly expressed support for colonized and oppressed people including Africans and African Americans.[13] Though without adequate financial means, Russia did influence the politics of several countries, including Germany and Britain. Russia realistically could not provide military assistance, but it did provide ideological support for revolutionaries. The Comintern disseminated information worldwide denouncing capitalism and provided theoretical foundation for worker protests and modest startup funds for propaganda, such as newspapers and education in economics and alternative political strategies. Thus Russia provided political alternatives and information to workers, peasants, and oppressed ethnic groups that otherwise may not have been available.

The catch was that Russia needed wealth to rebuild. The theory that revolution would soon pervade Europe was premature at best, and Lenin was in the awkward position of acquiring capital from the West. Despite this conundrum, Lenin used the Comintern effectively in international politics.

It took time, however, for communism to permeate African American politics, as black activists sought a useful affiliation to push their own political agenda. Before establishing camaraderie with the Comintern and other labor movements, African American activists advocated and lobbied for communists to realize that race was as serious an issue as class. African Americans invigorated the discourse on communism as the ideological answer for the poor and marginalized of the world. One of the first black activists to join the party, Otto Huiswood, argued that the communist perspective of American racism was flawed and that this error ultimately would derail the movement. He posited that racism had put black people at the bottom of the economic scale where they could be paid less than any other group of workers. As a result, he argued, industrialists could reduce their labor costs by hiring black people and simultaneously enervating the labor movement. It was crucial that the CPU destroy racism within its ranks in order to further the liberation of workers and the poor. Other African American activists saw no reason why communism could not be conjoined with nationalism: just as East Indians and Chinese had a right to self-determination, so did African Americans. These activists pressured the party to recognize the unique position of African Americans and accept that race and class were twin iniquities as opposed to race being simply a subordinate component of class. The bottom line for black radicals was that racism had to be eradicated in communist parties so that it could be vanquished in the world. Further, the party had to resolve conflicts caused by the fissure of the American communist movement; it had to incorporate black activists into leadership positions within the party.

There were obstacles to incorporating black Americans into the party. Lenin had submitted the question to the Second Congress, and an in-depth discussion was held concerning the possibilities that their unique struggle and location would lead to the facilitation of global revolution.[14] Lenin posited that African Americans could be developed into an excellent vanguard cadre in the struggle against European imperialism in Africa and among the other "darker" colonized races. He also wanted (some would say naively) racism to be eradicated from the American party. Lenin apparently believed that the African American revolution could be folded into the world revolution against capitalism.

Of course Lenin's assessment was inaccurate because the priority for African Americans was to eradicate racism and gain political incorporation and economic access. African Americans were attuned to political and economic issues of the day, and many were educated, well traveled, and active in international politics.[15] African diaspora politics had worked for over 100 years to end exploitation, racism, and African colonization. African Americans worked in unions from the late nineteenth century, sometimes with whites, as in the shipyards of New Orleans, or sometimes forming their own unions, such as sharecropper unions. Further, African Americans had lobbied at the Versailles talks as well as advocated for change in their own newspapers and organizations.

Black radicals continued to argue their points of view and were able to place the issue of race into the discourse. But disagreement with white American communists prevailed, and while black radicals kept working to educate the party and gain resources and support for their American struggle, they also developed radical political organizations outside of the U.S. Communist Party (CPU). Even though the party underestimated racism, black activists could see how the components of the ideology could be useful to them both in America and in international struggle against racism. These activists knew that they had to deal directly with this contradiction in communism while trying to convince the black masses of the possibilities of working within the party as it evolved to understand race as a political issue.

This differing view of race constantly plagued the relations between black and white communists, particularly in the early years from 1921 to 1925. Blacks felt that even those white communists who advocated equality often practiced paternalism and therefore alienated black members. White communists believed many black members to be reactionary and often surreptitious nationalists, and so both groups felt frustrated in attempting joint action. Thus racism and different political experiences obstructed effective multiracial organizing among communist elements in the United States in the early 1920s. But it did not stop black radicals from organizing black communities using some of the propositions of socialist and communist theory. As a matter of practicality, black radicals had two components to their political strategy: dealing with the evolution of the party and creatively incorporating the economic analysis of capitalism into their struggle in the United States.

An example of the growth of black radicalism in the CPU and in U.S. black communities is the African Blood Brotherhood (ABB). Initially, the ABB was a clandestine organization that fought for global black unity and the eradication of racism. The ABB had been allied with the UNIA; several of its members were also members of the UNIA. Cyril Briggs and Grace Campbell had been associated with the Socialist Party and had followed the Bolshevik revolution closely. In fact, Briggs was at the founding meeting for the U.S. Workers Party. Persuaded by Lenin's "Thesis on the National and Colonial Questions," Briggs sought to incorporate radical principles into the ABB nationalist program and also attempted to form a cadre within the UNIA with the goals of transforming the UNIA ideology from capitalist to his synthesized ideology that embraced black independence and communist principles. Members of the ABB began to move toward communism in early 1921. Since the ABB was a clandestine organization, not much is known about its programming and membership. However, several researchers put the membership around three thousand and believe that there were branches in American cities and the West Indies. These historical studies estimate that ABB founders Briggs, Campbell, and other members formally joined the U.S. Communist Party in late 1921 or early 1922. It has also been established that the party helped fund the ABB's news organ, the *Crusader*. Along with other black journals, the *Crusader* had a wide readership and was highly critical of the UNIA and especially the Black Star Line.[16] These black radicals continued and modernized the traditional collective activism and unionism of the nineteenth century. However, black alliances with the CPU did not become significant until 1928.[17] By this time, several black activists had studied at Russian universities and agreed upon policies and programs that were conducive to African American needs. These measures made the CP palatable to African American activists, and membership increased throughout the 1930s and 1940s.

Britain

Britain's domestic politics reflected the changes in the international political economy. The hostilities that were brewing between capitalists and socialists on a global level were evident in domestic party politics and policy formation as well. To curtail the influence of socialistic parties and Bolshevik penetration, several influential Conservatives and Liberals retained the coalition government that had guided Britain through World War I.[18] However, an important contingent of liberals also joined with the Laborites and strengthened the Labour Party. The young Labour Party insured that the concerns of disaffected workers and returning soldiers were represented within government. And while the political division impeded the development of precise reconstruction policies, it also influenced Britain's position in the international political order. Of the major European powers involved in the war, Britain suffered the least from infrastructure damage. However, during the war, Britain not only financed the upgrade of its own armed forces, but as hegemon, it had to provide significant resources to its European allies. To augment the Allied forces, Britain disposed of nearly $1 billion of its foreign securities and incurred total war debt of over $7 billion.[19] The war debt, along with inflation, forced the British off the gold standard. Policymakers realized early on that the financial indebtedness had to be relieved or Britain would suffer serious economic and social consequences.

Therefore the key goals of Britain had to include increasing the national income and finding additional means to retire its foreign debt. It also wanted to stabilize the international economy by reinstating the gold standard. Increasing national income required the expansion of money supply. The expansion of money supply, in turn, was dependent on the amount of gold held in reserve. A committee assembled to determine Britain's financial options concluded that financial stability and reconstruction could not otherwise be achieved.[20] Britain's concern with the gold standard was not limited to economics; it was a matter of prestige as well. Having substantial gold reserves enhanced independence and power in both international politics and economics. Increasing national income and returning Britain to the gold standard required emphasis on the acquisition of gold bullion. With intense management of its empire, this was an achievable goal. Great Britain controlled (or held interests in) a significant percentage of the world's gold mines in its empire and measures were taken to increase production to prewar levels.[21] Since two of its principal mining sites were in Africa, Great Britain would have been alarmed by any political and economic activity within the colonized population that would have affected gold mining and the shipping of bullion to the metropole.

Another way to increase state wealth was to increase exports. Unfortunately, war had reduced Britain's exports by over 60 percent,[22] and even the reclamation of the previous export level appeared impossible. There are several reasons why this was the case. First, approximately 35 percent of Britain's merchant marine had been destroyed during the war.[23] Second, the economies of many of its major trading partners had been severely damaged, while at the same time Britain's economic competitors, the United States and Japan, had taken market share. Finally, the wartime economy had to be converted back to civilian control. In the meantime, surviving corporations required government support to contribute toward national income expansion. Britain achieved this by augmenting these corporations' functionality and productivity. In the case of the African colonies, this entailed insuring expatriate corporations unfettered access to raw materials. For example, the Lever Brothers corporation relied on the unrestrained exploitation of palm kernels in West Africa, including the Gold Coast and Nigeria, to manufacture soap and cooking oil.[24] Such unscrupulous exploitation further curtailed African land ownership, property rights, and income capability.

MERCHANT MARINE PROBLEMS

Britain had been the model laissez-faire nation, exploiting its comparative advantage by specializing in industrial production and importing not only the raw materials for industrial production but a significant portion of its food supply as well. The war exposed a serious flaw in this policy. To defeat Britain, Germany merely focused on destroying British cargo steamers and stopping Britain's seaborne resupply. It was an effective strategy as it depleted the British fleet, although it did not win the war. After the war, reduction of Britain's merchant fleet impeded the import of food and the necessary raw materials for the industrial sector. It also meant a reduction in revenue, as shipping was one of Britain's primary "invisible exports." It is often argued that the so-called invisible exports (shipping, insurance, and banking) buoyed the British economy even when its other exports declined.[25] Reinvigoration of the British merchant marine had to be an integral part of increasing exports. The British government was able to augment maritime services because of its wartime shipbuilding program; soon new ships began coming on line. However, the command economy was still in force, and the government made several missteps in its attempt to get much-needed resources into Britain and simultaneously coordinate the shipping of exports stimulated by the consumer boom. Ports became congested as the result of government storage of supplies in port sheds and the disuse of smaller ports because the newer ships were too large to use them. In addition, shipping was impeded by dockworker strikes.[26] British ships could not resume serving fellow European states because many of its former shipping customers were nations hard hit by war. A result was that shipping revenue stayed low because freight tonnage was down.

MAJOR ECONOMIES DECIMATED

The decimation of so many economies decreased demand for British exports. Eastern Europe was devastated, relying on America and other philanthropic sources for an adequate food supply. Germany had targeted France's infrastructure during the war. Plus, France had depleted its funds and borrowed heavily from Britain and the United States. It had little ability to resume importing British goods. The situation was made worse by the prostration of Germany.[27]

Britain's second largest trading partner, Germany was economically devastated by the war and by the heavy reparations imposed by the Treaty of Versailles. Germany was an integral part of the Western European economy, being the principal supplier and customer of Eastern Europe and one of the largest economies in Western Europe. As a result, the rest of Europe could not recover in the absence of the German recovery. As Keynes observed, the demand for reparations crippled the recovery of Europe because Germany did not have the wealth to pay for what it had destroyed and the incremental partial payments it did pay were insufficient to fund the redevelopment of Western Europe. Havighurst agreed with Keynes's analysis, pointing out that Germany needed to sell, not buy, goods. So not only were Britain's exports negatively impacted, it was gaining no "income" from unattainable reparations.

STRONG COMPETITION

Britain also had lost global market share to the United States and Japan. Even in export areas that had been strongholds for Britain, such as coal and shipbuilding, U.S. competition was noted.[28] The United States aggressively pursued markets in Latin America and invoked the Monroe doctrine to discourage European competition in the area. Therefore, Britain had to be careful in resuming trade relations in Central and South America. Through its Caribbean possessions, it had access to the region, but exploitation of trade relations had to proceed slowly even as British need was immediate. Japan not only competed in the shipbuilding industry, but it won markets in Asia and exerted political control in German protectorate areas.[29] Finally, the wartime economy had to be converted and returned to civilian business interests. This would involve reintegrating soldiers into industrial employment, convincing women and minorities to relinquish jobs they had obtained during the war, and providing benefits to workers that could not be absorbed into the contracting industrial sector. The transition was impeded by serious and persistent strikes, often in key areas, such as coal production.

EMPIRE STRUGGLES

So it is clear that Britain needed to retain control of its empire to rebuild its economy and market share. Britain needed unfettered access to gold and other materials to reinstate the gold standard and fuel its industries. It needed to retain as much shipping business as possible. But while imperialism may have been beneficial for the metropole, it was devastating for the colonized states and territories, the so-called periphery. The empire was composed of people who wanted to reclaim their independence and improve their economic positions. From the "white dominions" to sub-Saharan Africa, subjugated people sought to renegotiate their positions vis-à-vis Britain. The comprador class and other West African political activists vociferously protested the dismantling of indigenous institutions, their role in commercial relations between West Africa and Western Europe, and growing economic colonization. They gained momentum after World War I, advocating self-governing institutions and African economic development. To increase pressure and protest land tenure violations, efforts were made to form regional political protests groups, that is, an alliance among activists throughout the British West African colonies. One group that successfully organized was the National Congress of British West Africa, formed by the educated elite.[30] More avant-garde efforts also were undertaken, concentrating on land ownership, independent development, and retention of African cultural and political institutions.[31] Both ideological groups considered broader coalitions and interacted with diaspora organizations interested in African development.

In South Africa, unionism was a primary protest vehicle. Two major strikes occurred in 1919 and 1920, resulting in numerous African casualties. Africans resisted land seizures and peonage, and also worked with diaspora and other pan-African political movements.

African resistance to repression was not confined to the African continent. African delegates tried to participate in the Versailles conference, and their news organs provided extensive reporting and editorial coverage of the European meetings.[32] In London, several political organizations lobbied for African issues. Continental Africans, West Indians, and U.S. African Americans pooled resources and developed newspapers, letter-writing and leaflet campaigns, and lectures to publicize colonial repression, racism, and land seizure. These organizations held conferences,[33] protested to parliament, and defended Africans and West Indian workers accused of rioting when defending themselves against attacks in London, Cardiff, and Liverpool.

Colonial officials noted this political organization and opposition. In an attempt to curb opposition, Britain introduced symbolic legislative participation in West Africa. Nevertheless, African colonies and émigrés were thought to lack the military technology or organization to resist imperialism. This analytic view was imbued by British racism; Africans were considered intellectually inferior to Europeans, and African protestations and issues were routinely ignored in policy-making decisions.[34] The British government took a Machiavellian position: there was no reason to negotiate with militarily powerless groups. Imperialistic policies remained in place, but political opposition would be monitored. Several researchers document that the British used repressive measures, including the banning of political and diaspora organizations and newspapers in African and Caribbean colonies.[35] In addition, surveillance kept the British abreast of political activities.

Far from being insignificant actors, both Russia and Britain had reasons to influence and direct African and diasporan political discontent. Black transnational activism was not a military threat to these powers but a variable to be considered in political competition and the rebuilding of international economic institutions. For Russia, these activists could be trained as a vanguard to facilitate communist encroachment on colonial empires. For Britain, black transnational activism was yet another colonized rebel force to be monitored and destabilized if it interfered with redevelopment of Western Europe.

4

Home Dock: The United States and the BSL

For many reasons, the politics and economic positions of the United States are important to this study. First, it is in the United States that the Black Star Line was launched. At the time, the U.S. economy was the rising industrial power in the world. As a result, it was in the United States that workers had the best opportunity to make stable wages. This was true for the black population, both native born and Afro-Caribbeans; and thus it is arguably the primary place where blacks could consistently buy stock for the Black Star Line. It is also the United States that took on hegemonic responsibility to rebuild the international economy; and it was the United States that spawned (through continued regional imperialism and market expansion) a great deal of the economic growth and discord in the hemisphere.[1] Therefore, a chapter is devoted to the United States and its political environment that allowed the BSL to be born.

Regional Integration

By the time the Black Star Line was established, the United States had established political and economic control over the Caribbean region. Beginning in the late nineteenth century, the United States had forced economic integration for its own interests, which included control over the region's resources and market expansion. Labor migration was facilitated by the United States seizing and consolidating the sugar and fruit industries in the area and occupying states that resisted its control. The United States also gained control over nascent oil production in Latin America.[2] Economic integration assured a major goal of dominating not only Central and South American markets but opening a gateway via the Panama Canal to dominate the Pacific as well.[3] The distinctly American approach to imperialism was not to permanently occupy the Caribbean and Central America but to retain indirect control of inconvenient government policies and markets. Through this method, the United States already controlled Puerto Rico, Cuba, Nicaragua, and the Philippines. So even before World War I started, the United States had grown into the regional power in the Americas, which included much of the African diaspora. However, not only African diasporans but most inhabitants of the Caribbean basin opposed U.S. imperialism and resisted in any way possible the increasing domination and economic repression in the region. Many of these states and people would become supporters of the Black Star Line, unionization, and many forms of resistance and infrapolitics.

In total, the United States loaned Europe over $10 billion during the war. The United States became a creditor nation and a major player in international politics. In addition, the United States expanded its exports significantly. The financial sector provided farmers with loans to purchase more acreage in order to meet market demands for food in war-torn Europe. Industrialists quickly replaced workers sent off to war. Indeed, expansion of exports had been a goal of the Wilson administration before the war. Wilson had come into power as the result of a split in the Republican Party and had honed a coalition of farmers in the South (cotton growers) and the western states and capitalists, all of whom were interested in increasing market share in the international economy. Because of its size, the United States produced a surplus that could not be consumed within its borders, regardless of the phenomenal growth of national income. Wilson understood that America's meteoric economic growth would stagnate if the surplus could not be exported: inventories would mount, necessarily eliminating the need for continued production, which in turn would lead to unemployment. As a result, economic growth and wealth accumulation would decrease, and in the turbulent political environment that would inevitably result, idle workers and farmers might rebel, causing additional economic and political dislocation. Therefore, Wilson saw an ever-increasing need for export expansion.[4] Wilsonians were convinced that one of the best ways to increase exports was to expand market share in Latin America and Asia; thus, regional integration of the Western hemisphere, favorable to US. economic growth, became an important goal of the administration.

The Wilson administration and many business leaders sought to improve the export potential by selling to Latin America's stable and growing economies. Although these economies were relegated to the European controlled periphery, these countries had stable incomes and could become customers of America's industrial products and provide a dependable supply of raw materials needed in U.S. industries. The latter was important because European imperial states controlled the production of raw materials within their colonial empires; South America, at least from a Wilsonian perspective, should address the raw materials needs of the American hemisphere. The United States would provide its industrial products, such as steel and railroad stock, to Latin American consumers. The United States' foreign trade position would be greatly enhanced. For these reasons, the United States sought to replace Europe in these profitable markets.

There were other equally important reasons that the United States sought to curtail Western European influence in Latin America. The most important was to ensure the absolute control of the new Panama Canal. The canal was the cornerstone of trade expansion policy because it afforded the United States not only the reduction of distance and therefore transportation costs in its foreign trade, it enhanced the possibility of capturing significant market share in Asia and Australia. The United States then would be in a position to compete with the world's most powerful nations. To achieve this, the United States had to secure all approaches to the canal. This involved not only the circumvention of European power in the region but minimizing political instability and independent development of the countries within the region, particularly those adjacent to the shipping lanes from the U.S. industrial corridor along the Atlantic seaboard to the isthmus through which the canal was carved. U.S. ships would go between Cuba and Haiti and pass just east of Jamaica. Only Jamaica was still a colonial possession, under the control of Britain.

Wilson achieved these goals by modifying the questionable Roosevelt corollary of the Monroe Doctrine to include the monitoring and the selective replacement of European economic activity in Latin America and the Caribbean.[5] One strategy to loosen European control was the establishment of U.S. financial institutions in Latin America. U.S. banks helped facilitate trade between the United States and Latin America by eliminating the need for London to process various administrative aspects of commerce, such as currency conversion and credit options. This transition of the financial infrastructure in Latin America was seen as crucial. Wilson's secretary of state summarized their position: "A European power in control of the public debts of an American state and also with large investments in transportation, agriculture and mining could achieve domination just as completely as if it had acquired sovereign rights."[6]

Thus, the United States rationalized its emphasis on regional integration as the need to stop competing economic colonialism within the Western hemisphere. Regional political instability was addressed in the same manner it had been in the late nineteenth century: by political and/or military intervention, financial inducement, and occupation when deemed necessary.[7] Though these measures were often characterized by U.S. officials as altruistic or in the best interests of the region's development, Latin Americans saw the same measures as paternalistic at best and imperialistic at worst. As a result, Latin American and Caribbean countries preferred trade with Europe to counterbalance U.S. influence.[8] However, the war forced Latin America to accept regional integration as German submarines sabotaged shipping and European trading partners diverted their spending and production to their military needs. Latin America had no choice but to increase trade with the United States. According to Gilderhus, by 1919 the United States controlled at least 90 percent of Latin American import trade with the outside world.

The U.S. Merchant Marine

Wilsonians realized that export expansion would be vulnerable without the development of a strong merchant marine. At the beginning of the 1910–1919 decade, the United States shipped only about 10 percent of its goods in its own vessels; for the rest, Americans relied upon the European shipping industry, particularly upon the British.[9] However, the critical importance of shipping was not seriously addressed until the European powers diverted ships from international commerce to the war effort. This left American goods in ports with no reliable means to acquire shipping space. Dependence upon foreign shipping underscored Wilson's argument that profitable foreign trade depended upon a reliable merchant marine; he argued that reliance upon one's competitors for shipping was contradictory to sound business practices and economic development. Nevertheless, it was America's entry into the war, rather than commerce, that was the primary cause of an intense shipbuilding program. The U.S. Shipping Board (USSB) was created by Congress to deal with the shipbuilding program that was not only to provide warships but also oversee the development and supervision of the U.S. merchant marine expansion. Perhaps because the U.S. shipping industry handled so little of the country's commerce, the USSB did not have experienced administrators to oversee this important project. Paul Zeis argues that the shipbuilding effort became a pork program.[10] Shipbuilding contracts were given to companies with no prior experience in the industry; contractors were overpaid and materials overpriced. Cursory design led to the building of inappropriate ships. Perhaps if the war had not ended abruptly, the USSB would have had the time to correct its mistakes and build a highly effective merchant marine. But the war ended before many of the warships were built. Technical logic would have called for the suspension of building warships because they were no longer needed. But political and economic realities dictated otherwise. The Wilson administration was concerned about the transition from the command economy formed during the war to a peacetime economy that reverted control to the private sector. The transition was expected to cause unemployment during the retooling of the economy; added to this was the probability of reduced exports because war materials and equipment would no longer be in demand. To minimize employment dislocation, the Wilson administration continued to build unnecessary warships, several of which were wooden and could not have been useful in future military action.[11] In addition, the inexperienced USSB paid contractors for capital equipment and for the real estate (for shipyards) that would not be used for the intended purpose.

Inefficient building and management caused problems in trade as well. As predicted, there was an economic slowdown immediately following the armistice, but unexpectedly, a boom increased demand for consumer goods, and production activity picked up throughout the economy, including the export sector. However, industry-wide ineffectual management meant insufficient shipping space throughout 1919, and once again U.S. goods were stalled in ports. Many available ships had to be used in postwar tasks, such as transporting food to a devastated Europe and returning soldiers and equipment. The shipping space shortage impeded foreign trade worldwide. U.S. business interests placed extensive pressure on the USSB to release ships for commercial use. While smaller ships (under 4,000 tons) eventually were released, freight rate controls remained. These factors—growing exports, shortage of shipping space, and controlled rates—meant that shipowners could make considerable profits from businesses scrambling to get scarce cargo space. The USSB encouraged this development and also leased ships to companies that were eager to pursue excessive profits in this manner. The Merchant Marine Act of 1920 returned the significantly enlarged merchant marine back to the private sector, but by that time, the boom was transforming into what turned out to be a prolonged economic slump. Declining demand meant fewer exports to be shipped, but it was at this point that all the new ships came into service. The consequence was predictable: "Beginning in midsummer 1920, reports began drifting in that commercial tonnage around the globe was having difficulty in obtaining cargoes. The bottom fell out in December. By January 1, 1921, for lack of adequate business, the Shipping Board had tied up 468 of its approximately 1600 vessels. A month later, the figure rose to 513. By March 1, close to 35% of the Board's ships were lying idle in American ports, and eventually this figure would rise to 70%."[12] The shipping glut meant profits fell throughout the industry. In fairness, it must be pointed out that the United States wasn't the only major power to experience a downturn in its shipping industry: Great Britain and Japan experienced serious declines in shipping as well. Nevertheless, one could argue that the United States stood to lose more because it had to compete with Britain, the most experienced shipper and the United States' principal competitor.

International Relations

Economic nationalism influenced the United States' role in the Versailles peace talks and the rebuilding of Europe. However, relative inexperience in international affairs may have caused Wilson to underestimate the negotiating skills of Europeans. Wilson reasoned erroneously that Europe was financially in America's hands, and would therefore acquiesce to U.S. solutions. But with a history of war and constant involvement in negotiations, given the condensed area of Europe, the European leaders were prepared to withstand American pressure. European leaders held restrained respect for the United States but were fully aware of the growing imperialistic tendencies of the United States in Latin America and its economic aggressiveness in Asia. Thus, while the emphasis of the peace talks was supposed to be on political and infrastructure reconstruction, there is evidence that nationalistic and mercantilistic concerns pervaded the proceedings. While Wilson was not adverse to addressing these concerns, his solutions were fundamentally different from traditional European armistice agreements. Rather than simply dividing the "spoils of war" among the most powerful, Wilson wanted to implement what he termed a new liberal-capitalist international system.[13] This plan included an international bureaucracy, the League of Nations, that would handle the economic relations and disputes of the member nations.

Wilson sought to distribute wealth and minimize disruptive imperialistic relations by giving Germany's colonial empire to the smaller European states. He also advocated self-determination for Eastern European groups freed from disintegrated empires and for the so-called dominions. Then Europe and the United States would be in a position to "manage" raw materials in colonized territories as well as stabilize global markets in an orderly, non-violent manner. These points were approved. However, the German colonies were mandated to a modified and attenuated League of Nations, thereby leaving them vulnerable to exploitation by the Allied powers.

What could not be resolved was the substantial debts of the participants. The United States steadfastly refused to cancel the debts of the European powers and would only grant credit for much-needed food supplies, except for the literally starving states of Eastern Europe. In Western Europe, however, Wilsonians wanted to expand or at least retain some of the market share developed during the war. But the economic strain imposed on Europe by debt retirement slowed down revitalization. As the result, the United States drained the gold reserves of Western European countries attempting to repay the loans; these payments may have impeded industrial investment, which in turn slowed production and caused unemployment to rise. This may have contributed inadvertently to strengthening socialist and other worker protests in Western Europe. However, the United States could see that Germany could not pay the immense reparations of $33 billion. Ultimately, the United States loaned money to Germany to pay reparations to Allies, who in turn paid for American "liberty loans."

The United States impacted its own financial system by continued deficit spending, which stimulated price inflation. Its credit position toward Europe caused exports to decline because cash-strapped Europe had to cancel orders. This contributed toward domestic unrest and global instability. Thus rather than retaining markets, the American economy was on the verge of market contraction. Throughout the first half of the 1920s, the United States and Europe negotiated the war debt until finally the United States cancelled it.

Domestic Politics

The United States' relationship to Russia was entirely different, and it was concern about communism that most aggravated domestic political unrest. Warnings from Russian dissidents helped convince U.S. officials that disgruntled American workers would decide to enlist in radical political initiatives. Thus,

American antipathy for Russia and communism spilled over into domestic politics. The U.S. government and key industrialists were concerned about Russian government influence on American workers' movements. In 1919, there were over 2,600 strikes in the United States, some critical enough to impede production and even the smooth operation of cities. In Seattle, a general strike of city workers brought the public services to a standstill. The national guard had to be called out in Boston when its police force went on strike; a steel strike impeded production in that critical industry.

The most militant movement was the Industrial Workers of the World (IWW). Principally a socialist organization, the IWW organized effective strikes and had begun to penetrate several industrial sectors. Even though its communist leader had been expelled, industrialists and government officials effectively used the strikes of the IWW and other unions to vilify worker movements. Defamation became much more effective when bombs were sent anonymously to several government officials and industrialists, and paranoia mounted in American politics. The U.S. Justice Department organized an antiradical unit in its General Intelligence Division. Headed up by the young J. Edgar Hoover, the unit led raids on several worker and so-called radical groups, including educational institutions such as the Rand School. Local governments violated civil liberties in a like manner. The Lusk committee of the New York legislature, which was charged with identifying and eradicating radicalism, raided several political organizations. These governmental institutions used informants to infiltrate any organizations suspected of being enemies of the state, including African American political organizations. Using legislation enacted during the war, many people were detained; some were actually deported.[14] The ongoing struggle between labor and industry, the latter augmented by government, nearly destroyed the union movement. Union membership in both wings of the movement—the more conformist AFL versus the radical IWW—declined significantly. Repressive measures affected socialist political parties as well; legally elected socialists were refused their seats in the New York legislature.

Because the gross national product (GNP) and foreign trade were strong in 1919, perhaps some Americans, particularly nativists, believed that strikes were unwarranted. However, with the exception of some railroad workers and skilled laborers, working conditions and employment security were dismal. For example, textile workers and steelworkers faced unsafe working conditions, long hours, and low incomes. Technological advances had led to consolidation in many industries, and over a million Americans lost their jobs.[15] There was fear that returning soldiers would unravel the artificially tight labor market and reduce wages further.

The literature indicates that worker dissatisfaction was justified, but inadequate political representation and growing inflation may have facilitated strikes. Until the rapid development of the industrial sector, which had been facilitated by the war, political power belonged to rural America. The farming constituency (primarily nativist) combined with small-town patricians to control Congress and the presidency. By 1920, the census proved that the majority of Americans were urbanites; however, the powerful rural constituency was able to prevent reapportionment of congressional districts, thereby denying urban workers effective representation in government. Strikes were one of the few avenues through which workers and the poor could voice their discontent and economic plight.

The union movement was divided irrevocably, however, and unable to combine resources to engage industrialists effectively. The American Federation of Labor (AFL), under the leadership of Samuel Gompers, repudiated socialists and would rarely work with unskilled labor, people of color, or women. Gompers was powerful, a staunch Wilsonian and a labor adviser to the administration. The IWW leadership, on the other hand, was socialist, dominated by workers, some militant. Very active in the western United States, many of its members were attacked and pressured by U.S. law enforcement agencies. There were also natural fissures within the labor movement. Racism was prevalent in many unions, and blacks that replaced striking workers were seen as scabs, which exacerbated dissension. But African Americans, understanding that industrial employment was the principal channel toward economic advancement, took advantage of these employment opportunities and defended themselves against white labor.[16] While black thrusts toward economic independence are understandable, these racial divisions in labor strengthened the political capabilities of the industrialists and interest groups, such as the National Association of Manufacturers (NAM) and the steel industry, who both supported the Justice Department's attack on labor and financed public relations campaigns designed to vilify labor movements.

But because the progressive movement straddled the major political parties, the Justice Department's questionable tactics eventually were renounced and flagrant civil liberties violations subsided. However, the antiradical unit was not disbanded, and infiltration of political and labor organizations continued. The election of 1920 returned government control to the Republicans. However, Wilson's push for export expansion remained a key goal, and government retained strong ties to business.

Xenophobia and Racism

Contemporary culture and institutions are imbued with past mores, myths, and traditions.[17] Often members of a cultural group hold internalized traditions, political positions, and preferences without accurate knowledge of the origins. Prejudices growing out of ancient geopolitical conflicts and religious differences inform the views held by distinct groups. These political and religious issues migrated to America along with the Europeans. Ingrained attitudes conjoined with distance and time created the nativist constituency, which dominated American politics well into the nineteenth century, over 140 years. Nativists were primarily agrarian Protestants, patricians and the wealthy, and American government institutions reflected their values and culture.

Later immigrants came from Southern and Eastern Europe. They spoke non-Germanic languages and retained cultural institutions that were different from those of nativists. The immigrants were impoverished and settled in congested urban areas. They became the workforce of the growing industrial sector. Southern and Eastern Europeans as well as the Irish and their cultures were defamed, often referred to as the "great unwashed." They were vilified because of their religions as well. The diverse American religious groups carried within their cultural memories dissension between Catholicism, Judaism, and Protestantism. For these reasons, Southern and Eastern Europeans and other non-Protestant immigrants were marginalized. Their low political and economic status went along with abominable living conditions.

However, these immigrants were in a better position than people of color. Asian immigrants suffered racism in addition to the conditions suffered by their Eastern European counterparts. To contain the growing Asian population, Congress passed legislation to terminate their immigration privileges and exclude them from the political process. Chinese and Japanese people were attacked vociferously and their cultures disparaged.

The customary repression of the U.S. African American population became more complicated after World War I. As one observer noted, "the equilibrium between the races" was destabilized. Transatlantic immigration stopped during the war, and black and white men became soldiers. Yet the industrial sector had to continue expanding, not only to support Europe but to take advantage of the profitability that the war created. Government assisted in the organization of labor to fuel the war machine by creating bureaucracies such as the National Labor Board, which facilitated the organization of labor and unions. There was also a Bureau of Negro Labor, which African Americans used whenever possible to improve their employment situation. In addition, industrialists encouraged the migration of African Americans to the northern industrial sector to replenish the labor supply. This expanded African Americans' earning potential greatly, and they were pulled into the industrialized economy. This labor diversification altered American economic relations irreversibly.

Arguably, African Americans were the most derogated racial group in the American political economy.[18] Yet black labor was once again necessary to insure the expansion of the American economy. However, this time, without absolute slavery or feudalism, the African American population did not acquiesce to inferior positions in the workforce. As will be discussed in detail in the next chapter, blacks assertively resisted poor conditions through protests, institution building, unionism, and limited political participation.[19]

Eastern European immigrants and African Americans each impacted the economy and politics of the United States. The former worked primarily through unions; the latter, although involved in unionism where possible, also formed grassroots social movements. Through combined political activism and perseverance, these two groups managed to impede the repressive administration of the economy and therefore fueled and protracted political dissension in the United States.

The International Political Economy during 1919–21

This survey of the hegemonic triad—the United States, Great Britain, and Russia—underscores four aspects of the international political economy of the era that are key to understanding the motivations and strategies of the United States, Britain, and Russia, and the ability of the BSL to operate. The four components are:

Economic volatility and collapse
Defensive nationalism
Integral role of shipping (to recovery and growth)
Repression as policy

ECONOMIC VOLATILITY AND COLLAPSE

World War I destroyed British hegemony. According to Alan Cafruny, hegemony entails the leading power "accepting restraints, orienting policies toward the achievement of systemic stability."[20] He argues that "the hegemon practices self-restraint in order to maximize self-interest, granting concessions to maintain equilibrium." The leading power in the postwar era was the United States; however, with the decline of Wilsonians, the American government seemed uninterested in granting concessions or resolving systemic trading problems. This meant that there was no single power to provide collective goods and coordinate economic activity internationally. Exclusive of the United States, major industrial nations were off the gold standard and there was no other dependable international foreign exchange. Economic development relied upon the U.S. currency position and British Commonwealth's unstable economic infrastructure. Revolutionaries looked to Russia for support. All of this meant that global economic activity was unpredictable.

Adding to the uncertainty were the direct consequences of the war. The aftermath of the first technological war wrought unprecedented human and economic devastation. Human loss cannot be quantified easily, but one can conclude that in addition to the pain and hardship inflicted on families and society, the loss of the industrial, technical, and bureaucratic skill had a profound effect on the international economy and the three states highlighted here. This could only have complicated economic recovery, by weakening governmental ability to evaluate economic needs and implement the appropriate retooling of the economies. The extent of devastation and financial drain were unique. As a result, government officials may not have been prepared for the arbitrariness that permeated their economies. They had been correct to try to adjust to an economic slowdown; but they were unprepared for the commodity boom. Starting in the second quarter of 1919, the boom was fueled by the need to replace consumer goods, clothing and shoes for returning soldiers, housing construction, and growing demand for automobiles.[21] With the possible exception of automobile production, however, demand subsided by the summer of 1920: by the time governments had geared up to exploit the boom, a slump hit.[22] The recession forced governments to adjust financial institutions and mechanisms in order to withstand economic contraction.

The United States had an additional impediment: inexperience. The country had barely become an industrialized nation. In fact, the transition was still underway when the war began. The destruction of Europe's agricultural sector stimulated agricultural growth in the United States, growth that could not be sustained after the war. The demand was temporary, but nevertheless the agricultural sector was allowed to borrow and purchase more acreage. When the demand subsided, farm income declined. Loans could not be repaid, and banks serving the agrarian sector suffered losses. The industrial sector underwent a similar decline. War orders were cancelled, so industrial production had to be reduced. The consumer boom returned some vigor, but once consumers had replenished depleted goods, the boom abruptly ended. Corporate consolidation only exacerbated economic contraction. Figure 1 shows that the United States' GNP dropped over 20 percentage points between 1920 and 1921. In human terms, the slump meant a loss of over 2 million jobs. Figure 2 illustrates that factory workers could not go back to agriculture, nor could farmers go to industry. Both sectors were severely impacted.

The U.S. government sought to increase market share in order to restart its economy. But recall that Britain sought the same solution. Russia, in dire need of wealth, needed to access the raw materials of adjacent states, and would have obstructed the expansion of capitalism into Eastern Europe by either Britain or the United States. Each state assumed a defensive stance to protect their contracting economies.

DEFENSIVE NATIONALISM

The lack of an exclusive hegemon and severe economic dislocation helped stimulate nationalistic impulses among the three leading nations. Both Britain and the United States wanted to resuscitate their economies via export expansion, which caused intense competition. Both had to quell disgruntled

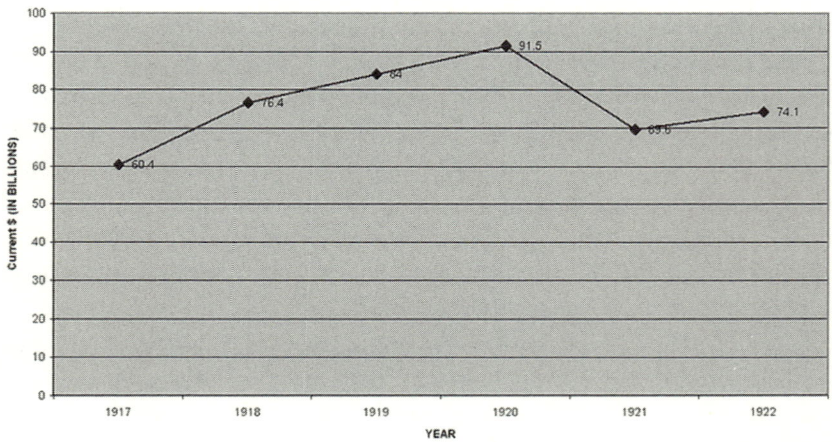

Figure 4.1. The American economy in 1920–21 suffered a slump, which was caused by a drop in exports to Europe for military supplies and food. This meant that production had to be decreased because there was no market for industrial and agricultural goods. *Source:* National Income and Wealth, Series F1–5, Gross National Product, Total and per Capita in *Historical Statistics of the United States, Colonial Times to 1970* (Washington, D.C.: U.S. Department of Commerce, Bureau of the Census), 224–25.

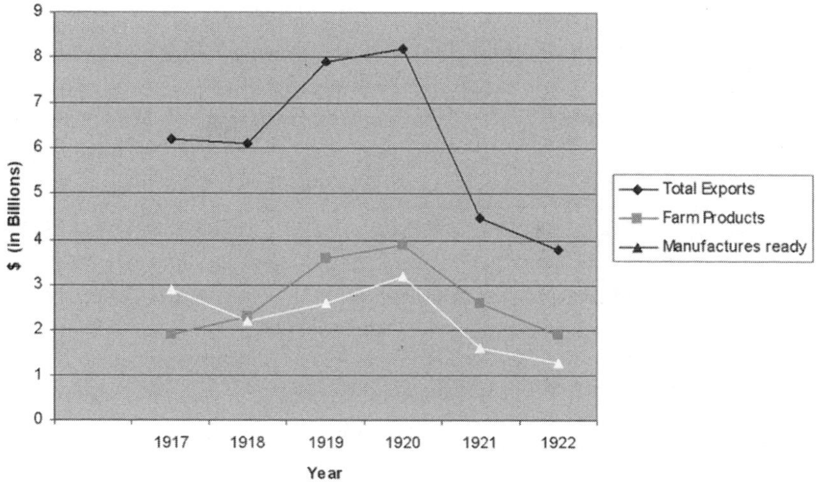

Figure 4.2. It was impossible for workers to transfer from industrial work to agricultural work because both sectors of the economy lost market share; thus unemployment rose considerably. *Source:* Exports and Imports of Farm Products, Series K251–55, and Value of Exports and Imports, Series U187–200, in *Historical Statistics of the U.S.*, 482, 884.

workforces, especially in the export sectors, to attempt expansion. They secured markets using all resources short of military force. They used clandestine activities, repressed weaker nations and organizations, and obstructed each other.

Britain and the United States were moving toward trading spheres, with British domination in Europe and Africa and the United States in Latin America, with plans to compete for markets in Asia. However, economic realities softened the rivalry. Russia and Japan presented serious impediments to Western European/American control of the world order.

Russia presented two problems. First, Russia inserted itself into European politics. It sought and gained a clandestine alliance with Germany. Russia allowed Germany to reassemble its military on Russian soil; in return, Russia learned from Germany and would acquire resources should a socialist regime come to power in Germany.[23] Other East European states gained from this alliance as well. Secondly, Russia could augment political instability in Western Europe and the United States by supporting political revolution and proselytizing economic conversion to communism to people justifiably protesting partisanship and inequity.

Despite racist theories regarding Asian ability, Japan proved to be a formidable competitor. Japan proved itself militarily against Russia, and its shipbuilding program was effective. Further, it was becoming an imperial power within Asia, and therefore could obstruct European and American penetration of Asian markets. With different cultural mores and economic organization, increasing Japanese economic strength would undercut the European-built economic structure.

Thus Russia and Japan presented similar problems for Western Europe and the United States, and may help explain the Red scare and reactionary racism. These possibly serious economic and political threats, combined with consanguinity, ensured an alliance, albeit fiercely competitive, between United States and Western Europe.

ADDRESSING THE SHIPPING PREDICAMENT

Before the war, industrial nations had relied on Britain for efficient maritime services. However, when Britain consolidated its maritime resources behind its war effort, international seaborne trade was impacted negatively. D. H. Aldcroft, a British economist studying this situation as well as postwar shipping, observed wryly, "All nations realized in the war that self-sufficiency in shipping was a thing to be coveted. The thanks Britain received for being the shipping servant of the Allies during the war was a recognition by them that their national fleets must be built up at all costs so that a greater proportion of their seaborne trade could be carried by ships under their respective national flags."[24]

Aldcroft accurately summarizes one of the reasons for the emphasis on the augmentation of merchant marines. Given the disorganization in the global economy and the need to retain domestic stability, industrial nations could not leave seaborne trade in the hands of the declining hegemon—which was now an experienced competitor. Another reason, of course, was to enhance ability to compete for markets and safeguard access to and control over raw materials. For the United States, this included maintaining control over the Panama Canal.

A strong merchant marine was also an important power symbol. In an article on the political economy of international shipping, Cafruny argues, "As a basic infrastructure of international trade, shipping is a key source of influence in world politics. The industry is an independent producer of wealth, an important lever of national industrial development, and a crucial element of military power."[25] In other words, a strong merchant marine facilitates preparedness for war. Germany and Britain had demonstrated the importance of naval vessels in modern warfare, and their naval power ensured the dependable acquisition of raw materials. Given the state of the international economy after the war, industrial nations had to be prepared to protect what they saw as their economic interests.

The United States was compelled by the same reasons as the Europeans to build up its merchant marine. In order to expand and retain market share, the U.S. merchant marine needed to outcompete the British in the eyes of future trading partners by exhibiting dependability, efficiency, and greater shipping capacity. To achieve this goal, the United States encouraged citizens, organizations, and businesses to not only expand exports but to consider entering the shipping business. This was one of the main purposes of the Merchant Marine Act of 1920.

However, this response may have proliferated inexperience throughout the U.S. shipping industry. The inexperience conjoined with political partisanship and mismanagement, documented by Zeis, and led to a glut in capacity. And because the U.S. merchant marine was second only to Britain in size, the shipping capacity glut may have contributed to the recession in the shipping industry and to American calls for complete privatization of the U.S. merchant marine.

To enhance its ability to increase market share in Asia and Australia, the United States had to have strong naval capabilities to protect its control of the Panama Canal. The canal enabled the United States to cut shipping time significantly and therefore allowed American companies to compete with the more experienced European traders.

REPRESSION AS POLICY

As discussed earlier, political chauvinism and racism were embedded within the ruling groups. This is true for all three states. Lenin tried to transcend historic Russian imperialism (Russification) in the area with more equitable alliances in the region. However, Russia continued to depend on the region's raw materials—a strong reason to retain political dominance over states such as Georgia and Ukraine.

In keeping with the Hobbesian argument that conquest entailed the right to colonize, Western European imperialism exploited several nonindustrial nations. Their imperialism was strengthened by their racist beliefs—both creationist and evolutionist. Floggings, land seizures, and serfdom were reported throughout the African colonies. The educated elite and nominal and traditional rulers were marginalized. Émigrés also experienced racism and repressive public policy in colonial centers. Returning white British soldiers rejected black economic competition as well as miscegenation, and racial violence erupted in several cities. In the British shipping centers of Liverpool and Cardiff, for example, racial violence led to deportation of black seamen and other industrial workers without due process and allegedly without pay.[26] In the West Indies, numerous strikes occurred to support the émigrés in Britain. They also protested income disparities and constrained economic opportunities due to racism within the colonial system.

The United States, developed in the same tradition, exploited and discriminated against the same groups as did Western Europe. Economic uncertainty in the post war era simply increased discrimination against marginalized groups, as returning white soldiers sought to displace black workers and reclaim industrial work for whites exclusively.

The repression that resulted from the violence produced undesirable (and perhaps unexpected) results for both the governments and industrialists. Industrialists, perhaps with government complicity, underpaid and overworked marginalized groups, including Eastern Europeans, Chinese, and African Americans. Goldfield, Link, and Kennedy all point out how some industrialists deliberately hired East Europeans and nativists to stop unionization.[27] During labor unrest, African Americans were hired as strike breakers, and they used this opportunity to establish themselves inextricably in the industrial economy. Fully cognizant of repression by experience, these African Americans realized that such actions weakened unionization. However, the reality was that African Americans were kept out of most unions due to racism and ethnocentrism. Therefore they took advantage of the strife between industrialists and unions to improve their economic growth and strengthen their communities. Thus unionists strengthened industry by excluding minorities. Knowing that East Europeans were disfavored in unions as well, employers deliberately and without fear of reprisal exploited workers to increase production and profits. Workers continued organizing; in the tight labor market caused by the war and brief postwar economic boom, strikes constantly dislocated production processes. As the union movement intensified, industrialists resorted to force and deportation. Government, focused upon expanded markets and repelling communism, supported industrialists.

The political discord between the U.S. government and business with African Americans was just as acute as that with communists and socialists. To prepare for the war effort, the U.S. government had passed legislation to manage industry to insure effective military production. African Americans lobbied to be included in this legislation and succeeded in gaining coverage under federal statutes that facilitated unionization and benefits to keep workers committed to the war effort. They were able to secure higher wages (albeit still lower than whites) in many industries, including steel, railroads, and government shipyards. Wartime legislation involving the railways helped African Americans to contend with unionists and white supremacists who sought to bar them from employment. When they could not join industrial unions, they formed their own. And since the wartime legislation enabled litigation, on occasion they employed lawyers to argue their cases. Having been involved in the labor movement since the 1800s, they understood capital/labor dynamics and deliberately served as strike breakers to achieve entry into the job market. As Orenic and Trotter point out, "Black workers fought to transform the federal government from an opponent to an ally in protection of their own interests."[28] Through lobbying, unionism (where possible), and political negotiations with local city officials, African Americans strove to improve their economic status and their society.

However, racism took more dangerous forms in the postwar period. Returning black veterans were attacked in an effort to discourage the push for political and social equality. But the equilibrium between the races had changed.[29] And when attacked, black people fought back, to the surprise of most Americans. Because of the rash of violence between the races, the summer of 1919 became known as the Red Summer. From the perspective of black people, these were the "Fight-Back" riots. For example, in Washington, D.C., Wilson's policies removed blacks from government positions, replacing them with whites. But in an ironic result, blacks found jobs in the private sector that paid higher salaries. Resentment over the pay issue, racism, and sensationalized journalism culminated in violence. Initially, blacks were attacked by white sailors, and without police protection they were vulnerable. But as it became clear that they were being attacked with impunity, the Fight-Back action unfolded. Blacks bought weapons and went on the offensive, meeting force with force.[30] There were injuries and fatalities on both sides. Officials finally restored order, but it was clear that black Americans would defend themselves both physically and through legal methods.

Most importantly, the way racism segued to unbridled violence showed that government and societal institutions did not provide adequate service or protection to black citizens. Because institutionalized racism was so embedded in American culture, bureaucrats did not require specific instruction to exclude black people. This is one of the principal reasons that African Americans strove to build institutions to meet African American political, economic, and social needs: integration into American society was not an option. Thus for their survival and growth, African Americans found collective investment in themselves to be imperative. The UNIA's Black Star Line was similar to other institution-building efforts undertaken throughout the black Atlantic.

Some political scientists theorize that it is during war and its aftermath that oppressed groups have a window of opportunity to improve their political and economic status. This is because the major powers are distracted and must focus resources and power on rebuilding and regaining strength and control of their states. Concentration of most resources within the home region greatly attenuates the capacity to control and manage colonized countries. The experience of 1919–21 lends credence to this theory. Cognizant of these circumstances, many groups, including Asians, East Europeans, Africans, and the African diaspora sought to reach independence, or at least improved political and economic relations with major powers. It is within this context that the Black Star Line project must be examined.

5

Charting the Black Atlantic: The UNIA and Its Location in African American Politics

Now we will survey the politics of the African diaspora, finally focusing upon the UNIA, the parent organization of the BSL. This discussion examines the UNIA's purpose and organizational structure, especially how it linked with and functioned in the African diaspora. This highlights how, with limited resources, the UNIA was able to finance and launch a shipping enterprise. This will be followed by the case study of the BSL, including its inception, structure, and performance. Contentiousness surrounded the project, even as it was embraced throughout the diaspora and parts of Africa. In the following chapter, I probe the case study, attempting to trace how it operated within the international economy given the interests of hegemonic states, opposition, and moderate resources. This project helps us gain insight into the dynamics of diasporan politics and how these resource-poor communities can impact international political and economic relations. A political economy approach is used to extricate the study from cultural aspects that tend to obscure the ongoing political and economic activism in the diaspora. With insight into political and economic institutional linkages, we may achieve a rudimentary understanding of how diasporas work in the contemporary, more complex global economy.

The UNIA emerged in the era when African American political options expanded considerably. Throughout the nineteenth century, African Americans were politically active throughout the diaspora. In both rural and urban areas, they resisted repression and found innovative ways to gain political voice and modest economic gain. Urban history research shows that even under terrorist conditions, they worked to protect members of the community accused of crime.[1] In such environments, they would challenge political authorities to uphold the law. As they interfaced with the mainstream, they became cognizant of the wide range of political ideologies and strategies. In the South, they built tight communities around their churches and lodges and defended themselves against economic repression. They formed mutual aid societies and farmers' cooperatives, worked within the Populist movement, and took their activist strategies and experiences with them as many migrated to the industrialized cities in the South and the North, and to urban areas of the western United States.[2] In their new homes, they continued to join political movements for racial justice and for workers' rights and to support black business development. While accommodationism, fathered by Booker T. Washington, still existed, community-focused activism was widespread. Black activists also joined the more avant-garde socialist and unionization movements when possible. They also modernized their conception of nationalism, often innovatively combining it with socialist or communist activism but especially reenvisioning the form the modern nation-state would take.

Consequently there was fluidity in early-twentieth-century political activism. Various ideological viewpoints were not as doctrinaire as past research suggests. Activists ventured to those organizations that seemed to be making political and/or economic progress for black people, making ideology a secondary issue. Throughout my research, I found activists moving from one ideology to another based on the effectiveness of the organizations that pursued those ideologies. As Michael Dawson points out, black activists tailored ideologies to combat the political and economic problems that faced them.[3] This study highlights the connection between supposed political adversaries. For instance, activists who had been a part of the Tuskegee machine became associated with the UNIA and used their connections to the Republican Party to address political and legal obstacles.

African American Politics, 1914–25

The era in which the BSL emerged was fascinating in terms of the metamorphosis in African American political options, which was caused by changes in the international political structure, which in turn can be attributed to structural changes in the economy. The first of these structural changes occurred in British economic policy. The largest colonial power, Britain dropped its protectionist policies for importation of sugar from its colonies.[4] This led to a fall in the profitability of sugar production in the British West Indies, which meant that black islanders had to look for better opportunities. The profit loss coupled with growing unrest among underpaid black West Indians led to completely restructured economic relations in the islands. West Indian blacks migrated to more successful sugar plantations in Cuba and Central America; some tried to subsist as farmers, specializing in banana production, which was less capital intensive but was a profitable cash crop. West Indians also worked on the Panama Canal and other Central American colonial economies. Those with professional training migrated to the United States and Britain.

In the United States, similar migration was evident also. Here it was not agribusiness but industrial development and segregation that fueled black migration from the agrarian south to industrial cities in the south, north, and west. In larger urban areas, in both the United States and Britain, comingling occurred between previously disparate black populations. In London and Manchester, colonized blacks from the West Indies and West Africa shared communities and race-based challenges. In New York, Harlem was home to a diverse black population: most were American born, but there were a substantial number of West Indians and a smaller group of West Africans. The specter of war only stimulated these migratory patterns and interaction of groups because industries needed workers. While some intermingling had always existed, even during the antebellum era, it did not permeate social classes and regions to the same extent. In the post–Civil War era, for instance, interethnic contact was dominated by transnational relationships between black journalists, scholars, missionaries, and political activists. Of course, black newspapers from various urban areas also circulated throughout the diaspora, and religious orders retained close associations. A plethora of research documents transnational relationships between these groups.[5] The structural changes in economic relations simply amplified and prolonged these relationships.

Nevertheless, the black responses to the politics described in the previous chapter were varied and were embedded in the political ideologies and the economic structure of the era. In the United States, the responses were entangled within political ideologies, while in the Caribbean, political responses seems to have been proscribed by economic relations. Because of this divergence in strategies, Caribbean and the U.S. responses will be discussed separately.

CARIBBEAN RESPONSES

In the early twentieth century, black political participation in the Caribbean did not extend to partisan politics. Although slavery was prohibited in the 1830s, the colonial political structure limited political privileges to white islanders and the educated colored caste. Racial discrimination was not officially responsible for this outcome, nor was it customary to acknowledge racism. Rather, racial discrimination was embedded securely in the economic structure in ways that excluded the black population from political equality and material resources. The economic structure was based on a peonage system made possible by denying reparations and education to the manumitted slave population. Destitute, most of the freed black labor force worked for pitiable wages, supplemented by subsistence agriculture. Caribbean economist Eric Williams explains the black workers' predicament: "It meant a change from chattel slavery to peonage, or, as has been said in another connection, a change from the discipline of the cartwhip to the discipline of starvation. The slave was raised to the dubious dignity of a landless wage laborer, paid at the rate of twenty-five cents a day in the British islands. Sweet were the uses of emancipation! To free the Negro it was necessary not so much to destroy slavery, which was the consequence of sugar, as to alter the method of production in the sugar industry itself."[6] And sweet, too, were the profits of the absentee investors and plantation owners. The United States' business profit alone in the Caribbean during the interwar years has been estimated at over $700 million annually on average. The principal colonial power's profits probably were much higher. Such profitability would have discouraged the elimination of the peonage system; no steps were taken to assist impoverished black workers to gain political voice. This structural poverty circumscribed ownership of already scarce arable land and obstructed political participation. There were black landowners, usually with small farms or banana plantations, but these were rare. Again, Eric Williams elaborates:

> In the British West Indies high property qualifications disfranchise all but a handful of colored and white voters. In Trinidad one must earn over $300 a year before he can be registered as a voter; the agricultural laborer gets 25 cents a day. Prospective members of the Legislative Council must own real estate to the value of $10,000 or derive an annual income of $1,000 therefrom. This is true, with variations, for all the British islands, with the exception of Jamaica, which has a 10-shilling vote . . . The privilege of voting, of membership in the Legislative Councils is restricted to the handful of whites and a fraction of the colored middle class.[7]

Ironically, this economic segregation ultimately provided blacks with access to political action. Overall, the archipelago is predominately black; they were the principal workers in agriculture, raw material production, and public works. Whites were landowners; the small professional class was dominated by the mulatto caste. The production and infrastructural workforces were therefore overwhelmingly people of color. The avenue into politics was organized worker strikes. Between 1919 and 1921, several strikes occurred throughout the islands.[8] The Trinidad Workingmen's Association caused significant economic dislocation in that oil-producing island nation. In Jamaica, strikes were coordinated between rail workers, dockworkers, and agrarian elements. Britain had to respond at least to their pay-increase demands. In Panama, where canal workers were segregated and wage inequality was severe, strikes turned violent.[9] Small farmers formed cooperative organizations and tried to develop independent access to export markets, particularly for bananas. Protests were taken directly to Britain, lobbying for political representation and economic progress. The ultimate protest was immigration to ameliorate structural poverty. Unskilled laborers immigrated to Central and South America in search of land and better employment opportunities. Professional workers and artisans went to industrial centers, including the colonial metropole, Britain, and the nascent industrial power, the United States. In these industrial centers, islanders became involved in a variety of political organizations, as they had in the islands.

U.S. AFRICAN AMERICAN RESPONSES

In the United States, the responses can be categorized in four political strategies. The first of these strategies was the pursuit of political equality or at least reasonable representation and participation in governance through traditional American liberalism.[10] This avenue was pursued through continued involvement in the Republican Party, which was still regarded as the party that had brought about emancipation and reconstruction. First, clientelism (accommodationism), the traditional institution through which black-white political relations were handled, began to decline. To understand the metamorphosis in racial political relations, one must go back to the refashioning of clientelism at the beginning of the twentieth century. Theodore Roosevelt had augmented clientelism to control the political participation of black Republicans. He had managed this by selecting what Michael Goldstein calls a national black power broker to control black politicians and their access to the Republican Party structure and therefore to power.[11] Booker T. Washington and the infamous Tuskegee political machine served this role by managing black Republican patronage in federal and state government for the Roosevelt administration and attempting to dispel black activism through the control of major black newspapers.[12] However, Washington's effectiveness was decidedly diminished by the work of independent and radical activists. Further, the Taft administration disenfranchised black voters in the electorally rich south in order to lure dissatisfied white southern Democrats to the Republican Party. Taft accomplished this by acquiescing to the demands of southern white Republicans for a "lily-white" party.[13] This reduction of black patronage positions further reduced Washington's ability to quell the activism among African Americans. By joining with political rebels and socialists, black politicians and activists in the North and South increased independent political activity. Though much research has focused on electoral politics in the North, urban historians have found that activism was deeply ingrained in black communities throughout the country.[14]

Blacks formed groups to affect electoral outcomes within their communities. This was possible because of demographic changes facilitated by industrialization, which had pulled together black workers with European immigrants to form a new kind of workforce in America's urban areas, particularly the North. With segregation placing blacks in contiguous neighborhoods, they came to dominate several electoral districts and could influence political outcomes or possibly win office and patronage as it related to government jobs and other public resources *without* the assistance of white Republican patrons. Their growing numbers in industrial cities like Detroit and Chicago augmented their ability to defend themselves and establish stable communities.

But yet another structural change influenced African American electoral politics. Patronage agreements between emboldened black politicians and the debilitated Republican Party were eroded by the growing political strength of the Democratic Party among northern constituencies composed of not only African American workers, but European immigrants and Catholics allying for political power. The Democratic Party first captured northern urban centers and then won the White House in 1912. Democratic machines, like the reinvigorated Tammany Hall in New York, controlled urban centers and began to make inroads in the growing black political electorate by the use of patronage and symbolic politics.

Blacks used the political recognition to their advantage. Goldstein suggests blacks had learned the value of territorial control and coordination: voting power, collective action, and lobbying, at least in the North, could increase direct access to the government. As a result, blacks began to diversify their political strategies. Lobbying and service-oriented organizations were fused with traditional collective protest strategies and became substantive vehicles for change in urban black America. These included organizations such as the NAACP[15] and the Urban League. Organizations of this political genre presented their positions and strategies to the public through newspapers: the NAACP in the *Crisis* and the Urban League in *Opportunity.* The activists most associated with this group of organizations were W. E. B. Du Bois and Charles S. Johnson. Note that the dismissal of partisan politics is not implied here; on the contrary, these organizations tried to influence the electorate by evaluating candidates and analyzing political issues and positions. Rather, these organizations put a creative spin on clientelism and legal activism. The NAACP, for example, achieved some judicial victories. Intervening to help black sharecroppers accused of murder and rebellion in Elaine, Arkansas, the NAACP managed to get their death sentences overturned and stopped the extradition of another black farmer charged in the incident. The case reached the Supreme Court, which concluded that the farmers had not received a fair trial, and eventually they were exonerated.[16] The NAACP also held marches in New York to protest lynching. It was the NAACP that tried to shepherd the Dyer anti-lynching bill through an illiberal Congress during this era and engaged the accommodations on the importance of political representation.

In the international arena, the NAACP and other black organizations organized transnational black activists and challenged racism at the Versailles conference and the League of Nations. It clearly was the forerunner of more efficacious pan-Africanism in the 1940s. At Du Bois's request, the NAACP underwrote Pan-African Congresses (PACs) in 1919 and 1921. These gatherings were sponsored to forge alliances with other diaspora and African activists and influence the administration of the colonies and the treatment of black people globally. Again, correspondence occurred with the highest government offices, including officials at the peace conference. But no meaningful concessions were won, although diasporan links were strengthened. News coverage of the PACs insured that colonial powers and revolutionary movements alike were educated as to the political aspirations of black people. Though the UNIA was interested in diaspora politics and African liberation, the NAACP and the Urban League disapproved of its nationalist position and joined other critics in deriding its programs.

The second political strategy involved coalition with the international workers movement through unionism and support of the Socialist Party. The strategy was to analyze economic relations and expose capitalism's role in the exploitation and repression of black people. African Americans explored socialism as far back as the establishment of the Colored National Labor Union in 1869 and continued to do so throughout the latter half of the nineteenth century with organizations such as the Afro-American Council and activism in the Populist movement.[17] Blacks participated in dock strikes at strategic ports in Louisiana and Pennsylvania.[18] Activists like George W. Woodley joined the socialist movement perhaps as early as 1896 and worked to convince the American working class and African Americans in particular of the merits of socialism through lectures, writings, and agitation. He advocated the benefits of socialism in both unionism and in the electoral area by giving a series of lectures in cities throughout the North. Thus, African Americans were aware of socialist theory before the mass migration from the South, and supported socialist candidates that advocated the elimination of racism and increased economic opportunity.[19]

Hubert Harrison was one of the most eloquent socialist activists in the early 1900s. He was one of the best-known and respected of the "soapbox" orators of Harlem. Active in various venues—education, journalism, organizing—Hubert Harrison chided American socialists for not championing the cause of the African American worker. Because of the hypocrisy and heated debate he witnessed over the issue, Harrison eventually left the party. While he kept his socialist principles, he went on to found the Liberty League, clearly the forerunner of the UNIA. The league put "race first" but retained Harrison's views on the usefulness of socialism and class analysis in the African American political struggle.

Other black activists involved in the socialist movement included A. Philip Randolph, Chandler Owen, and W. A. Domingo. With financial assistance from the Socialist Party, they advocated their strategies through their well-known monthly publication, the *Messenger,* and by participating in public discourse and supporting any program that either taught collectivist strategies or implemented programming embodying their goals. However, it was difficult to win black converts to socialist ideology during the early 1920s since it was often white workers who attacked black workers for various reasons, including for strikebreaking activity, just as Harrison had charged.[20] White workers wanted to eliminate black competition in the industrial sector, which was expected to contract with the demise of the temporary market for machinery and equipment created by the war. Not only was European demand for equipment and machinery expected to decrease, but once its industrial sector was rebuilt, it would resume competing with the United States for market share. Successful European competition would mean the United States' market share would shrink, especially if Britain regained its customer base, as they were certain to do in their colonies. This would translate into fewer American jobs for a larger labor pool. This structural change would drive down wages, and therefore the quality of life for all workers. For these reasons, white workers were the principal instigators in the riots during the infamous Red Summer or the Fight-Back riots.

American demography had been irreversibly altered. African Americans had attained resources, and their understanding of and participation in the American political system had been accelerated. African Americans had participated in the war effort and expected the promised amelioration of racial conditions in the United States: if there was to be self-determination for European states and dominions, then there should be for African Americans as well. Blacks had served as soldiers in Europe and had become more experienced in military tactics. In addition, they had become acclimatized to urban America, working in the industrial labor force and experiencing a more tolerable political atmosphere than existed in the South. Thus when attacked, black people fought back and refused to reenter the peonage system or abandon entry into industrial employment. With such tension and antagonism between black and white workers, unionism and alignment with white workers was not viewed favorably during this era.

Du Bois succinctly explains why black socialists faced difficulty attracting African Americans to unionism and the Socialist Party: "Theoretically, we are part of the world proletariat in the sense that we are mainly an exploited class of cheap laborers; but practically we are not part of the white proletariat and are not recognized by that proletariat to any great extent. We are the victims of their physical oppression, social ostracism, economic exclusion, and personal hatred; and when in self-defense we seek sheer subsistence we are howled down as scabs."[21]

Despite this criticism, black socialists advocated unionism but not uncritical support for the union movement. A. Philip Randolph and others agreed that racism existed in the movement, but they argued that African Americans could intelligently distinguish those unions that were not racist and focused upon the elimination of labor exploitation for all workers. For these reasons, they encouraged support for the Industrial Workers of the World (IWW). Randolph explained this position in the *Messenger:*

> The IWW is the only labor organization in the United States which draws no race or color line. . . . There is another reason why Negroes should join the IWW. The Negro must engage in direct action. He is forced to do this by the government. When the whites speak of direct action, they are told to use their political power. But with the Negro it is different. He has no political power. Therefore the only recourse the Negro has is industrial action, and since he must combine with those forces, which draw no line against him, it is simply logical for him to throw his lot with the Industrial Workers of the World.[22]

Black socialists also worked with community groups and initiated direct action (such as organized protests) where possible. They supported organizations that included some form of economic radicalism, whether on a domestic or international scale. These values led black socialists initially to support the UNIA. However, the development of the UNIA's merchant marine program affected this alliance as they clearly disagreed in economic philosophy: from a socialist standpoint, African Americans could ill afford to commit scarce resources to "speculative" economic development. The UNIA had chosen a capitalist strategy. Persistent reports of financial problems within the UNIA only increased socialists' resolve to safeguard black economic interests. These intractable differences were to sever the alliance. History emphasizes Randolph's and Owens's role in the coordinated offensive, which facilitated the dismantling of the BSL and skepticism concerning the UNIA's programming.

The third political strategy, affiliation with the Communist Party, was an outgrowth of African Americans' experience in nationalist and socialist political activism. It was clear that racism was prevalent and used to circumvent black advancement in all aspects of society: economic, social, and political life. But it was also clear that the transformation of the American economy called for attention to new economic opportunities and perils. Thus, all activists looked for ways to adapt their political activism to the changing economic and geographical space in which a growing number of blacks lived. Two advocates who saw the need for the conjunction of race and economic issues in the emerging industrial nation were Hubert Harrison and later A. Philip Randolph. Another group that saw the changes in the political sphere was the African Blood Brotherhood, which was co-founded by Cyril Briggs. The ABB was an outgrowth of the Hermitic League, a pan-African organization dedicated to the formation of a black nation-state and international coalition among African-descended peoples. The news organ of the Hermetic League was the *Crusader,* and it was to become the voice of the African Blood Brotherhood. Briggs and his associates retained the general nationalist ideology of the Hermetic League but added to it the radical position of the new Bolsheviks, who—from their perspective—had achieved a spectacular revolution in Russia. This embrace of communism put the ABB on the radical side of the split of American socialists, but the ABB was still at odds with the Comintern because they advocated for the recognition of racism as an issue as serious as classism. Thus the ABB carved out a new node on the spectrum of black activism. On the one hand, they agreed with Harrison and the UNIA that racial uplift was central to political activism, but on the other hand, they agreed with the radical position of the Comintern that capitalism is pernicious to the interests of working people.

The ABB incorporated some of the political strategies of the Comintern and accepted the latter's support for its newspaper. Using a strategy attributed to Communists, the ABB sought to "burrow within" the UNIA and become the core cadre of the organization. But even though the UNIA accepted strategies such as unionism in the Caribbean, it did not adhere to such strategies in its U.S. branches because of the rabid racism in America's unions. The result was that the ABB's overtures to the UNIA membership were rebuffed; however, interest in the Communist Party did take root. Nevertheless, it was well past the zenith of the UNIA when communism began to emerge in black politics. Some researchers would argue that it was not until the 1930s that black communists gained voice in the community.

At the same time that Briggs was working to inject communist theory into black political struggle, ABB members worked to change the Communist Party, constantly advocating the addition of racism as an insidious problem for workers in America. The members of the ABB were instrumental in the efforts to convince the Comintern that racism was a corrosive force just as bad as white labor exploitation. In later years, the Comintern would become involved with the black workers' dilemma in America and establish several programs including the American Negro Labor Congress. Further pressure and lobbying by black communists led to the Com intern's thesis of a "nation within a nation," and activists worked to operationalize that black nation in America's South based on Communist principles.[23] Briggs also became a vitriolic critic of the UNIA in his newspaper the *Crusader;* during the imbroglio that followed, the federal government was able to use black activists' charges of fraud and totalitarianism to prosecute the BSL directors.[24]

The fourth strategy, black nationalism, historically construed, fits the basic archetype of Western nationalism.[25] The primary goal is to build a nation exclusive of other races and based upon a specific ideological position, usually Western in origin. The UNIA's paradigm was born out of the Western nationalist tradition and embraced an industrialized economic structure. Black nationalists associated with the UNIA did not wish to remain within a white-dominated or even a multicultural state. Ultimately, complete separation was required although some laws and institutions would be Western in tone.

The UNIA's ideology evolved over time, progressing from confraternity as the primary aim to a "pan-African" position, and finally to the goal of building an exclusively black westernized nation. In fact, it could be argued that, more than a state, the UNIA intended to build an empire because its agenda called for the absorption and transformation of the entire African continent to the political ideology and economy of the UNIA.[26]

Most studies on the UNIA focus on Marcus Garvey, the principal founder of the organization. But the mass organization could not have been and was not built by one person or personality. This is not to say that in-depth character studies are not useful in helping researchers to understand a political era. Nor is it to discount the legendary organizational skills of Garvey. Rather, it is to point out that studies focusing only on the recognized leader of an organization or movement discount the fundamental necessity of experienced manpower, skills, and commitment among members to organize political activism and programming.

Garvey was the chief spokesperson; he was the authoritarian (but absentee) manager of administrative affairs and programming at UNIA headquarters. His main role was creating and holding the interest of the black public in the organization and its programs; because of his eloquence and appeal he was the major fund-raiser, and he traveled extensively. These two crucial jobs kept him out of the UNIA headquarters, and others had to take care of daily administration, map out programs, and plan events. Most importantly, seasoned lawyers and journalists kept both the New York district attorney and attackers from competing organizations—via their newspapers—at bay.

Garvey was no preordained messiah, with African Americans throughout the diaspora waiting with baited breath for him to come and rescue them. On the contrary, there were many political organizations and respected spokespersons well established not only in Harlem, but other parts of the country and throughout the diaspora. So Garvey had to find a way to get his positions heard and his programs considered in an intensely competitive political arena, just as his rivals did. He had to work with others; he had to win the trust and respect of politically seasoned African American activists, who by this time had over fifty years of experience with the Republican Party, Populists, and Socialists as well as linkages with nationalists throughout the diaspora and in West Africa. There were also liaisons with diasporan organizations around the black Atlantic, including in Britain, Africa, and the Caribbean.

The Backbone of the UNIA: Veteran Activists

The validation of veteran activists was key to the Black Star Line being considered worthy throughout the diaspora. In particular, black journalists/

activists based in the United States corresponded with their counterparts abroad to help to sell the BSL venture. For example, John Edward Bruce, a popular journalist and UNIA advisor, corresponded with Dr. Robert Love in Jamaica about the venture as well as with Caseley Hayford, an African lawyer and activist, in the Gold Coast. Gold Coast activists did not embrace the UNIA's political program, but they did embrace the Black Star Line.[27] Seraile points out the importance of men like "Bruce Grit," a newspaper columnist's pen name that alluded to his acerbic style and reputation for truth-telling, to the internationalization of the UNIA and its Black Star Line: "This point cannot be underestimated. Bruce was able to bring into the Garvey movement many race-conscious men and women because of his contacts in West Africa and the Caribbean."[28]

Another important activist to the BSL effort was Henrietta Vinton Davis, an elocutionist and actor. She had been in several plays and had spoken at many events before joining the UNIA: she was a popular performer who would draw many people to mass meetings featuring her and the BSL Choir. Their performances would be followed by speeches of UNIA politicians and administrators. Davis was also a key international organizer for the BSL, raising thousands of dollars for the effort in the Caribbean. Further, she served as Garvey's lead administrator after his deportation in 1927.

The black lawyers on retainer for the UNIA and BSL were indispensable. In 1919, attorneys circumvented the New York district attorney's efforts to stop the organization's programs. And it was these lawyers, William Matthews and Wilfred Smith, who outmaneuvered Hoover and other political officials who tried to keep Garvey out of the country after he had completed a fund-raising tour in the Caribbean. These attorneys had worked within the Republican Party and/or for other well known activists such as Booker T. Washington. They interacted with black Republicans and arranged for Garvey to return to New York. Had they represented him at his trial, rather than him representing himself, he may have won the case or at least avoided deportation.

Because it was to be a thoroughly black venture, black ship captains were invaluable. In the entire shipping industry, there were only three black captains, and all of them volunteered to work on the BSL. They eventually became critical of the effort because of the authoritarianism of the UNIA leadership. However, one captain, Joshua Cockburn, may have misrepresented himself, as he served as a broker for the sellers of the *Yarmouth,* meaning that he earned a commission from the sale. It is Cockburn who suggested that the line buy the Yarmouth.

There was an international facet to African American politics *before* the advent of UNIA popularity; even in the rural sections of the islands and America's segregated South, there is evidence that people received a variety of newspapers on a regular basis.[29] There was a plethora of black newspapers from all regions of the diaspora, all giving different ideological perspectives on contemporary politics. Further, in larger cities such as New York, Chicago, and Boston, blacks avidly consumed mainstream newspapers and journals; the same is true for black populations in Western Europe. So while some assume that blacks were politically unsophisticated and ready targets for fraud, the historical evidence suggests a politically informed African American population. Others point to the UNIA as causing divisions between educated and lower-class groups, but the tension between middle-class black leadership and working-class blacks was well entrenched before the Black Star Line existed. African Americans were not naive nor were they homogeneous—especially in Harlem, which was the location of the UNIA's headquarters and center of most of its activities. There was an intermingling of blacks from different parts of the United States, with varying levels of education and different cultural norms. Further, there were people from the Caribbean and those who had gone first to Central America or England before migrating to the United States, as had Garvey, and finally there was a sprinkling of West Africans among them.

This is the political environment into which the UNIA launched its merchant marine, the Black Star Line. Given the political suppression, new (albeit limited) economic freedoms, and unprecedented access to information in black communities, the politics were intense, and from varied perspectives. At times interaction between African American political organizations was confrontational, but there were also coalitions since for the most part their goal was the same: for black Americans to have political and economic parity with white citizens.

A discussion of the political history of the UNIA will help the reader to better understand the political goals, development, and challenges of the UNIA. And grasping these variables is key to understanding the operation and problems of the Black Star Line.

UNIA Goals and Structure

Because of the political climate of the beginning of the twentieth century, in particular intensified economic discrimination, black "nationalist" advocates were attracted to the UNIA's ideals and programming. Initially, the UNIA was a Jamaican "confraternity" established to ameliorate the obstacles impeding the freedom and development of the entire "Negro" race. The organization was founded in 1914 in Jamaica and concentrated primarily on apolitical goals of education and etiquette of its membership and supporters.[30] The largest documented UNIA project in its Jamaican era was a plan for a vocational school modeled after the Tuskegee Institute, a noted black vocational college located in Alabama. The search for funds for the vocational school brought Marcus Garvey to the United States in March 1916. Consequent touring of the United States enhanced Garvey's understanding of the political and economic problems and possibilities of the African diaspora beyond the situation of British colonized blacks.[31]

Perhaps convinced that confraternity could be facilitated in the United States, Garvey relocated the UNIA headquarters to Harlem, New York. With the support of Hubert Harrison, a noted Harlem political activist, Garvey became involved with U.S. black politics in the Liberty League. The first U.S. chapter of the UNIA was inaugurated in 1917. Within a year, fraternal objectives evolved to uplift goals through political and economic means. Educational programming was modified to focus on psychological rejuvenation, with lectures on African history and poignant explanations of the economic determinants that had caused African slavery and continued oppression of black populations into the twentieth century.

The solutions, Garvey and other UNIA spokesmen emphasized, involved organizing institutions that reversed economic dependence and facilitated political freedom. In keeping with these goals, the UNIA purchased a one-story structure that became known as Liberty Hall. Political and social programming was held in the building throughout the week and on weekends. Programming was well organized and involved talented speakers and educators, always with a political message that either addressed contemporary political problems of the race or focused on the historic (or contemporary) events believed to have contributed to them. Often both were covered during one event.

One of the attractive elements of UNIA programming was the inclusion of music and literary arts: programs always included musical selections, professionally presented. Acclaimed dramatist Henrietta Vinton Davis often performed dramatic readings and served as the introductory speaker for the programs' orators. Her popularity with black audiences nationally insured reasonably large audiences at UNIA events. The performances usually were followed by an address by a well-known minister or professor; the message here was usually motivational in terms of spirituality or racial pride. Finally, the principal speaker, often Marcus Garvey, would speak. Known for his oratory, the well-read Garvey would analyze contemporary political events, focusing on the issues detrimental to black progress. His analyses frequently demonstrated an understanding of complicated political and economic matters. His eloquence permitted him to offer provocative, very detailed but theoretical UNIA solutions and programs that would achieve independence for black people.

Other tactics increased the UNIA's power base in the black community. For example, Garvey often sent telegrams to world leaders and noted activists and would read the responses (usually from social secretaries or public relations officers) at UNIA events.[32] Further, he would permit political activists, some of whom received regular news coverage, to present their cases and movement ideology to the audience.[33] African American activists including Ida B. Wells, A. Philip Randolph, and African activists addressed the audiences. Even white revolutionaries were allowed to speak, including socialists and Irish representatives of Sinn Fein. These spokespeople demonstrated the possibility of revolution among marginalized populations, the necessity of escalating political struggle to attain racial equality. UNIA spokespeople often compared the plight of the African diaspora to that of the groups that these guest speakers represented or to historical plights that racial or ethnic groups overcame—against seemingly impossible odds—to attain sustainable nationhood and power. For example, Garvey spoke about nineteenth-century Germany and how it overcame seemingly insurmountable obstacles to be an industrial power:

> When we can as a race settle down to business with honesty of purpose, we will be on the way to the founding of a permanent and strong position among the nations and races of the world. Commerce and industry were the forces that pushed the great German Empire to the front. As it can be remembered, during the first Napoleonic era, Germany was regarded as the pauper nation of Europe, whilst England and France had reached a high state in commerce and industry, having their merchant marines sailing to and anchoring in every port of the world; Germany was without steamships. The German was looked down on then, even as the Negro of the South is looked down on today. . . . These are fair examples of how a people can rise to greatness when they apply themselves to any one good thing without faltering.[34]

The Japanese, as an example of a people of color making a successful transformation into an industrial power, were often used as a model to emulate. These illustrations supported the UNIA argument that the reinstitution of independent black political and economic status were achievable goals, given adequate time, organization, and resources. This commitment to political and economic independence may have added prestige to Garvey personally and to UNIA programs generally.

Surely the inclusion of artists was an ingenious move. One cannot proselytize to an empty venue; one must first attract potential followers. Even the UNIA constitution called for music and choir performances at all organization functions. Such organizational methods seem to have facilitated the UNIA's ability to establish divisions and recruit and retain membership. The methods paid off: it became the first mass political movement in the African diaspora.

Constitution and Bylaws

At its inception, the organization actually had two components. One, the UNIA, was responsible for the fraternal and social programs. The second component was the African Communities (Imperial) League (ACL), which was to develop the organization's commercial wing, linking black communities throughout the diaspora and Africa. According to Hill, the African Communities League was to be "the umbrella wing of the organization under whose auspices the Black Star Line, the Negro Factories Corporation, the Negro World [journal], the leasing of Liberty Hall and UNIA offices, and the establishment of other UNIA and ACL endeavors (restaurants, laundries, hotels) officially operated."[35] Perhaps due to their disparate functions, these institutions were incorporated in New York separately. But for all practical purposes, they melded into one organization, which most referred to as the UNIA. The growing membership was forged into a well-oiled machine made possible by a meticulously written constitution.[36]

The UNIA also provided services. Meals were provided for impoverished and unemployed black citizens. Temporary shelter was available in Liberty Hall. A death fund was institutionalized for the families of deceased members. The Black Cross Nursing Corps was established to teach health. As commercial programs were developed, an additional benefit was that they employed UNIA members.

The UNIA constitution is invaluable in dissecting the political and financial structures of the UNIA. It also underscores the transcendent influence that Western political institutions, particularly British ones, had on the UNIA leadership. The constitution reutilized organizational activities and clearly outlined the chain of command. Article 5 vested political and administrative power in the potentate and the president-general/administrator, with the latter having the operative power. (Marcus Garvey was the president-general/administrator of the UNIA.) Other important officials include the following:

The counsel-general was responsible for the legal affairs of the organization.

The secretary-general, who also managed branch secretaries, handled all correspondence.

The high chancellor was the highest-ranking financial officer, with primary custodial responsibility for UNIA funds. All treasurers and assistant treasurers of chapters and branches were his subordinates. Audits were to be conducted twice yearly and financial officers were bonded.

The executive council included these and other high-ranking officials. The council resolved disputes, developed policy, and addressed political issues.

Finally, procedures were incorporated governing modification of the constitution. Such amendments were to be considered only during the UNIA's convention held annually in August, to which each chapter and branch could send a delegate. Because of the transnational reach of the UNIA, the conventions were international in scope. Attendance varied between three and five thousand annually throughout the 1920s.

The UNIA established chapters in most major cities, including New York, Chicago, Boston, Philadelphia, Los Angeles, and New Orleans; most states had chapters, including the southeastern United States. According to the constitution, a charter would be granted if at least seven people of "intelligence and good character" were committed and willing to safeguard the principles and goals of the UNIA. If more than one chapter was established in a state, then the original chapter would be the "charter chapter" and, as such, was assigned a supervisory function for all subsequent chapters in said state. During the UNIA's high point, when some cities reportedly had over 5,000 members, hierarchical structure became even more stratified, being organized into principal regions.

Administrative distinction had to be made between *chapters* in the United States and *branches* in colonial areas because of colonial policy regarding civic organizations. Branches were established throughout the Caribbean, both British- and Spanish-speaking islands; there were also branches in West Africa and in South Africa. Often branches were interlinked with labor organizations. For example, the UNIA was intermixed with the Industrial Workers and Commercial Union in South Africa.[37] But even with this administrative complication, branches were thoroughly integrated into the UNIA government structure and participated in its programs. Chapters and branches were structured to link with the UNIA's headquarters in New York. Each had a president, secretary, and treasurer working in unison with their superiors in New York. These factors speak to the membership management capability of the UNIA and to the strength and unifying efficacy of the constitution. Effective management and discipline ensured vital communications links for uniform policy implementation.

Two additional factors further enhanced this communication. The establishment in late 1918 of the *Negro World* assured consistency and standardization in the information delivered to the membership, supporters, and the public.[38] Thus membership could conform to policy and ideological positions of the UNIA executive. While effective information delivery did not quell rumor or criticism, it may have diffused the impact of both. The *Negro World* extended the UNIA's ability to educate its members as well as interpret breaking news events for them. Finally, the *Negro World* proved to be an effective recruitment tool and sales instrument for the UNIA's commercial ventures, particularly BSL stock.

The second policy that facilitated the UNIA's stability and strength was that each chapter own or rent a building (Liberty Halls) in which to conduct organizational business and hold meetings and other functions. Such ownership may have deterred interruption of UNIA programming by government and other oppositional forces. This proved to be important because the federal government did discourage building owners from renting halls or auditoriums to the UNIA; in other instances, building managers were encouraged to inform government authorities of all dates that UNIA functions would be held.[39]

Access to relatively stable funding cannot be overemphasized in any explanation of the UNIA's effectiveness and durability. Membership dues were 25 cents per month, of which one-fifth was forwarded to headquarters to finance ongoing programming. Members also paid 10 cents per person for a death benefit, and it too was forwarded to New York. Fund-raising and donation revenues were divided between locals and headquarters. At the height of its popularity and legal entanglements, the UNIA established a $1 annual tax to meet the growing bureaucratic, legal, and financial needs of the organization.

Evolution from Organizational Activism to Nationalism

The UNIA's Jamaican programs seem to have been apolitical, focusing on educational and social development. Once established in the United States, the organization began to enter political waters. In 1918, the UNIA supported the political efforts of the Liberty League founded by Hubert Harrison.[40] Outraged by racial pogroms and continued disenfranchisement, the league aggressively and independently organized self-defense efforts and lobbied Congress to prohibit lynching through federal statutes. Concern for employment and economic exploitation was also addressed. The league's impact seems to have been minimal, and within a year many league members had become a part of the UNIA. Harrison became an effective editor for the *Negro World.* The organization became more focused on independent development, as there was little indication that government would alleviate the growing economic and political discrimination against black people. Elements of self-determination began to be integrated into UNIA's agenda for mitigation of these problems.

These modifications in outlook may have increased their interests in the Paris peace conference. The conference's imperialistic approach to the African colonies focused the UNIA's attention on the need for independent African and diasporan economic development. The UNIA lobbied against the peace treaty for these reasons. And as returning white soldiers displaced black industrial workers, the UNIA also began to prioritize business development and trade possibilities between black populations:

> If we are to rise as a great [people] to become a great national force, we must start business enterprises of our own; we must build ships and start trading with ourselves between America, the West Indies and Africa. We must put up factories in all the great manufacturing centers of this country, to give employment to the thousands of men and women who will be thrown out of work as soon as the nation takes on its normal attitude. In these factories we must manufacture boats, clothing, and all the necessaries of life, those things that the people need, not only our people in America, the West Indies and Africa, but the people of China, of India, of South and Central America, and even the white man. He has for hundreds of years made a market for his goods among Negroes and alien races; therefore, Negroes have the same right to make a market among white people. . . . When we can as a race settle down to business with honesty of purpose, we will be on the way to the founding of a permanent and strong position among the nations and races of the world.[41]

Here, we begin to detect the kernels of a rising aggressiveness in the UNIA's political and economic intentions. This passage does not discuss voting, and it seems to indicate movement away from lobbying as a tool to protect and develop their constituents' interests. Independent development began to emerge as the exclusive remedy.

I would argue that the organization of the UNIA began its metamorphosis toward nationalism at this point. It moved beyond defending the race against violence and discrimination and began to take the offense. That is to say, rather than working to develop an independent economic and political structure within the U.S. political economy, and working toward entry into the international economic structure as an American business, it began to argue for complete separation from the governance of the United States or Western Europe and toward the development of its own economy within an African empire. Comparing the UNIA's goals as explained in its constitution to its actual modus operandi—the goals of its projects—after the Great War substantiates this point. The constitution states in section 3 that the UNIA's policies toward black people internationally would be beneficent and politically supportive:

> The objects of the UNIA&ACL shall be: to establish a universal confraternity among the race; to promote the spirit of pride & love; to reclaim the fallen; to administer to and assist the needy; to assist in civilizing the backward tribes of Africa;[42] to assist in the development of independent Negro Nations & Communities; to establish Commissionaries or Agencies in principal countries and cities of the world for the representation and protection of all Negroes, irrespective of nationality; to promote a conscientious spiritual worship among the native tribes of Africa; to establish Universities, Colleges, Academies and schools for the racial education and culture of the people; to conduct a world-wide commercial and industrial intercourse for the good of the people; to work for better conditions in all Negro communities.[43]

Section 3 stops short of calling for the development of an independent state over which the UNIA would govern or participate. But the allied powers' decision to grant administration of the former German colonies in Africa to the League of Nations, along with the growing violence against returning black soldiers and intense discrimination in the employment sector, raised such ire in the UNIA ranks and leadership that the rhetoric moved beyond the original goals of the organization. Again, Garvey:

> They called us out but a few months ago to fight three thousand miles away in Europe to save civilization, to give liberty and democracy to the other

> peoples of the world. And we fought so splendidly, and after we died, after we gave up our blood, and some of us survived and returned to our respective countries, in America, in the West Indies, in Central America and in Africa, they told us, as they told us in the past, that this country is the white man's country. What is but menial opportunities for you where you live in contact with white men? Because they have told us that in America, because they have told us that in France, because they have told us under the government of Great Britain that our opportunities are limited when we come in contact with white men, we say the war is not over yet. The war must go on; only that the war is not going on in France & Flanders, but the war will go on in the African plains, there to decide once and for all in very near future whether black men are to be serfs and slaves or black men are to be free men.
>
> We have decreed that black men are going to be free as white men are free or as yellow men are free. We have declared that if there is to be a British Empire, if there is to be a German Empire, if there is to be a Japanese Empire, if there is to be a French Republic and if there is to be an American Republic, then there must be a black republic in Africa.[44]

It is duly noted that many of Garvey's contemporaries and modern researchers have characterized Garvey's oratory as bombastic. But this evaluation must be contextualized to prevent the rash dismissal of the political understanding of the UNIA rank and file. Recall that many followers had previous political experience in all venues of African American political expression, including the populist movement in the agrarian south and in the western states. And while most of the membership can be classified as proletariat, such categorization must consider that the discriminatory economic and employment practices classified them as such, regardless of their education, political activism and understanding, and economic capabilities. Even those recently freed from feudal relations had been exposed to political activism through reconstruction and participation in populist politics, as peasants in the Tuskegee machine and through the black media. Further, religious institutions often incorporated political news and strategy in programming.

The political alternatives desired by the UNIA seemed improbable to achieve by any means given the recalcitrance, racism, and formidable resources of the dominant political powers. But irrational desperation is not implied here. The UNIA's goal was revolutionary change, not escapism as has been alleged; and the UNIA's membership supported the overall plan of separation and nation building just as others sustained the NAACP or struggled for unionism. It was the status quo that seemed irrational and futile from most African American perspectives, regardless of ideological stance. Rather than dismissing them as grandiloquent, Garvey's (and other UNIA leaders') public speeches can be better evaluated by classifying them into three categories: analytical, evangelistic, and promotional.

When analyzing international politics or the UNIA's political goals, Garvey's oratory skills enabled him to present clear, well-reasoned arguments, which were supported by press reports. UNIA rhetoric, while revolutionary or militant, remained on par with other strategies espoused during the era. Illustrating this view allows us to present simultaneously the basic UNIA nationalist strategy, which is key to understanding the strategies employed in the implementation of the BSL. The premise underlying the UNIA's acceptance of nationalist goals was its analysis of international politics.

It was believed that two formidable challenges to imperialism and capitalism would unravel Western European and American dominance over the international political and economic structures. The first challenge was the belief that Japan's growing militaristic stance and imperialism would serve as a counterforce to European imperialism. Garvey often alluded to a possible alliance with Japan, wherein Japan would provide military support and other resources to the UNIA, including equitable agreements for the purchase of ships.[45] Indeed, Bureau of Investigation (BI) agents reported that Japanese did visit the UNIA headquarters, though it is unclear if the visitors represented the Japanese government. There also may have been interaction on the West Coast. Japanese insurgency in Asia, along with uprisings in other colonized regions, were expected to weaken Europe militarily. European racism and imperialistic tendencies would inevitably lead to war against Japan and other militant populations, but, already weakened by the Great War, European resources would be attenuated and military intervention in Africa against the UNIA (while simultaneously combating other colonial uprisings) would not be sustainable.

The second challenge to Europe that the UNIA believed helpful to its plans was the anticipated communist revolution restructuring economic relationships. The communist movement would cause further dislocation in the international economy as well as in the domestic politics of the imperialist states. This attenuation of political power would be particularly debilitating because conventional warfare by European powers and the United States would prove untenable against their own workforces. Thus in chaos, the imperialistic powers would not be able to prevent the disassembly of empire, not only in revolutionary areas such as Ireland and Egypt, but in West Africa as well. This was seen as a window of opportunity for Africans to ally with Japan and other revolutionaries against Europe and seize African land.

Another major component of the nationalist goals would be met by establishing UNIA government apparatus in Liberia, the only "free" West African state. This involved helping to free Liberia from European creditors, most accumulated during the war, then working to build the Liberian economy, preparing it to serve as the homeland for diaspora returnees. Contrary to the commonly held view of the "back-to-Africa" movement, no mass exodus of black people to Africa was planned. Rather, agricultural and industrial settlements were to be established by UNIA technical specialists.[46] These settlements would facilitate economic development and help establish trade links between diaspora communities and Liberia as well as create coastal trade among countries along the West African coast. Once economic relations were established, gradual migration was to occur over several decades. An excerpt from one of Garvey's speeches addresses this point:

> This African idea, this African proposition is one that you must understand thoroughly. We of the UNIA are not endeavoring to repatriate at the present moment—immediately—twelve million Negroes of America, or twelve and fifteen million from the West Indies. We are first trying to organize these twelve and fifteen million together with the twenty-five millions in South and Central America, with the one object of a free and redeemed Africa, and we are saying all the millions organized in this Western Hemisphere can be organized until we are ready, until Africa finds a Napoleon. . . . It means therefore, that we have years before us. *It might be five years . . . it might be a hundred years.* But whensoever the time comes we want to be ready here, sixty million strong.[47]

Diaspora-based political strategies were espoused by many different activists and groups in the era, including Arthur Schomburg, William Ferris, and Henrietta Vinton Davis. West Indians and West Africans in Europe formed diaspora-based organizations such as the Society of Peoples of African Origin and the African Progress Union in London.[48] Many others, including Kobena Sekyi, a West African barrister and activist, and Duse Mohamed Ali, a political activist, journalist, and entrepreneur in London, preferred an economic nationalism similar to that espoused in the UNIA's agenda. The writings and ideological stance of these activists were well known and may have influenced the creation of the Black Star Line. Even W. E. B. Du Bois, highly critical of the UNIA, acknowledged the credence of some of the economic tenets of the UNIA, especially the establishment of the BSL.[49]

The international character of UNIA projects was aided by activists such as John E. Bruce and Schomburg, who helped authenticate the UNIA in black areas outside the United States.[50]

When UNIA spokespeople extolled the superior virtues of the race, predicted UNIA control of the entire African continent, or linked the liberation movement with what can be described as Christian determinism, they ventured away from analysis into evangelistic speech. In fact, some publicity for programs in the *Negro World* made statements like "come hear Garvey preach."[51] Political resolution couched in evangelistic speech may have sounded eloquent but often cannot be considered cogent. It is in this realm that UNIA spokespeople give credence to charges of grandiloquence. The charge is also supported when one points to the UNIA's promotional speech, when spokespeople publicized a particular UNIA program or compared their capabilities to those of competing ideologies or organizations. In this promotional mode one finds statements such as "400 million Africans supporting the UNIA." I would argue that the UNIA rank and file was able to distinguish between these forms of speech and were not as gullible as Bureau of Investigation reports implied. I further would submit that it was the analytical speech, which drew upon past nationalist theories and was informed by intensified racism, that made the UNIA a candidate to be the first black mass organization in the United States. Its candidacy won a metaphorical victory upon creation of the Black Star Line. And establishing the Black Star Line led to formidable opposition to the UNIA and its political future.

6

Shipping Politics: The Case of the Black Star Line

Up to this point, this book has been setting the stage for the UNIA's effort to launch a race-based shipping line that would connect the diaspora both politically and economically, and then link the diaspora to its homeland, focusing specifically on Liberia. Readers are now prepared to examine whether diaspora theory conjoined to a political economy approach facilitates a more clear understanding of how blacks practice transnational politics within the African diaspora. Thus, this chapter is not only a historical digest of a UNIA program, but an example of how a resource-deprived group can participate in transnational politics, even though nation-states and international institutions threaten such attempts.

This chapter provides a history of the Black Star Line placed in the international political economy, allowing the reader to understand why events unfolded as they did.

We will see the steps necessary to bring the shipping line into being, how the effort was organized, and how the UNIA navigated international institutions and skirted the concerns of nation-states. The UNIA was able to build international support for the line among its members. A later chapter is devoted to the analysis of the BSL as an instance of political activism in the African diaspora and explains its meteoric rise and the reasons that it ultimately did not survive.

Origins of the Black Star Line

It is difficult to determine whether the UNIA leadership or the rank and file first suggested a shipping venture. In her memoir, *Garvey and Garveyism,*

Amy Jacques Garvey states that black seamen and businessmen urged the UNIA to start a shipping service to alleviate discrimination faced by black passengers and exporters.[1] Discrimination impeded the travel possibilities of black people regardless of nationality, occupation, or income level. Black producers and exporters had access to shipping services only after all white exporter and passenger needs had been met. In the federal court trial of BSL officials, UNIA member Jeremiah Certain said that UNIA membership including seamen and engineers interested in shipping, and that it was they who began raising money for the effort. Theodore Vincent suggests that the Black Star Line was first mentioned in a speech Garvey gave in Pittsburgh in April 1919. He suggested a fleet of black-owned steamships to carry African Americans back to their homeland. The idea was well received and was repeated in other cities. Garvey saw the fleet principally as a way to coordinate black commercial enterprises throughout the world, but his listeners found the prospect of returning to Africa more attractive and the UNIA office in New York was flooded with ticket inquiries.[2]

However, the *UNIA Papers* first document plans for a shipping venture in a letter written in January 1919 that was intercepted by the U.S. postal service, still operating under the Espionage Act. Eliezer Cadet, a Haitian who served as the UNIA delegate to the Paris peace conference, wrote the letter to a fellow Haitian illuminating the role of shipping in the UNIA's plans for the amelioration of economic opportunities in the black world: "If our peace propositions are accepted, we shall assemble the great Negro capitalists of the U.S. and establish a line of ships between the West Indies, America and Africa to facilitate the exchange of raw materials for manufactured products."[3] In April 1919 the *New York Call,* a socialist paper, reported that the UNIA would launch the BSL. At a mass meeting to announce the Black Star Line, UNIA spokespeople outlined the plan, which was to be funded via a traditional economic cooperative model of raising project funds, simply collecting donations from members and supporters. The BSL version differed from the traditional cooperative in that it involved multiple urban and rural communities in the United States and was secular as well as transnational. In part, the plan entailed raising approximately $2 million by seeking a targeted contribution from each community of the African diaspora and those regions of Africa with which the UNIA had contact. The proposed targets seemed to have been based on each community's earning capability. The U.S. black population, as part of the richest and most stable economy, could make the largest individual contributions, and here the UNIA hoped to raise 60 percent of the capital: one dollar from each of 1.25 million black Americans. In the West Indies, with a much more volatile economy based on raw materials production, it was hoped to raise $250,000; Central and South America would provide $300,000 to be accumulated by fifty-cent contributions; and Africa would raise $200,000 from modest twenty-five-cent contributions.[4] Several intelligence reports suggest that the UNIA believed that this traditional fund-raising would be augmented by Japan's support.[5]

Rather than immediately entering the shipping business, the plan was to accumulate sufficient funds to first *charter* a ship.[6] With this successfully completed, financial backing would be pursued from Japan and, according to Cadet's letter, also from black businesses. Including pledges, the initial collection was a modest $7,000.

The initial plan did not reach fruition for at least two reasons. One problem was the internal financial operating procedures of the UNIA, and the other was governmental intervention. The UNIA constitution delineated procedures to protect the organization against financial mismanagement; the most effective safeguard was automatic audits. When the audit committee evaluated the financial records, it did not condone the expenditures made with the BSL donations. In published reports, the committee implied malfeasance and referred to them as "concealed expenditures." In particular, the committee was concerned that the donations for the BSL had been used improperly to pay UNIA salaries and to augment the financial status of two new, but as yet unprofitable, UNIA business ventures, the restaurant and the newspaper.[7] The UNIA leadership questioned the real motivation behind the charges, suggesting that they were designed to discredit the organization and proved that enemy saboteurs had infiltrated the organization. The allegations of both parties were plausible. American financial rules were that donations collected for a specific purpose must not be directed to other organizational uses, but small community-based organizations often do combine donations in order to extend limited funds. UNIA revenue, regardless of source or designation, was used for the most pressing organizational needs, regardless of which subdivision was in need of a cash infusion. This custom was continued with the Black Star Line, as will be documented in this study. But it also was true that the UNIA had been infiltrated by the federal government and that some members had divided loyalties.

While the exact date is unclear, around the first of June, the audit committee reported its financial concerns to the New York County assistant district attorney, Edwin P. Kilroe. The audit committee was an internal operation staffed by UNIA members Uriah T. Mitchell, Joseph E. Johnson, and Norman Robinson.[8] With competent legal counsel who was to shield the UNIA from governmental and other critics, Garvey was able to postpone the inevitable interview with Kilroe. Over a three-month period, Kilroe would interrogate several UNIA members and hold meetings with UNIA counsel. While Kilroe did not find substantive evidence to bring charges against Garvey or other UNIA officials,[9] he did compel the incorporation of the Black Star Line. Kilroe ordered the UNIA to either incorporate their shipping program and purchase ships by June 1919, or return the donations to contributors. Indeed, several witnesses during the federal trial, for both the defense and the prosecution, testified that Kilroe cautioned that he would charge UNIA officials with commercial fraud if the Black Star Line was not incorporated.[10] Although the African Communities League (ACL) was the commercial arm of the UNIA, its charter did not cover shipping nor does the paper trail indicate the UNIA's intention was to place the BSL under the ACL management. One must keep in mind, however, that Kilroe's intervention may have changed any intention of doing so.

Kilroe's monitoring and warning necessarily changed the original plans for the BSL, and probably the pace at which it was supposed to develop. With legal help, the Black Star Line was incorporated in Delaware in June 1919. Hill suggests that Delaware was chosen because minimal wealth requirements, experience, or documentation of business expertise were required: "the state of Delaware became particularly attractive for businesses due to its simple procedure for incorporation, its low corporate income tax, and the special privileges that it offered corporations for enlarged capitalization and the authority to adjust their internal management and financial organization."[11]

Organization of BSL and Financial Difficulties

While a board of directors and officers were selected, the BSL relied upon the parent organization, the UNIA, for personnel as well as organizational and financial support. UNIA officers also served as BSL officers, and UNIA branches included BSL promotional presentations in weekly organizational meetings. The BSL sales force often included the treasurers or secretaries of UNIA branches, and BSL stock-selling efforts were conducted through the fund-raising institutions of the UNIA. In this way, BSL had captive audiences to which they could do sales promotions.[12] In other words, from its inception, the BSL was enmeshed with the parent organization both administratively and financially.

After incorporation, the initial sales promotion plan was to sell stock in two locations, New York and Newport News, Virginia.[13] Garvey, BSL treasurer George Tobias, and Henrietta Vinton Davis went to Newport News and other Virginia locations. Edgar Grey and Richard Warner conducted a stock promotion initiative at a mass meeting at the Palace Casino in New York. The UNIA's transformation from a financial cooperative to a stock company proved difficult. The loss of a stock book in Virginia and the alleged underreporting of contributions at the Palace Casino combined to fuel further discord within the UNIA and continued government inquiries into fund-raising practices.[14] Perhaps these initial missteps led to the institution of additional financial reporting procedures. The *UNIA Papers* and the trial transcript suggest that in this time period financial procedures seemingly separate from UNIA began to be developed for BSL.[15]

Initially, Black Star Line contributions had been processed by the UNIA. The secretary recorded the total amount and the UNIA treasurer would handle the bank deposit. Once the stock company was formed, the BSL instituted the same official positions (secretary and treasurer) but eventually adopted more detailed procedures than those of the UNIA. A daily report system was developed, which supposedly included reports on all stock sold through the mail, in the BSL office, and in the field. In both her testimony and memoir, Amy Jacques (who would become the second Mrs. Amy Garvey) provided a glimpse of the chaotic Black Star office after the project's popularity had inundated the office with money and requests for BSL stock. She discusses Garvey's exasperation with the inefficient office operations and his quandary of balancing office management with the necessity of wide travel to publicize and build the UNIA and BSL.

Financial management was impeded by the rule that mail could not be opened in Garvey's absence. Amy Jacques Garvey provides a vivid picture of an organization that grew faster than it was prepared to administrate: "He opened a large cabinet in his office and showed me stacks of mail. Said he, 'These accumulated while I was on a speaking trip. I haven't the time to help and teach someone to open, sort and put notations on them, before handing the moneys enclosed to the treasurer.'"[16]

The staff was inundated with cash to process and deposit. The accumulation of unprocessed cash would have provided opportunity and perhaps temptation to embezzle, and certainly there were continuous charges of theft against officers involved in processing. Sexism also seemed to have impeded financial operations. Amy Jacques was to supervise financial processing during Garvey's frequent absences, but the male officials routinely ignored her authority and requests. The headquarters seemed well organized on paper (that is, in its constitution and bylaws), but in reality it often lacked effective coordinated supervision.

The BSL field stock sales agents were supervised by the chief salesperson, who reported to the Black Star Line secretary. The link to the UNIA was that the chief salesperson was also the traveling UNIA secretary, which enabled him to coordinate the two organizations' efforts to arrange joint meetings to disseminate information on UNIA's ideology and economic programs, increase membership, and raise funds. Salespeople had specific procedures as well.[17] Sales agents were responsible for filling out the stock certificate and turning funds and stock stubs over to the appropriate UNIA branch secretary or to the chief salesperson. They also arranged promotional programming such as mass meetings featuring the UNIA's principal spokespeople, including Marcus Garvey, the Rev. George A. McGuire, Henrietta Vinton Davis, or Dr. William Ferris. Because these spokespeople were well known, they ensured large turnouts, particularly when presentations were accompanied by musical or artistic performances.

The duties of sales agents necessarily generated expenses. Authorized expenses could be deducted from the sales proceeds by the agent and then the net revenue forwarded to the appropriate officers. Stock salespeople received on average a 3 percent commission, and those who were UNIA staffers were authorized to deduct their UNIA salary with appropriate documentation. Other authorized deductions included travel expenses, such as rail fare and accommodations; promotional expenses, such as advertisement and printing pamphlets; and program expenses, such as renting an appropriate venue or paying musicians and other entertainers. In many instances, some expenses were defrayed by charging an entrance fee of fifty cents, and the UNIA branch in which the mass meeting was held would supplement the costs.

While this method of promotion was successful in that attendance often reached into the thousands and stock sales were considerable, the related costs consumed a significant portion of stock sales revenue. For an example, in a major forty-day promotional tour designed to rejuvenate the Black Star Line in late October 1920, over 50 percent of the stock revenue may have gone to overhead.[18] This nationwide tour raised approximately $10,000 and involved most of the UNIA's principal speakers, a thirty-member band, and singers. Needless to say, maintenance of this large troupe was expensive. While these arrangements seemed to facilitate the sales effort, lenient documentation and presigned stock certificates also provided temptation and opportunities to at best embellish expenses and at worst conceal embezzlement by those so inclined.

Overseas contributions and stock sales were handled through three channels. First, the *Negro World* augmented overseas chapters' efforts to promote the Black Star Line. The *Negro World* carried the effective speeches given at mass meetings as well as editorial letters by Garvey and columnists such as John E. Bruce and William Ferris. These persuasive arguments went far in selling the need for a shipping line. Also the newspaper included UNIA division reports, which fostered camaraderie between the branches and helped to strengthen a sense of unity in political mission throughout the diaspora.[19] *Negro World* coverage also indirectly explained the difficulties of the BSL by covering the tribulations of British and American shipping. Such coverage assuaged concerns about the BSL's ship the *Yarmouth* in particular because it indicated that management and mechanical problems occurred with more experienced shipping lines as well. During the era of the Black Star Line, the *Negro World* became one of the leading black newspapers in the diaspora, distributed throughout the Caribbean, Central and South America, and West and South Africa. As the result, the transnational UNIA membership had access to explanations that countered critics' arguments regarding the troubled operations of the Black Star Line.

Secondly, promotional tours in the Caribbean bolstered stock sales. Henrietta Vinton Davis led successful tours in the Caribbean and Central America. Her success was insured not only because she was a well-established artist and speaker, but also because she traveled aboard a BSL liner, when possible. In addition to holding mass meetings among the workers, she met with public officials in both Costa Rica and Cuba.[20] The *Negro World* covered these trips, and the newspaper's enthusiastic reports surely increased interest in more distant regions of the black Atlantic. This political and economic success was repeated and increased when Garvey toured the Caribbean in 1921.

Finally, considerable stock was purchased through the mail. This is illustrated in a BSL Daily Transaction Report, which lists the names of senders of letters processed in one day.[21] While one cannot infer from one list the extent of external investment, the list does suggest significant investment from outside of the United States. Fully 91 percent of the investment on this list came from overseas, particularly Cuba and Panama. This perception may be skewed because stock purchases on the list totaling $225 came from just two Central American investors, but only 7 percent of the persons listed give U.S. addresses. Also it must be remembered that in the United States, a great deal of stock was sold at mass meetings rather than by mail.

Of course, mail purchases were influenced by the tours, mass meetings held at branches, chapters, and churches, and the *Negro World* coverage. But also mail processing probably facilitated the purchase of subscriptions, thereby allowing investors to make a down payment during meetings and complete the purchase through convenient installments. These methods explain the UNIA's ability to accumulate over $750,000 for the BSL between spring 1919 and August 1921.

Entering the Shipping Business

From the UNIA's perspective, owning a shipping line was a reasonable tool toward independence and growth. However, the shipping industry was (and is) extraordinarily complex and expensive; in the era under discussion it was not only important to conduct business, it was the exclusive means of international travel. To be competitive, ships had to be immense, with diverse, airtight storage space that could accommodate large as well as perishable cargoes. In addition, ships had to be as fast as technology would allow. As a result, ships were complex machines with technical equipment that required specialized crews and maintenance. Fuel could be costly, requiring tons of coal for one round-trip voyage. Other necessary costs included insurance, salaries, taxes, and provisions. Successful shipping and fleet management requires expertise in a number of areas.

For all these reasons, an intricate set of institutions had evolved in the industrialized states to facilitate shipping relations and trade. Two key institutions that affected the life of BSL concerned classification and the ship purchasing process. BSL interaction with both institutions demonstrated its inexperience and its vulnerabilities. As in real estate, the shipping industry uses brokers to facilitate the purchases of ships. Each party in a purchase has its own broker. But because of the sophisticated mechanical systems and the perilous nature of shipping, it was customary to have ships classified and inspected before the sale was finalized. Industrialized nations have classification societies that not only determine classification status for insurance purposes but also "established uniform standards to determine the seaworthiness of vessels and also certified that a vessel met the structural and mechanical conditions needed to safeguard the lives and cargoes aboard. Based on considerations such as design, materials, age, maintenance, and other occurrences in the life of the vessel, the classification society placed the ship within a specific class and by means of periodic surveys determined whether that particular class status remained valid."[22] Because ships need insurance to serve international ports and therefore remain competitive, vessels usually seek to be considered seaworthy by a classification society; but while classification is highly recommended and routine, it is not required. Shipowners display certificates of seaworthiness for their vessels, but since the frequency of surveys for specific systems of any given ship can range from annually to once in several years, the actual condition of a ship can and often does differ from its classification status.[23] Proficient brokers customarily involved surveyors in the purchasing process to scrutinize the vessel's classification record and perform inspections of the crucial equipment, such as boilers, on the ship.

Available evidence suggests that the BSL looked at several ships before settling upon its first purchase, the *Yarmouth*. Two supporters with maritime service looked for vessels.[24] Wright's testimony is vague as to the outcome of his search. The record shows that he looked at two vessels, the *Montara* and *Corona*, in early 1919. Much more is known about Joshua Cockbourne's search. Cockbourne was a *master* (a captain in U.S. parlance) in the British merchant marine. He testified that after reading about the problems BSL experienced with the county prosecutor, he volunteered to help establish the shipping line. The first ships he suggested for BSL purchase were priced well over $400,000 each, and since BSL did not pursue these ships, Cockbourne concluded that they were too expensive. It was during this search that Estrada, a black American who was interested in selling his ship to the BSL, approached him. Estrada's vessel proved incompatible with BSL needs, but Cockbourne learned of the *Yarmouth* from him. The *Yarmouth* was to become the first vessel of the BSL.

With Estrada serving as the principal shipbroker, the *Yarmouth* was offered for sale at $175,000, notably less than the first ships considered for purchase. The North American Steamship Line, a Canadian subsidiary of Harriss, Magill and Company, owned the *Yarmouth*.[25] They were cotton brokers who owned only one ship, the aged *Yarmouth*, which they had used to transport their product. Subsequently, the government had used the *Yarmouth* during the war. During their negotiations, the price was lowered to $165,000; however, international shipping protocol and regulations impeded the purchase.

Because the North American Steamship Line was incorporated in Nova Scotia, it was under British registry. In order to avoid the complications that an international purchase agreement would engender, the BSL board was advised by Harriss, Magill to incorporate a shipping line in Canada. Settling upon a down payment of $16,500, the Black Star Line of Canada entered a tentative agreement with the North American Steamship Corporation, Ltd., in September 1919, but it soon became clear that BSL had not sold enough stock to cover the down payment. The contract was not finalized until October, when sufficient funds had been accumulated.[26] The next step was to transfer the registry to the United States and thus to the Black Star Line. But the Canadian shipping bureaucracy frustrated this plan. Hill explains, "The Canadian Department of Marine refused to register the bill of sale to the *Yarmouth* when the BSL of Canada could not satisfy the department as to its financial condition. The BSL of Canada, therefore, operated the *Yarmouth* under a charter agreement with the North American Steamship Line."[27]

The Canadian Department of the Marine made an important point, not only concerning the Canadian subsidiary of the BSL but about its parent company. The Black Star Line had to rely upon stock sales to make the payments on the *Yarmouth.* In fact, it was necessary to amend the agreement so that BSL had more time to raise sufficient funds: in October 1919, the BSL agreed to pay an additional $3,500 to defer payments on the *Yarmouth.*

As a result, the BSL had two powerful incentives to increase stock sales. First, it will be remembered that the assistant district attorney of New York, Kilroe, had given BSL a deadline whereby a ship had to be in evidence; and secondly, stock sales had to finance the payments in order to retain the ship and organizational support. Added to that pressure was the problem of the transfer of registry so that BSL could take official ownership and acquire the bill of sale. Interviewing Harriss and reviewing evidence of the agreement eased Kilroe's threat, because Kilroe could not find anything illegal about the purchase agreement even though the BI discouraged approval. British intelligence reported that Kilroe could not deter Harriss, Magill from selling to BSL.[28] Questions were raised about price inflation for the ship, but the agreement was within the law.[29] It is unclear whether BSL directors knew that the federal government also was trying to prevent the purchase. Of course, Harriss knew this because of his meetings with District Attorney Kilroe, and he put a premium on the price charged. During the trial, his lawyer shared a statement Harriss had made that paraphrased a statement allegedly made by Garvey in one of their negotiation meetings for the *Yarmouth:* "Since Garvey was going to collect 'a dollar from every Negro,' he (Harriss) would get his share."[30] Through their lawyer, Leo Healy, Harriss, Magill and Company arranged a charter agreement for the *Yarmouth* provided that the BSL obtained insurance coverage by the date of physical transfer of the ship. The formal transfer of registry, from British to American, proved to be a protracted problem.

As serious as these obstacles were, another issue turned out to be the single most pernicious impediment to the success of the BSL. That problem was the condition of the *Yarmouth* itself. While the seller, North American Steamship, had deemed the ship seaworthy, this was largely pro forma.[31]

Before sailing under a national flag, a ship theoretically had to be inspected for safety by the government under which registration was sought.[32] Key elements such as the hull and boilers had to be inspected periodically. Rigorous as shipping safety protocol may seem, in reality it is prohibitively expensive for governments to inspect vessels each time they are sold. Instead, government inspectors performed surveys on critical nautical systems on a varied schedule. Thus boilers may have been inspected every two years while the hull may have been examined annually. If a ship was sold at some point after the inspection, the protocol called for the parties of the purchase agreement to facilitate important inspections and inform the appropriate agencies of any problems uncovered.[33] But given the profit motive, one can conclude that this reporting protocol was not often practiced. Rather, ship purchase relied on private negotiations between informed parties; thus professional inspections and meticulously drawn contracts were critical to insuring reasonable purchase of a seaworthy and mechanically efficient vessel.

For whatever reason, the BSL representatives did not employ a marine engineer to perform an inspection on the *Yarmouth,* as was the custom, but rather bought the *Yarmouth* after a cursory inspection and recommendation by Cockbourne, who received a share of the broker's commission.[34] During its period of ownership, the BSL spent a disproportionate amount on retrofitting the ship for passenger service and constant repair of the *Yarmouth.* Worn boilers were the primary source of the *Yarmouth*'s mechanical failures. These expenses were one of the driving forces behind the intense stock selling campaigns.

When put into service, the *Yarmouth* had two assignments. One was to initiate the UNIA's plan to cultivate trade relations within the diaspora. The second was to facilitate stock sales in order to accumulate enough revenue to pay the installments on the *Yarmouth* and to keep the Black Star Line in business. It is tempting to prioritize these goals; however, they were inexorably intertwined. The UNIA had to appease its membership because it also was competing with several other political and business organizations for African American support and contributions. These competitors were highly critical of each other, and each had to demonstrate constantly not only capability to address problems but actual progress. Thus, the UNIA had to assure its membership and investors that the organization could indeed enter the shipping business and help black people improve economically. The UNIA had to keep the *Yarmouth* viable, attract exporters, and link with various diasporan communities in order to keep investors who were not members of the UNIA. This could not be done if it could not pay for the *Yarmouth;* without payment, the ship would have been repossessed.

Thus the UNIA had to do three things simultaneously: keep competitors at bay; convince its membership, investors, and exporters of its shipping competence; and attract ample business in order to pay Harriss, Magill and Company. From the perspective of the board, the *Yarmouth* had to become the principal stock seller. From the perspective of the *Yarmouth* captain, on the other hand, the primary goal was to carry cargo and passengers. Captain Cockbourne could not concern himself with economic exigencies; rather, he had to stay within nautical regulations—especially safety regulations—manage the crew, and make the actual journeys.

Nevertheless, the maiden voyage began on November 23, 1919, in a celebratory mode, with cargo and passengers bound for Cuba. It received wide news coverage and seems to have invigorated black people throughout the diaspora. In his memoirs, Captain Hugh Mulzac best described the impact the ship had on blacks and the kind of reception the *Yarmouth* received: "The *Yarmouth*'s arrival had been heralded by Cuban agents of the UNIA and sympathizers flocked from all parts of the island toward the docks to greet the first ship they had ever seen entirely owned and operated by colored men. They came out in boats when we arrived, showering us with flowers and fruit."[35] Beyond the symbolism, business interest was expressed that could indicate the BSL's potential profitability. Again Captain Mulzac: "President Menocal honored us with a banquet at the Presidential palace and expressed his great pride in seeing colored men make their own opportunities in the field of commerce. Before the evening was over he promised the support of the Cuban government for the ventures of the Black Star Line. Many other Cuban businessmen and landowners also pledged their cooperation."

Yet indications of cleavage between BSL administration and seagoing staff were present from the inaugural voyage. The *Yarmouth* carried cargo to the islands, but while there, Cockbourne was ordered to visit other islands in ballast to allow UNIA members to see the ship and purchase stock.[36] The *Yarmouth* did carry passengers on these inter-island trips and eventually obtained cargo for the return trip to New York. The cargo was coconuts, a perishable product. Cockbourne protested to Garvey that he could not continue to make stops in order to augment stock sales, as the produce would deteriorate. Cockbourne proved correct, and the exporter sued. Expenses not only increased due to the lawsuit but because the *Yarmouth* needed repair throughout the voyage; personnel costs increased because the crew had to be paid for the longer trip and more coal was necessary to fuel the ship for the unplanned stops. Therefore no net revenue was accumulated on the maiden voyage, and the BSL entered a vicious circle of trying to meet contradictory goals. This circle was made more turbulent by the lack of understanding of shipping protocol and maintenance practices. Of course, the unrelenting criticism of black political organizations was also a factor. Organizations such as the NAACP and black socialists were not only competing for membership but eventually formed a coalition to dismantle the BSL.

This observation is substantiated by the most controversial yet potentially most profitable voyage that the *Yarmouth* was to make.[37] Before the *Yarmouth* could be thoroughly evaluated and repaired after its maiden voyage, BSL management signed a contract to move whiskey worth over $5 million from the United States to Cuba. The advent of Prohibition (the Volstead Act) created an urgent need for the Pan Union Company to get its whiskey out of the country. Thus a shipper would have to be able to move quickly to get the job. On the one hand, the economic situation of BSL dictated bidding for the job. However, the poor mechanical condition of the *Yarmouth*, its unsuitable hold,[38] and crew exhaustion indicated the opposite.

Unfamiliarity with pricing standards and shipping protocol aggravated the fissure between BSL management and ship personnel. Given the value of the cargo and the urgency of the delivery, the management charged a relatively small amount for its services. Further, while it may have been customary for bonuses to be given to ship's captain to insure efficient delivery, Cockbourne receiving such an incentive raised suspicion about his loyalty within BSL management. Dissension and suspicion were heightened with the initial failure to deliver the cargo. It is unclear whether the *Yarmouth* was damaged in storm winds or if it was incapacitated in an effort to highjack the valuable cargo. Cockbourne maintained that he had to jettison some of the whiskey to stabilize the vessel. The Green River Whiskey Company charged theft by unnamed crew members and possible accomplices who pulled up next to the ship to receive the "jettisoned" cargo. Pilferage concerns remained throughout the voyage and the whiskey company sued the BSL.[39] Even on its arrival in port, however, problems arose that increased BSL costs. The consignee did not meet the ship, and according to marine law, the *Yarmouth* could not unload the cargo. According to custom, ships detained beyond the time specified in the contract have the consignee cover crew and provision costs under the terms of a demurrage clause in their contract. The *Yarmouth* did not have a demurrage clause and as a result had to absorb the cost.

On its third and final voyage to the islands, the *Yarmouth* crew demonstrated its potential by assisting a stranded Japanese freighter off the coast of Jamaica. Payment for this rescue could have reduced its debt substantially, but again, inexplicably, the BSL agent in Jamaica charged only a small fee. The *Yarmouth* made its final voyage between May and August 1920, after which its condition rendered it unusable unless extensive repairs could be managed. This was never accomplished.

The BSL's second ship purchase was the *Shadyside*. The *Shadyside* was an excursion boat, which the BSL planned to operate along the Hudson River during the summer and in the islands during the winter. The plan was to provide recreational transportation for New York's black population and for UNIA members in New York for the annual UNIA convention. Profits would provide the sorely needed revenue for the BSL. Purchased for $35,000, the *Shadyside* had been thoroughly renovated, records indicate, and therefore was in better condition than the *Yarmouth*. Previous historical accounts have suggested that the excursion boat was overpriced, but the insurers valued the *Shadyside* at $45,000.[40] However, operating costs exceeded revenues and thus the *Shadyside* again added to the BSL debt. The principal problem was the cost of fuel and entertainment on the excursions: the fare charged did not cover these expenses.[41] This may have been a rectifiable problem; however, during winter storage, the ship was irreparably damaged in an ice storm.[42] This pattern of mismanagement and misfortune (that is, breakdowns, cost overruns, and minimal profits) was to cascade, imprisoning the BSL in perpetual debt.

By the time the *Kanawha* was purchased in May 1920, the BSL had depleted its capital—at that time approximately $396,000.[43] The UNIA needed to intensify its efforts to rehabilitate the shipping program in order to retain the confidence of its investors. Because of the financial quagmire and the need to minimize mistakes in the abstruse shipping industry, Garvey was advised not to purchase the *Kanawha*.[44] The *Kanawha* had been the yacht of a Standard Oil executive and subsequently had been used by the American government during the war. The aging vessel required specialized equipment and extensive renovation to meet its planned use in the BSL. Although it would carry cargo, its primary purpose was passenger service and as a status symbol, meant to attract potential investors and exporters.

However, the extensive refurbishment and continual maintenance needs of the *Yarmouth* and *Kanawha* caused stock sale revenue to go directly into their repair and to pay for salaries and provisions of crews stranded on these intermittently incapacitated vessels.[45] A memorandum from O. M. Thompson to another BSL administrator poignantly underscores not only the maintenance issues but the concomitant financial woes:

> the *Yarmouth* has not been placed for repairs yet and it does appear as though it will consume all over eight weeks to get her in seaworthy condition at the cost of $73,000. . . . Captain Richardson did all in his power to get the *Kanawha* to Cuba but the ship is a bad purchase, in fact after the fourth attempt to cross to Cuba, the *Kanawha* is now at Wilmington, Delaware, on her way back to New York and we have a salary list of the crew of 39 for over three months without making a single trip.[46]

Given their financial straits, it became increasingly difficult to find repair vendors willing to contract with BSL, and declining revenue meant that cash up front for repair work was impossible. In order to gain access to cash and credit, Thompson resorted to creative financial maneuvers, as he further explained in the memorandum:

> With reference to my mouth being libelled (I guess you meant the *Yarmouth,*) yes, it is true and in addition to that the accumulation of funds is much too slow to retire the obligations at maturity. This makes the future of the Black Star Line just a little doubtful (of course this is confidential). In order to retain business however, another Corporation is being organized namely the *Black Star Steam Ship Co.* Don't let this get out in Cuba, work as hard as ever, I still believe that we have a wonderful opportunity.

But the BSL's financial problems were already widely known. The BSL's shipping operations had been excoriated in the mainstream press, as well as in the radical press and by ideological opponents in the black press for its mismanagement of both the shipping line and the scarce resources of its African American investors.[47] Although their understanding of shipping and investment was as limited as that of most Americans outside those industries in that era, attestation of distressed BSL investors, vexed former UNIA/BSL employees, and rumors from within the shipping industry gave credibility to their news reports. Such protestation coupled with rising unemployment further reduced investment in the BSL.

As Thompson's memorandum implies, many UNIA members and supporters still believed that the BSL could be established, despite what they may have presumed was interim financial indebtedness. They thought that given time and experience, the BSL could be the transportation link within the diaspora and between the diaspora and Africa. The market was undeniable from their point of view: racism only insured BSL market share. Supporters believed that if they could have obtained a qualified transatlantic vessel, economic progress would have commenced. In his testimony, BSL treasurer George Tobias articulated this belief: "Had we acquired the ship, it would be a great possibility of a great recuperation of the BSL, whereby we would receive freight and take trade throughout the world, and there was a possibility for the BSL to get lots of financing from its active operation."[48] The plan enacted to recoup funding and their reputation included a fund-raising trip to the Caribbean. Using the *Kanawha,* Garvey along with a few board members and stock agents had planned to spread out in the islands selling stock and reinstating the BSL as the answer to the diaspora's transportation problem. The long-planned Caribbean fund-raising tour was to take approximately three weeks. Taking potential investors and exporters to potentially lucrative business sites and visiting islands in the attractive ship, the *Kanawha* was expected to bolster both stock sales and enthusiasm. Garvey's fund-raising efforts in the Caribbean might have been successful if not for two obstacles.

The first obstacle had been predicted. The *Kanawha,* even with extensive renovation, required constant repair, and its condition prevented Garvey from using it on his tour. The revised plan was to have the *Kanawha* meet him in the islands, and he would triumphantly complete the tour in a vessel that symbolized the economic growth of the UNIA and therefore the black race. The ship did indeed get to the Caribbean after BSL stock agents on the tour wired money directly to the stranded *Kanawha* rather than following the stock sales reporting procedures.[49] At one point, funds were withdrawn directly from the bank to sustain the transport capabilities of the *Kanawha.* On a few occasions, the fund-raising group attempted to travel on the *Kanawha* only to get stranded and in the process contradict the image of BSL that they had worked tirelessly to create. Further, these travel delays meant that unbudgeted funds were used for cohort travel expenses involved in the Caribbean tour. While there is no detailed record, court testimony suggests that some associated costs of the tour were exorbitant.[50]

But some of these expenses may have been caused by the second obstacle. Garvey's movements were circumscribed throughout the trip: *Negro World* and labor unrest throughout the islands had convinced colonial authorities to monitor his movements closely. Further, he had problems obtaining visas. The United States resisted his reentry, and as a result, he did not return to the United States for five months, until July 1921, when his lawyers finally acquired visa clearance. As might be imagined, his detainment created several problems at UNIA/BSL offices because Garvey was the principal leader, motivator, and easily the most popular speaker. Thus while revenue and enthusiasm were increased in the West Indies, funding and commitment may have decreased in the United States, along with the effectiveness of its workforce. In the end, a significant portion of the money meant for the acquisition of a transatlantic ship never left the islands due to the immediate financial needs of the *Kanawha* and provisions for the fund-raising group.

The BSL administrative offices in New York faced insolvency; partially paid and unpaid employees understandably were becoming restive. Their agitation was combined with demoralization over the deficient performance of the BSL ships. Amid this tension and Garvey's absence, O. M. Thompson, vice president of the BSL, and Elie Garcia, BSL secretary, worked diligently to acquire the transatlantic ship, which would be christened the *Phyllis Wheatley.* They did so not only for political reasons but to prevent bankruptcy and the ensuing demise of the Black Star Line.

Table 6.1 summarizes the troubling financial history of the Black Star Line. Over the course of 2½ years, the BSL accumulated a deficit of over $475,000. In addition to ship purchases and operations, this includes administrative and stock selling expenses.

Table 6.1 Summary of BSL Financial History

Ship Name/ Rechristened	Purchase Price	Outstanding Principal	Estimated Income	Estimated Operating Expenses	Date of Purchase	Dates of Service
Yarmouth/ Frederick Douglass	$168,000	$25,150	$58,120	$194,803	Sept. 1919	Nov. 1919– Aug. 1920
Shadyside	$35,000	$15,000	$6,189	$17,142	Apr. 1920	May– Aug. 1920
Kanawha/ Antonio Maceo	$60,000	$0	$1,207	$134,681	May. 1920	Mar. 1921 Aug. 1921
Orion/Phyllis Wheatley	*$32,000	N/A	N/A	N/A	N/A	sale not completed
Total	$295,000	$40,150	$65,516	$346,626		
Administrative Expenses						
Office Expenses	$139,749					
Stock-Selling Expenses	$90,428					

This table was developed from summary reports compiled by the Bureau of Investigation's lead forensic auditor, Thomas Merrilees. See *Statement of Total Income and Expenses, July 1, 1919 to January 5, 1922,* in Hill, vol. 4, appendix 4, p. 1079. These figures are confirmed in Merrilees's testimony in *Garvey vs. U.S.*, pp. 1029–69.

Note: When adjusted for income and partial stock repayments, the overall deficit was $476,169. The ending date is January 5, 1922, because this is the date when the records were confiscated by the Bureau of Investigation.

*downpayment

The Elusive "Africa" Ship

Because the primary task of the transatlantic ship was to link the diaspora to Africa, facilitating the development of a black settlement in Liberia and of a black enclave economy, the *Phyllis Wheatley* was often called the "Africa" ship. Anticipating the ownership of a vessel capable of reaching West Africa, some UNIA members and supporters made deposits on passage to Africa. Documentation suggests support in Africa also. West African exporters were interested in independent means to transport their goods, increased control of the market, and flexibility in travel possibilities. West African political activists and media were divided on the viability of the UNIA. The National Congress of British West African States (NCBWA) wanted to regain its past comprador position in the colonial economy. Until the advent of quinine, which cured malaria and allowed the British to permeate the interior, many educated Africans had been an integral part of the comprador class of the colonial economic system. Thus, while they supported the economic goals of the Black Star Line, they did not accept the political agenda of the UNIA. J. Ayodele Langley, in his discussion of an NCBWA activist, cogently highlights this: "He thought there was something to be said for the commercial aspects of Garvey's Pan-Negroism, especially the project of the Black Star Line, but advised British subjects against participation in UNIA politics 'as conditions in both hemispheres differ altogether from each other.'"[51] According to Langley, the NCBWA decided that the UNIA's politics should be disregarded but the Black Star Line patronized, "it being a Negro undertaking and its object being solely for the purpose of facilitating and giving us more and brighter prospects as Africans in our commercial transactions."[52]

Another component of Africa's elite, however, advocated a more nationalistic agenda; and while they embraced segments of the UNIA political agenda, they rejected as naïve the notion that Garvey was the provisional president of Africa or that African Americans thoroughly understood African politics. Kobina Sekyi articulated this well:

> What Marcus Garvey and any other leader of Afro-American thought has first to appreciate before he can present a case sufficiently sound for Africa to support in the matter of combination or cooperation among all Africans at home and abroad, is the peculiar nature of the African standpoint in social and political institutions. The salvation of the Africans in the world cannot but be most materially assisted by the Africans in America but must be controlled and directed from African Africa and thoroughly African Africans.[53]

Like the comprador class, these more independent-minded Africans embraced the Black Star Line. And in at least three African states, Liberia, Sierra Leone, and Nigeria, there were BSL investors and supporters.[54] Documentation shows that Nigerians may have wanted to open a BSL office, but conflicting reports from Nigerian supporters may have made difficult a decision to do so.[55] The combination of continental African interest and investment (albeit prudent) indicated that there was support on both sides of the Atlantic to warrant the purchase of a transatlantic ship.

To select this ship, Thompson engaged the services of a shipping agent.[56] This may have been an indication that the BSL administration had learned experientially the importance of following shipping protocol and engaging professionals knowledgeable about the shipping industry. Heretofore, the BSL had relied upon lawyers to advise them on political, legal, and some business matters; but shipping was beyond the professional experience of these attorneys. Of course, they had also consulted ship captains Cockbourne, Mulzac, and Richardson, but the knowledge of the ship captains obviously lay in ship operations, not purchase and finance. Some BSL board members may have been convinced that white representation might improve the chances of getting a better ship and price.[57] Nevertheless, BSL still experienced difficulty finding a company willing to sell a transatlantic ship to the line. Thompson explained this in his testimony: "When we talked of buying a ship whom we interviewed or whom entertained any desire of selling us a ship said that they could not think of selling a ship to a corporation that was in so much debt and had so much notoriety."[58] The BSL retained the services of the New York Shipping Exchange operated by A. Rudolph Silverston; he was the sole proprietor, but stated he had silent partners. To escape the BSL's debt record, they used the BSL's New Jersey subsidiary corporation to purchase the transatlantic ship. Perhaps these changes would have been sufficient to change the poor performance of the BSL's management, but inexperience was not the only obstacle it faced.

Because the *Yarmouth* had been idle for at least a year and the *Kanawha* was disabled in Cuba, there was no revenue from the ships. The negotiations with the U.S. Shipping Board further protracted the time period in which no ships were operating for the BSL. Their inability to complete the agreement with the USSB undermined the establishment of the transportation infrastructure for the economic enclave envisioned by the UNIA. Those who had invested for the line's potential profitability logically began to question the management decisions.

This in turn dissuaded potential investors: monthly stock sales surpassed 6,000 shares only once during 1921, during the month of July 1921 (15,371 shares sold) when it seemed the *Phyllis Wheatley* purchase was imminent. When the Africa ship did not materialize, stock sales soon dropped again. With such discernible evidence to augment the black press's criticism, community supporters were disheartened.

While the UNIA attempted to subsidize the shipping line until the *Phyllis Wheatley* reinvigorated interest, it was itself facing financial distress. The BSL had been the UNIA's largest and most successful program, and their conjoined income financed the staff that served both organizations. With the BSL's losses, staffing and programming were negatively impacted and the constant bombardment of criticism effected membership growth.

At the 1920 convention, members had displayed a willingness to continue to support efforts to stabilize the shipping line. However, by the 1921 convention, some investors and disgruntled members established a committee to develop a full financial report on not only the BSL but also the UNIA.[59] This probing contingent included influential members such as Noah Thompson from the Los Angeles Division, Rev. George Weston, and Captain Hugh Mulzac. And their concerns over the financial status were valid.

Thus three groups—capitalistic investors, nationalists who were Garvey detractors, and nationalists who were Garvey supporters—were vocal at the 1921 convention. In the detractors camp was Rev. George Weston, who had

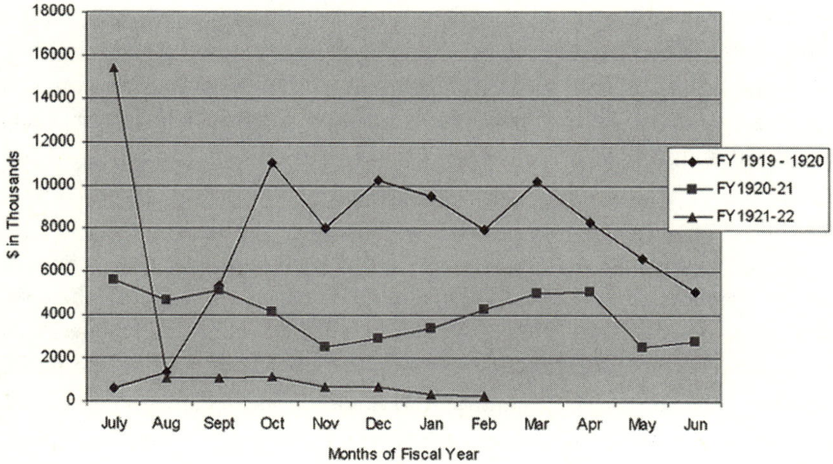

Figure 6.1. BSL shareholders understood the economic realities faced by the black merchant marine. Investors responded to the launch and bought over 10,000 shares. Stock sales dropped as they reacted to the incessant problems plaguing the Black Star Line. *Source:* "Finances of the Black Star Line," in Hill, ed., *UNIA Papers,* 3:775–76, 4:1082–83.

been a key adviser to Garvey. Weston and others questioned how, with the various forms of funding received, the UNIA was nearly insolvent. Investors wanted answers surrounding not only the obstruction to the *Phyllis Wheatley* purchase but an explanation for the allocation of funds from all sources.

It must be noted that the comingling of funds per se does not seem to have been an issue at the 1921 convention. Remember that within the organization there was no operable distinction between the UNIA and BSL. Such formal differentiation was the result of the forced incorporation of BSL imposed by the New York prosecutor and the attendant American regulations of such financial institutions. Rather, it was the minimal progress in launching the line and inordinate expenditures that were at issue among the delegates. One disconcerting expenditure may have been the use of the death fund. The auditors report submitted to the 1921 convention revealed that these monies were misappropriated for expenditure by the UNIA and perhaps BSL needs. Of the $19,000 collected during the fiscal year for this fund, only $1,275 had been paid out in death benefits, yet the UNIA's year-end balance was less than $3,000 in all funds except the African Redemption Fund. This was a separate account dedicated to the building of the Liberian settlement, but $34,000 from the fund was used to buy BSL stock.[60]

Finally, there was the question of BSL management, including the continual purchase of impaired ships and the concomitant renovation and repairs required, which exhausted the funds. Ultimately, some financial improvements were incorporated into financial procedures, such as salary scales for employees; Garvey and his supporters ultimately retained control but not without sustaining substantial impairment to the UNIA's reputation and organization, damage that the *Negro World* could not dissipate.[61] Recriminations and financial decline continued, and by the end of 1921, BSL staff had been laid off and the *Yarmouth* had been sold to address a lien against it by a repair company.

It was rumored widely that Garvey's arrest was imminent, and in February 1922 he and three BSL officers were indicted. By the end of February, stock sales were stopped and by March 1922 the negotiations for the *Phyllis Wheatley* were cancelled.[62] These acts formalized the end of the Black Star Line. However, these calamities did not end the allegations of financial malfeasance or efforts to recoup investments and deposits made for African passage. Most importantly, they did not destroy the UNIA or its interest in the establishment of a black-owned shipping line. Perhaps an excerpt of a Garvey editorial may help explain the organization's survival and its position on the failure of its premier program:

> But the idiots do not seem to realize that the Black Star Line is but a small matter compared with the bigger object of the Universal Negro Improvement Association; that the Black Star Line bears the same relation to the Universal Negro Improvement Association that the Shipping Board bears to the United States Government, and that even though $300,000,000 may be lost in the Shipping Board the government will still conduct the affairs of that corporation for the benefit of the nation. And so, even through the tricks and dishonesty of a few employees of the Black Star Line, the corporation cannot be permanently damaged, because there are 400,000,000 Negroes who are determined that the work of the Universal Negro Improvement Association shall go on, and nothing like a million dollars, or even ten millions, can permanently interfere with its mighty program. All the loyal stockholders of the Black Star Line have nothing to fear, because the Universal Negro Improvement Association will, if the enemies try to do anything to the corporation, make every effort to secure the interest of every loyal stockholder, who believes in the cause of Africa for the Africans and an emancipated Negro race.[63]

This statement suggests that the UNIA considered itself a government as opposed to a mere political organization. Several speeches throughout the *UNIA Papers* by various UNIA leaders support this observation. From this viewpoint, the BSL was considered an errant agency that had to be reorganized and funded with additional stock receipts, which they seemed to consider analogous to public funds. As a result, loyalists at the 1922 UNIA convention established a Black Star Line Redemption Fund, which was charged with raising money to reimburse the investors.[64] An excerpt from the *Negro World*'s convention coverage illuminates their reasoning:

> The Hon. Clifford Bourne, of Guatemala, said the subject was one on which the life of the UNIA depended. Were it not for the Black Star Line, there would not have been the UNIA. The Black Star Line had lost, but, taking it as a whole, they had not lost, because it had accomplished many things for them and had improved the morale of the people. He thought it a very simple matter to devise ways and means of asking members to buy redemption shares. One suggestion was, if possible, that every member of the association should purchase one share of stock in order to resuscitate the company.[65]

The loyalists' efforts and stepped-up political participation in the electoral process helped raise funds for Garvey's defense and delay the trial until May 1923.

The experience of the Black Star Line did not eliminate the UNIA's goal of building a transnational shipping business. Another shipping venture, called the Black Cross Navigation and Trading Company, was established in 1924. One ship was purchased, and it performed more effectively than its predecessors. However, there were crew-related impediments, and it was attached for the debts of the BSL and confiscated.[66]

This is the brief history of the UNIA's attempts at running an international shipping concern. In the next chapter, we will analyze the venture to discover what strategies enabled the organization to engage in political and economic activism in the international economy, and what mistakes and forces marooned the project.

7

Stormy Seas: Government Obstruction of BSL Transnational Goals

Purchasing a ship through the shipping board minimized the deceptive selling practices the BSL had experienced in the private market. Tedious USSB bureaucratic processing delayed procurement, however. Any ship purchase had to be approved by several departments, including the ship sales division, the legal department, the insurance department, and finally the board of directors. Further, given the BSL's financial history, the USSB also demanded financial reassurance before finalizing the transaction. These conditions put additional pressure on the BSL because they had to make the down payment on a $350,000 vessel, pay for a performance bond, provide insurance, and be prepared to make payments. On the other hand, the ship was more likely to be classed and seaworthy.

There were two other reasons for USSB's slow response. The USSB was coming under increasing pressure for its own performance. Its primary goal was to sell U.S. and German vessels efficiently into the U.S. merchant marine. Rigorous competition in the international economy demanded that the United States go beyond the advantage of its large production capacity to wield power in the efficient transport of its goods and improve its competitiveness for greater market share. To do this, the USSB was created in part to assist U.S. exporters in purchasing and operating ships. However, businesses complained about the USSB's incompetence in marketing and some questionable unprofitable leases of ships, which led to charges of patronage politics. The *New York Times* reported that foreign ships were carrying more American cargo to parts of South America than U.S. ships, and that on the Atlantic coast foreign ships carried over 70 percent of U.S. freight. Indeed, the USSB was losing over $4 million a month, and ships were reportedly rusting in port.[1] Thus in late 1921, the USSB management was replaced, and new management probably was trying to improve the agency's effectiveness and avert growing criticism by thoroughly scrutinizing buyers to insure better revenue intake.

Another reason for the USSB's lassitude may have been a Bureau of Investigation (BI) memorandum to USSB, which stated:

> The Bureau has been advised by a strictly confidential source, that MARCUS GARVEY, president of the Universal Negro Improvement Association, and head of the Black Star Line, is negotiating at the present time for the purchase of a boat from the U.S. Shipping Board.
>
> I am sure that you will recall the activities of Marcus Garvey and I am therefore, referring this information to you for such attention as you may deem advisable.[2]

The Bureau of Investigation, the forerunner of the Federal Bureau of Investigation and housed in the Justice Department, had been watching the UNIA and its auxiliary organizations since early 1918.[3] The federal government was concerned about the rising political activity and resistance of black activists and organizations. Their surveillance covered all organizations regardless of ideology. They hired black informants to report on African American political activity across the nation. The UNIA was considered one of the most dangerous because of its caustic rhetoric and ability to mobilize its membership to follow UNIA's agenda nationally. Surveillance was conducted in four tiers. There were informants placed within the organization; informants and agents observed the interactions between black organizations and within the community; UNIA divisions around the country were monitored, particularly when Garvey or other officials visited; and finally bureau administrators set and implemented policies, as well as interacted with other governmental surveillance units, in order to contain UNIA activities and influence.

The quality of the informants and agents' reports was varied. Reports with obviously incorrect information are discounted in this study. Most of these seem to have been reports from outside the New York area, when a local police officer in a given city was dispatched to cover a UNIA speech or meeting. Many names were confused or misspelled, UNIA organizational structure was misrepresented, and so forth. Such reports are useful in a few ways, however; they substantiate the attendance numbers and show the extent of surveillance. They also offer insight into systems used to collect contributions in UNIA meetings across the country. I also treat cautiously reports that contain biased or subjective statements. For example, descriptions of participants as "ignorant workers or Negroes" or continuous personal political commentary demonstrate a priori conclusions rather than professional observation. Nevertheless, there were reports that stand up as professional, descriptive, and confirmable; other documents corroborate many of the situations or conversations detailed in these reports. Taken together, the BI reports are a useful source of information and convey the extent to which government surveillance may have affected the Black Star Line.

Informants inside UNIA headquarters were highly valuable to the intelligence-gathering apparatus. The BI informants were remarkably close to the heart of the UNIA organization. Two in particular, known as Agent "800" and Agent "P-138," were in positions to acquire information that may not have been accessible by any other means. This fact lends utility to their reports; but corroborative documentation is not always available, particularly for private conversations and isolated activities.[4]

Agent 800 became a key assistant to Garvey, who was the head of all UNIA operations. Agent 800 was assigned the task of opening mail for Garvey; thus he was able to glean information even before Garvey and also to initiate effective subversion within the organization and between the UNIA and other black organizations. An excerpt from one of his reports suggests how much leeway he had to evaluate incoming mail: "I had this letter in my possession but upon second thought, thought it best to let it go in Garvey's files. Will keep a look out for further communications from this man. . . . If I can only hold this job of registering the letters I expect sometime to get some real good information."[5]

Agent 800 also reported on his relationships with other UNIA members, including those who later became opponents of the organization. One competitor in particular, Cyril Briggs, a leader of the ABB and later the black communist movement in New York, was to become estranged from the UNIA and instrumental in compiling evidence for the fraud trial. Using his newspaper, the *Crusader,* Briggs was highly critical of the Black Star Line, and he and Garvey often waged battle through the court system.[6] At one point Agent 800 joined Briggs's organization, the African Blood Brotherhood, and ingratiated himself with Briggs as a valuable tool against Garvey. This enabled Agent 800 to facilitate effective sabotage, which ultimately may have hurt both organizations. Agent 800 gave a UNIA mailing list to Briggs, which allowed the latter to mail his newspaper with criticism of Garvey to key UNIA leaders. Again, Agent 800:

> Briggs is very worried for fear that someone in Garvey's crowd will find out that I am a member of his organization and tell Garvey and Garvey will fire me and he has no position to give me. He warned me tonight to be careful. I will take care of that. Briggs told me that each president of Garvey's divisions would receive a copy of his magazine, but he would not say how he got the names and addresses, but by that statement I know that he received my anonymous communication. He seemed to be very much elated over it.[7]

This machination may have succeeded in deepening the fissure between members of the UNIA and the ABB. It most certainly increased mistrust within the UNIA administration. Damaging leaks suggested that a UNIA staff person or director had disclosed important organizational information that could be used against the executive and thwart program plans. Coupled with payroll issues, the leak fueled accusations that facilitated the dismissal or resignation of several disgruntled or stressed administrators and clerical personnel.[8] Several of these former UNIA administrators and staff, along with aggrieved investors, were to become government witnesses in the trial. Agent 800 also reported on all visitors observed and fragments of conversations or meetings overheard. It was Agent 800 who reported on the development and training of the esoteric African Legion, the military wing of the UNIA.

Agent P-138 has been identified as Herbert Boulin, a Jamaican widely considered to be Garvey's close friend.[9] In addition to reporting on UNIA activities, P-138 served as a barometer of the stress level of the UNIA's strategists and especially of Garvey's disposition. For instance, P-138 alleged that Garvey confided suicidal thoughts over the financial problems of the Black Star Line.[10] He also reported a conversation upon Garvey's return from the Caribbean tour that implies Garvey was unaware of the protracted negotiations with the USSB for the transatlantic ship, the *Phyllis Wheatley.*

Both Agent 800 and P-138 documented the meteoric ascension of the BSL and its financial downfall. The reports indicate how a fissure grew and broke the UNIA into at least two camps. While the informants generated weekly reports about the UNIA offices, BI agent James E. Amos interviewed competing political activists and the disgruntled employees of the UNIA. The accumulated information from these three agents was used by Special Agent Mortimer Davis to interview material witnesses, such as *Yarmouth* owners Harriss and McGill, ship repair companies, and disgruntled captains, including Cockbourne and Richardson. This information was passed on to the federal prosecutor and a forensic accountant.

The Bureau of Investigation committed surprising levels of resources to the surveillance of the UNIA. However, the UNIA was considered one of the most seditious organizations of the era.[11] Hoover had become convinced that the UNIA was a tool of the British government, which is why he tried to convince the State Department to deny Garvey reentry into the states after his Caribbean tour. "I have been under the impression for some time, although with limited amount of proof, that Garvey's movement in this country is subsidized to some extent by the British government, further, that he through his emissaries, has been responsible to a considerable extent, for the negro disturbances. . . . In view of the above it is my desire, should Garvey leave this country, that he be denied entry in the future."[12]

The U.S. consuls abroad monitored Garvey's movements in the Caribbean and forestalled his return to the United States for five months. Ultimately, the State Department allowed Garvey to return, arguing that there was no law to prevent it and the perceived martyrdom of Garvey would only escalate black discontent. BI agents, including Agent 800 and P-138, reported that Garvey's lawyers used their links to the Republican Party to achieve Garvey's reentry. Reportedly, a bribe of $5,000 was paid through a prominent black Republican, Henry Lincoln Johnson.[13]

The Bureau of Investigation was not the only governmental unit interested in the UNIA. Both the State Department and the Military Intelligence Division monitored the UNIA's activities, not only because of anti-communist paranoia but because of strikes and protests threatening economic instability in the Caribbean. The seriousness of the Military Intelligence Division's concern is made quite clear in a directive written to the assistant chief of staff for intelligence, Eastern Department: "In addition to the foregoing, it is desired that you apply the Strategic Index in all four factors to this movement with a view to providing us as soon as practicable with a complete basic monograph of this movement, which we look upon as being one containing grave possibilities to the United States through the opportunity that it may afford our future enemies to strike us in our weakest point."[14]

While Hoover suspected that UNIA was a British instrument, Great Britain theorized an alliance between the UNIA and the Irish Republican Army. No concrete evidence was found to support either allegation. Britain was the colonial power in Ireland and in regions of Africa and the Caribbean, the home of substantial UNIA/BSL membership including Marcus Garvey. Coalitions had been formed in other parts of the British Empire, and it was plausible to the British government that another revolutionary alliance was emerging within its empire. Their surveillance seemed to uncover a connection between Sinn Fein and the UNIA. One link had been Magill of Harriss, Magill and Company, the owners of the *Yarmouth.* A British military intelligence report commented upon the *Yarmouth* purchase:

> We are informed that Garvey got his boat through under peculiar opposition. The District Attorney used all power to have the sale cancelled, but Harriss, Magill & Co., S.S. Agents, would not listen to any proposition made. Mr. Magill, it is stated, is now in Europe. He is said to be an Irish sympathizer and is selling boats to Irish syndicates. From the fact that he is selling boats to Irish syndicates and to Negroes, and that they [blacks] got Trotter to the Peace Conference, it would appear that there is something doing.[15]

Another sign of a link for Britain was speaking engagements for Irish radicals at UNIA mass meetings; other socialist and communist activists spoke in New York in the earlier period of the organization. Misunderstanding the nuances between nationalists and radical black activists, Britain conflated the possibilities of black uprisings and labor unrest.

Given the decline of its economic position, Britain was cautious about any movement that could disrupt its labor resources as well as the business climate in and around South America and the Caribbean. Thus Britain monitored and exchanged information with the United States regarding the activities of the UNIA and BSL in the region. Britain needed to regain market share in South America but had to be conscious of U.S. interests because America was not only its principal creditor but its main competitor. Political unrest in West Africa was important, too, due to British need for an undisrupted flow of resources, especially gold and palm oil from the region. Britain and France also may have had an interest in Liberia's rubber trees, and therefore would not want a UNIA stronghold there. British competitors in West Africa (mainly France) did not have superior power or a financial hold on Britain as did the United States. Nevertheless, Britain monitored the UNIA and BSL actions in West Africa, particularly in Nigeria. I have not uncovered documentation that Britain disrupted UNIA or BSL operations, although one might surmise it a strategy that would have been approved.

It was widely believed at the time that Garvey not only had to bribe U.S. officials but also agree to tone down his revolutionary rhetoric in order to get back into the country. While Garvey was contesting his passport status and trying to stabilize the *Kanawha* situation, Thompson and Garcia were trying to purchase the *Phyllis Wheatley.* Without Garvey's presence, time-consuming consensus had to be reached among key officers and advisers in order to move the purchasing process forward. Growing distrust among board members may have aggravated this problem. The negotiations with the USSB further extended the time period in which no ships were operating for the BSL.

As it turned out, the end of the shipping project came when the Bureau of Investigation and the Post Office brought charges of mail fraud against four BSL officers.[16] Embezzlement does not seem to have been considered the primary charge since no personal bank accounts or transactions were reported for any of the defendants.[17] At one point, the federal government looked at Garvey's travels with Amy Jacques in order to charge him with violation of the Mann Act, the "White-Slave Traffic Act" intended to combat interstate prostitution. Instead they decided to prosecute four BSL directors for fraud through the U.S. mail; the formal charge was violating section 215 of the U.S. Criminal Code.[18] The case built against the BSL directors included newspaper advertisements for investment in the *Phyllis Wheatley* transatlantic liner before it had been purchased. Stock promotions had included pictures of a ship, and the implication was that the ship had already been purchased. These promotions had been mailed to potential investors, and the government charged that this was deliberate fraud. Yet the prosecution's case highlighted financial mismanagement and ineptitude in maritime business rather than mail fraud. Negligible evidence was presented that spoke to corporate fraud. This evidence centered on one envelope mailed to a UNIA supporter; the trial transcript suggested that the recipient of the letter was flustered and did not make a convincing witness.

Two incidents strengthened the government's chances for a favorable verdict. First, Garvey fired his lawyers because they advised him to make a deal on a lesser charge; he thought the charges baseless and decided to represent himself. With no legal experience, he was unable to argue a coherent case or get into evidence information that he thought vindicated him and the BSL project. Second, Rev. James Eason, an elected official in the UNIA, was murdered in New Orleans before the trial began. A venerated activist and "race" man, Eason had become critical of the authoritarianism and mismanagement in the organization and was rumored to be a key witness for the prosecution. He was killed after giving a highly critical speech of the UNIA movement, and the assailants arrested were UNIA African Legion members. Critics asserted that the order had come from the UNIA leadership, which proved to be quite damaging to the UNIA and by extension to the defendants on the trial.[19]

Yet the trial validated what an arduous task the BSL was. The forensic accountant's analysis of the money collected and spent showed that a majority of the money had gone to pay off the loans for the ships and to the endless ship repairs. The trial also illustrated how difficult it was for the UNIA to maintain an international membership and withstand competition and criticism. The complexities of shipping and the misadministration were clearly demonstrated as was the inexperience and idealism of the BSL board and supporters.

Government institutions impacted the BSL project on many levels. First the local government of New York forced the UNIA to incorporate or repay money donated to the merchant marine project. The New York prosecutor also tried to stop the purchase of the *Yarmouth*. The federal government through informants and agents sabotaged the UNIA administration by intercepting the mail and aggravating discord between various African American political organizations. The American government also pressured members of the UNIA to report information on the organization's operations.

On the international front, the American government suppressed the distribution of the *Negro World* in the Caribbean region. And various agencies, especially the Bureau of Investigation, worked to keep Garvey out of the United States. One of its reasons was the belief that the UNIA and/or Garvey was an agent provocateur of Great Britain. Another important reason was the concern over labor disruption in the Caribbean, especially at fueling stations that were to support travel through the Panama Canal.

Britain's rationale for suppressing the UNIA/BSL was similar to that of the United States. It could not afford for labor and therefore production to be disrupted in African and Caribbean colonies. Seeing the UNIA as a revolutionary group, Britain surveilled the UNIA and suppressed the newspaper in its colonies. It shared information with the U.S. intelligence community but also proscribed UNIA settlements and growth in Liberia.

There is no evidence that these powers sabotaged the ships, but because BSL was incorporated, the American government could monitor its activities. And because one ship was under the British flag, it could be scrutinized by the British.

The fraud trial put an end to the merchant marine venture; however, the evidence that a crime had been committed was tenuous at best. Seeking investors for a corporate venture that turns out to be unsuccessful is not in itself fraud; by its definition, investment embodies risk taking. Investors were free to pull out of the venture. As information revealed that the project was failing, investors did pull out, transferring their economic and political activism to more effective strategies. Others who believed that the company's literature misled their investment decisions supported the government's prosecution of the BSL directors. Activists from other organizations supported the prosecution because of the belief that African Americans' scarce resources were being squandered in an undercapitalized, mismanaged venture that showed no indication of profitability or improvement. In this larger sense, it was fraudulent; it prevented limited resources from being invested in promising political activism and local politics and economic projects. Government motives were not as noble; they used the discontent within the African diaspora to repress not only the BSL, but the UNIA movement.

8

Marooned: The Rise and Fall of the Black Star Line

The Black Star Line's performance can also be evaluated as a diaspora project designed to ameliorate political and economic problems. Sheffer highlights characteristics that I found useful for analyzing this venture: ideologies, political structure, financial base, education/skill levels, mobilization strategies, channels of influence, and impact upon international political arena. Close consideration will be given to the advantages and disadvantages of each attribute in light of the international political economy operating in the era. The UNIA's actions regarding each attribute can be integrated and organized to see what the UNIA did that led to the rise of the Black Star Line, and what strategies and deficiencies led to its fall.

Ideologies

Many "race" activists were committed to survival and self-defense first and then stability in their communities. But their activism brought them in contact with mainstream political ideologies, and as they worked for change, these ideologies were tapped. In the black community, one could find adherents of integrationism, socialism, and nationalism, and activists became involved in larger organizational movements such as the ABB and the UNIA. Initially, the two operative ideologies in the UNIA were socialism and nationalism. These distinctly western ideologies were conduits through which black activists operationalized their existential goals to find ways to liberate black people from exploitation and participate in the building of a healthy, equitable society. Yet they were constrained by the tenets of their chosen ideologies. The differences between socialism and nationalism led to a fundamental schism among the most educated and experienced activists within the UNIA. The appearance of the BSL and the decision to embrace capitalistic goals for it deepened the fissure to such an extent that the more doctrinal socialist activists left the UNIA and became the primary critics of the BSL.

Another ideologically based challenge for the BSL was from those black activists who accepted the capitalistic component of BSL but eschewed its nationalistic base. These were the activists of the integrationist school, many of whom supported NAACP programming and the Pan-African Congresses. Thus, diasporan activists were divided between two transnational movements, attenuating scarce economic and human resources.[1]

Ideological difference conjoined with competition for members and political power among these three groups initiated intense journalistic criticism of the BSL. These competitors were prominent actors in their own right and their news organs reached large audiences. They were therefore capable of curtailing BSL's pool of potential investors. Socialists and communists argued that it was improbable that capitalism could be adapted to eradicate the economic problems of black people. This argument gained cogency as BSL faltered. The *Crisis* carried in-depth analysis of the UNIA's financial and political organizations, which raised concerns about the competent operation of the shipping venture. Such criticism influenced the development of the BSL. While it is true that New York district attorney Kilroe pressured the UNIA to incorporate BSL, incorporation and purchase of a ship also served to quell the criticism of black competitors and critics. The UNIA had to divert significant resources to combat their competitors, subdue opposition, and allay the concerns of its membership and investors regarding the BSL's financial problems. Thus the UNIA's management decisions about BSL were as much influenced by ideological battles as they were by economic conditions and opportunities.

Another important point must be made that does not emerge from formal ideological difference: the altruistic kernel motivating a substantial share of black political activism. The essence of the political philosophy of black activism was the political and economic rehabilitation of the black race through whatever reasonable methods available. Ideology simply was grafted on to that seed. So strong was this position a phrase was coined for its practitioners: they were termed "race" men and women. A primary responsibility of these activists was the protection of the masses of black people. And activists in each of the ideological groups—beyond competition—may have sincerely believed that they were protecting the race from misusing resources and time, which were all too often ephemeral. Thus, activists formed an alliance against the UNIA, and the UNIA in its stead believed itself to be defending black people from ineffective activism. This same commitment caused dissension within the organizations as well. For example, BSL activists disagreed with the ways in which the program was operated and made their complaints heard at the 1921 UNIA convention.

And although one cannot categorize opportunism as an ideology, it most certainly operated within the BSL. One of its most deadly forms was theft of resources. Embezzlement only exacerbated mistrust in a highly charged environment.

Nationalism was the primary ideology operating in the UNIA, but the membership was not homogenous. One cleavage was between socialists and nationalists. But a prime cleavage was that each group believed its ideology the sole protector of black political rights. Mismanagement and probable embezzlement intensified simmering animosity.

The African diaspora is not politically monolithic. Ideological difference was one basic reason for dissension both within and outside the BSL organization. Ideological diversity among all diaspora activists led to criticism, with some black activists including some diaspora activists aligning with the government to dismantle the shipping line. For example, Cyril Briggs, who became a black Communist activist, and others helped the federal government assemble possible prosecution witnesses.[2] Trying to withstand the onslaught led to some of the misguided management decisions of the BSL—not having the ship examined by an engineer, accepting cargo at a lower price than profitable to deliver, and ignoring the captain's advice—exacerbating structural problems in BSL management.

Political Structure

As stated in BSL minutes of July 26, 1920, "The policy of the UNIA is to control this corporation to help the Parent body in achieving its objects."[3] The first UNIA objective for the BSL was to link the diaspora via a transportation network that would facilitate political and economic interaction. Secondly, BSL was to stabilize that transportation network and link it to West Africa, not only to expand a black enclave economy, but also to provide a bridge to the perceived homeland, where a nation-state would be established and then expanded.

The UNIA political structure stood on a foundation of black nationalism as codified in its *Declaration of Rights of the Negro Peoples of the World.*[4] The

UNIA not only claimed the continent of Africa as the home of black people but called for human rights and equitable treatment of blacks wherever they were, and renounced the League of Nations for its role in black servitude. The organization was committed to eradicating colonialism and reclaiming the entire continent. This ambitious agenda was to be carried out over decades and would result by building a military force and by allying with other revolutionary groups fighting against colonialism. And if we are to believe Bureau of Investigation (BI) reports, the UNIA wanted a coalition with Japan, considered by anticolonial activists a power capable of contending with European military forces, particularly if augmented by revolutionary groups.

These are not the goals of an organization but rather of a nation. I submit that the UNIA's political structure was that which they perceived necessary to support a germinal nation-state. The primary goal was to transplant the state to a safe location within the African homeland. Therefore, a key component was internationalism, forming an alliance with the only free West African nation-state, and engaging forces considered unreceptive to its nation-building plans. The organizational structure therefore included posts that did not exist in domestic political organizations. There were ambassadors to represent them at the League of Nations, regional leaders for the West Indies and for the United States, a civil service, and an international convention. A church was also established. In light of the UNIA's internationalist bent, the *Negro World* followed international political events and emphasized the transnational character of the UNIA and treated its shipping line as its merchant marine.

The political structure combined several political institutions from the United States and England. Institutions from the United States and England were selected because it was under their educational and political systems that diaspora activists had been schooled and with which they were experienced; the majority of UNIA members and BSL investors were subject to American or British laws, even continental Africans. Most of those who were not under Anglo political systems were subject to the French and Belgium systems. Their political discourse indicates that the UNIA leadership had little information on indigenous African political institutions, and the political structures reflect this.[5]

From the American political system, the UNIA adopted two fundamental documents. First, the UNIA's Declaration of Rights with its demands for freedom and equality with all other groups is reminiscent of the U.S. Declaration of Independence, as highlighted by its similar title. The tone of the Declaration of Rights is similar, demanding equal rights, independence, and representation boldly in writing. Secondly, its political philosophy includes the principle of democracy, as presented in its paramount organizing document, its constitution. The UNIA constitution laid out the chain of command, rights of members, financial structure, and bylaws. As spelled out in the constitution, UNIA chapters were to elect their leadership, and each chapter and branch was to have representation at the annual convention. The incorporation document for the BSL indicated that the shipping line was to be managed by a board and shareholders were to be informed as well as participate in decisions.

Though integrated into the constitution, the British political institutions adopted are more numerous. The titles of UNIA officers and their political relationships are modeled after Britain's, beginning with the power dichotomy between the potentate and the president-general. As in the modern English political hierarchy, the potentate had no material power in the UNIA; it was a symbolic and ceremonial office. The UNIA potentate was to be a continental African,[6] perhaps to symbolize the veneration of Africa as the homeland in their political beliefs.

Material power and control was vested in the president-general as the "working head of the UNIA"; this is reminiscent of the prime minister's control over British government. Other offices described in chapter 2, such as the high chancellor, arose from the same model.

The keystone for the UNIA political structure was authoritarianism.[7] This may seem to contradict the assertion that the UNIA adopted American democratic institutions, but a closer examination will show that it does not. The formalized institutions were practiced, but the authority lay with the New York headquarters. The hierarchical structure insured this. Each chapter had administrative officers who managed the UNIA's affairs in their jurisdiction. These were elected offices, but election granted the authority to make chapter decisions within the structure of the constitution and bylaws; membership entrusted decision making and program planning to administrators who supposedly reflected their views. And in turn, headquarters made decisions for chapters and branches. At the top of this hierarchy was the president-general, who dominated the structure.

I distinguish here between *authoritarianism* and *autocracy.* Authoritarianism creates dominance through administrative offices, but cannot enforce unmitigated control over its members, as would be the case with autocracy. In fact, an organization or regime needs loyalty and trusting members to encapsulate its power.

Trust in leadership receded when BSL problems emerged, and even nationalist ideologues called for changes. Some even called for new leadership.[8] In addition, members used formal and informal channels to influence the management of the BSL in particular. The annual conventions of 1921 and 1922 were used to try to force changes, and though the UNIA/BSL leadership retained control, their position was destabilized because an ample and varied proportion of the membership became disillusioned. Members and supporters were free to exit the organization (or conceptual state) at will.

The exit option particularly hurt program management. High attrition of BSL administrators accompanied authoritarian governance of the UNIA. This added to instability of the BSL because new officers would not only have to learn about BSL's version of shipping administration and adapt to indifferent economic realities, but institutional memory in key administrative positions could not be accumulated and drawn upon. Authoritarianism hurt program management in another important way. The charismatic Garvey had to travel extensively to insure the continual inflow of capital, and no other administrator was able to command the respect or support to manage office operations effectively in his absence. This deferred crucial policy decisions and implementation as well as impeded the large international bureaucracy. Effective performance in these two crucial roles—major fund-raiser and state executive officer—kept Garvey inundated with work. The execution of these major responsibilities along with his serving as a frequent editorialist may help explain his legendary imperious management style. In his presence, sycophancy was often in force, but in his absence cooperation and therefore production was diminished.

Authoritarianism did have one benefit to African diaspora economic activities. Authoritarianism contributed toward effective centralization of transnational administrative and communication systems. This led to focused management that caused the UNIA political structure to function like a machine. The constitution spelled out how funds were to be collected and how to submit funds. This insured uninterrupted collection of dues, stock revenues, and donations to the treasury. Authoritarianism meant that restrictions on the processing allowed the UNIA/BSL flexibility in the allocation of investment funds to the needs of the organization as a whole, rather than to the program to which the funds were dedicated. The UNIA treated all streams of revenue as tax revenue meant to finance its state apparatus and programming.

The *Negro World* used the international network not only to advertise the shipping line and educate its membership regarding UNIA programming and positions on political issues, but it inculcated its membership against the charges of financial mismanagement and other criticisms. For example, the

Negro World ran stories of other shipping companies and countries having problems with their merchant marine. Du Bois and Briggs faced formidable opponents in editorialists such as Ferris and Bruce. Ferris took issue with Du Bois and the 1921 Pan-African Congress: "the so-called pan-African Congress was far from being what the term implies. Of the fifty-seven delegates at the congress, only fourteen were Africans—less than one-third. From this it will be readily seen how far short the congress was of being Pan-African . . . It was the poet rather than the scientist in the learned Dr. Dubois that caused him to call a congress, not representative of Africa, a Pan-African congress."[9]

Ultimately, however, authoritarianism may have helped defeat the BSL. As we will discuss in a later section, shipping and accounting knowledge were limited within the UNIA, and the few with such knowledge, such as Captain Mulzac and Clarence Curley, an early BSL director and an accountant, were kept outside of the leadership circle. As a result, nescient decisions by the BSL board led to the rapid depletion of funds and eventually confidence in the shipping venture. It is true that other obstacles impeded BSL's furtherance, but inexperienced management encased in an authoritarian political structure was not the least of these.

Financial Base

Without financial resources, linking the African diaspora via shipping would have remained an idealistic theory. The acquisition of independent financial resources was the bedrock, the essential substructure, upon which the shipping effort could be built. The indispensable kernel of the acquisition plan was the UNIA's decision to rely upon small contributions. This made the plan plausible to black people at all income levels, which gave the venture a chance. Plus, casting the net over the entire black Atlantic made it possible to amass larger numbers of contributions, which meant a realistic chance at capital accumulation. Internecine disagreements, which were referred to law officials for resolution, forestalled this plan, however.

When unable to convince organizational leadership otherwise, the UNIA's audit committee complained to the New York district attorney about the misuse of BSL funds for other UNIA programs. Rather than state intervention dissolving the BSL idea as it may have intended, it inadvertently provided a better capital accumulation alternative. By presenting an ultimatum to UNIA leaders to choose between dissolution and incorporation of the shipping venture, the New York district attorney gave the BSL better procedures for capital accumulation. This enhanced the program in several ways, two that are particularly important here.

First, incorporation professionalized the procedures that the BSL employed for capital accumulation. Professionalization called for a separate administrative structure for BSL, which included a board, financial administrators, and stock sellers. Procedures were codified for selling stocks, handling the incoming money, and managing the salespeople. Incorporation required providing a record of sales, which was a management tool for the BSL treasurer. Ongoing records of sales meant that fund calculations were simplified and sales projections could be made. The BSL also knew how many stock certificates were outstanding. Secondly, incorporation provided a terminology that enhanced the sales pitch of the sales force. The use of the terminology suggested an understanding of investment, which may not, in fact, have been present. The financial terminology provided phraseology for promotion purposes that had not been available previously. Using concepts such as capitalization, BSL administrators and sales agents may have conveyed a financial competence that did not exist. Initial capitalization was $500,000, but this merely meant that the company was authorized by the state in which it was incorporated to amass that much capital. Capitalization did not indicate the amount of capital possessed or within immediate reach. Yet reports, correspondence, and news articles suggest that neither the press, opponents, nor government agents adequately understood this distinction. This suggests that working-class investors likewise may have misunderstood the actual financial position of the company. Ironically, W. E. B. Du Bois was one of the few writers who tried to explain the financial language correctly.[10]

With the small-contribution focus and impressive financial language, the Black Star Line became of interest to a community beyond the political allies and membership of the UNIA. The result is that several streams of money flowed into the New York headquarters from very different types of BSL investors:

Ideological supporters, independent and nationalistic activists throughout the black Atlantic

Those choosing to relocate to Africa for both political and economic reasons

Black capitalists investing primarily for profit

Caribbean and West African businesspeople looking for an efficient shipping alternative for their goods[11]

These fund-raising strategies enabled the BSL to raise approximately $800,000 over a ten-month period; estimates range from $750,000 to nearly $1 million. Therefore incorporation clearly presented the BSL the opportunity to use more lucrative inroads to capital accumulation.

However, inadequate financial management diminished the impact of fund-raising. First, the accounting system, while intricate, was inefficient. Reporting procedures were detailed, but report development and submissions were lax. In addition, BSL stock receipts were not always deposited separately but were combined with the revenue from other UNIA programs.

I am not convinced that this was the result of incompetence, miseducation, or inexperience. Rather, it was an intentional and inventive way to reconfigure an American financial institution into a tax-raising devise. The investment monies were deposited with other UNIA revenue and used like general revenue funds for operations and special programs. The BSL, while the most lucrative, was only one of these programs. Remember, the UNIA considered itself a government, not an organization under the jurisdiction of the United States. Thus the configuration of its financial system may have been considered its responsibility and its inherent sovereign right. I do not believe that the UNIA or the BSL board of directors saw their actions as criminal but as efficient use of resources to meet the perceived state's needs.

Previous studies point to the inflated price of the *Yarmouth* as another example of financial ineptitude, and as we have seen, the UNIA's unfamiliarity with shipping administration and the unscrupulous selling practices of some shipping agents make this a reasonable conclusion. However, the political economy operative at the time also influenced that sale price. The *Yarmouth* purchase agreement was in sync with economic realities in 1919. Recall that there was a shortage of ships in 1919, so the price for shipping capacity went up. This meant increases in the cost of ships regardless of age and quality issues. Aldcroft and Zeis both point out that several companies earned large profits from the lucrative market in selling shipping space. Two additional variables probably would not have affected a mainstream buyer: the UNIA was underfunded and a marginalized group. The BSL had to reduce expectations of ship size and quality in order to purchase, just as marginalized people have to economize on housing and other goods. Thus, the price for the *Yarmouth* was influenced by economic realities and customary cost inflation faced by marginalized people for goods and services.

The UNIA's view of itself as a state government may explain its peremptory management of its financial administrative staff. The secretive, authoritarian leadership did not give administrative staff adequate information to efficiently manage the financial system or personnel. These administrators were to follow orders and not attempt to force compliance to American law and accounting regulations, which may have caused a disconnection between the leadership and the financial administration of its program. Consequently, the ability to monitor revenues was compromised, but likewise leadership's ability to plan and operate its programs was compromised. Inadequate supervision meant inaccurate records, both of which are conducive to embezzlement.

From the federal government's perspective, the UNIA was a subversive and fraudulent organization subject to penalty, not a sovereign state. Incorporation necessarily invoked American legal constraints to the UNIA's financial administration and expenditures. To the epigram "He who has the gold makes the rules" might be added "He who writes the laws defines criminality."[12] Incorporation meant that the government could legally monitor BSL activities and charge it with commercial fraud and other criminal offenses if it did anything outside the rules of incorporation. Thus through incorporation, BSL amassed more funds but lost flexibility in the usage of the capital. Corporate regulations forbade the use of the capital outside the strictly defined parameters of the project for which stock was sold. The use of BSL funds in any UNIA programming—even though it was the parent company—was illegal. Further, corporate law gave the government parameters to intervene legally in BSL affairs. This meant the UNIA policy of using investment funds like tax revenue was unthinkable under U.S. jurisdiction: from the government perspective, there was no such thing as UNIA jurisdiction.

There was another interesting finding that not only speaks to the financial character of BSL, but also highlights its distinction from other African-American political organizations. The BSL takes on characteristics of entrepreneurship.[13] The UNIA diverged from the normative functions of a black political organization concerned with equality and/or independence and sought to lay the foundation of an enclave economy. It did so by attempting to found what Casson calls market-making service. First, a shipping line was an equitable and efficient method for black businesses to move goods and services into the marketplace. Secondly, the venture was to offer another mechanism to independence: it was to provide the transportation to an independent nation, where economic institutions could be developed and employed to facilitate autonomy in the international political economy. It was clear that discrimination had alienated many black customers in need of dependable shipping service. Therefore organizing and efficiently serving this market was expected to pay for itself once the line was established. The challenge was to create the line and develop dependable service.

The UNIA used entrepreneurship in an innovative way to alleviate social derogation and economic discrimination. Clearly, this was not the first time that entrepreneurship had been applied to the economic challenges faced by the Africans throughout the Black Atlantic. But heretofore, it had been individuals beginning business enterprises, even as those proprietors may have been politically motivated.[14] Such ventures had not been undertaken by political or social organizations. The UNIA tried to merge classic corporate entrepreneurship (as defined by Casson) to political pan-Africanism. Like the often-stereotyped entrepreneurship of the nineteenth century, the UNIA had a vision of meeting a specific unmet need of black people in an innovative way; serving this market would net financial profits. At the same time, the UNIA thought that it could facilitate the realization of its twin goals of economic independence and the establishment of a free state. They seemed to have envisioned themselves as the fourth factor of production, that savvy entrepreneur that could effectively assemble, organize, and manage goods or services in such a way as to not only meet the needs but eventually turn a profit for BSL shareholders and its political parent, the UNIA. In the *UNIA Papers*, there is a continuing discourse on what I would call a captured market. Stock-selling hyperbole aside, speakers and members were sincere in their belief that if a shipping service was offered, there would be ample black customers for it, coming to it out of need and racial patriotism. Therefore they were willing to risk shareholder funds along with membership revenue (such as dues and the annual tax) to implement the project. Theoretically, it may have worked were it not for twin contaminants in the black Atlantic: miseducation and assimilative effects, both of which limited entrepreneurial possibilities within the diaspora. The following two sections elaborate on how these effects worked against liberation.

Education and Skill Level

History suggests that the education of Africans in the diaspora was conducted in such a way as to be useful to the colonial powers and U.S. labor interests first and foremost, and secondly to meet the basic human needs of the subject populations. There was diversity in the education and skill levels of the activists involved in the BSL, but their expertise was in areas unrelated—at least directly—to shipping. They were confined at the poles of the employment spectrum as will be shown.

At one pole were those proscribed to physical labor and support services useful to carry on raw materials production, commerce, and urban maintenance, such as sanitation services. In the early twentieth century, the majority of black workers were still in agriculture, but the migration to other forms of physical labor was underway because of continuing industrialization and the development of a transportation system to support especially international trade. Many had migrated to Panama to build and service the canal that was expected to facilitate trade with Asia. The U.S. economy's expanding industrial sector during the war consumed all available labor; West Indians and black Americans built the infrastructure of both of these economic transformations. They were plantation workers for Central America's increasing fruit exports and sugar production concentrated in Cuba. Blacks stoked furnaces in American factories and transported raw materials at building sites in the emerging industrial economy. Others worked in the merchant marine as seamen, cooks, and stevedores. U.S. blacks also went west to work on the railroad and in mining.

At the other pole were the college educated and entrepreneurs. Their specialties, however, were confined to supportive professions. Black colonial subjects were educated to handle basic colonial administrative systems in the Caribbean, Central America, and West Africa. They served as clerks and bookkeepers in colonial administration, were permitted to work with printers, and worked as teachers among the masses. A few were licensed medical doctors and lawyers. The U.S. black population's access to education and careers was similar. Their education was geared toward providing teachers and administrative staff, usually for limited state and federal government clerical assignments, a remnant of the reconstruction era political clientelism with radical Republicans. A relatively few lawyers and doctors were trained to service the black population; rarely could they practice in the mainstream. And although higher education was limited, there was still an overflow of educated blacks for the few jobs available due to racial discrimination and the limited income in the community for what may have seemed extraneous or luxury services. Perhaps this fueled entrepreneurship; here again, however, the fields into which they could venture were proscribed. The areas where their skills were most developed involved language, both written and oral skills. Rarely were they educated in the sciences and technological fields such as engineering. Such education would have made them economically competitive and enable independent development, which were not required for industrial manual labor and in colonial American economies. Many of the educated chose what I would call entrepreneurial journalism, starting black newspapers or making arrangements to contribute articles for pay to black or liberal journals. As Hanchard points out, many black activists, particularly transnational activists of the era, were journalists. I would add ministers, missionaries, and academicians to this coterie with a platform to speak from. These professions were outside the closely supervised labor forces and therefore had some independence and flexibility.

The array of skills displayed in the UNIA/BSL leadership reflects these educational and employment experiences. The visible UNIA leadership, that is to say, those most in the public eye, were the orators and the editorialists. These would include Garvey, Ferris, and Bruce. The latter two were respected journalists and "race" men; they were close advisors to Garvey. Ferris was assistant president-general in the UNIA.[15] Next in visibility would be ministers, who often were division leaders, and noted performing artist and activist Henrietta Vinton Davis, who served as principal speaker at mass meetings and eventually became the UNIA vice president of international affairs. Hubert Harrison, another highly respected activist, lent prestige and intellect to the *Negro World*'s educational function. These orators and writers interpreted domestic and international politics for UNIA members and made the case for the BSL, which was first advocated by the many black seamen who supported the UNIA.

Educated in the liberal arts and informed because they were journalists and academicians, these activists developed political plans that they believed would diffuse exploitation and begin the redevelopment of a healthy black society. This was the essence of the UNIA's political goal, and the BSL was a crucial component of it. Although the outcome envisioned was commendable and may have seemed achievable, those involved in the project may not have realized the skills and resources required. Liberal arts, medicine, and law ill-prepared them to build the economic and transportation infrastructure to support an enclave economy, much less a nation-state. The few among them with practical training in accounting and business were isolated from the mainstream economy because of racism. Confined to clerical work, few had the opportunity to hone skills in the internal mechanics of economic administration. So while they may have known basic financial principles, they had no experience as to their application in actual economic world. It was not intelligence or ability but inexperience and inappropriate education that accounts for much of the incompetence demonstrated in the BSL shipping administration.

In the areas where there was some experience and competence, it was insufficient. This is illustrated in the experience of purchasing the first ship for the line. Speeches and editorials indicate that the leadership and spokespeople understood the importance of shipping, not only to UNIA's goals but also its indispensable role in the international economy. However, they did not understand ship operations or the complicated business culture of the shipping industry.

To Garvey's credit, the evidence suggests that he did turn to a ship captain, Joshua Cockbourne, for assistance, and the trial transcript reveals that he relied on UNIA members with shipping experience to look for appropriate vessels. But their experience was confined to ship operations; there was no expertise as it related to ship purchasing or ship quality. An analogy might help to emphasize the importance of this deficiency. Today, no professional airline would rely on a pilot to determine either airplane procurement decisions or the quality or types of planes required to meet its criteria for profitability and utility. At most, pilots' opinions and concerns would be factored into the choices recommended by aeronautic engineers, mechanics, lawyers, and financial professionals. The Black Star Line needed expertise in shipping procurement, engineering, and administration. The records do not indicate that this was sought until after the negotiations for the *Yarmouth* began. The nautical engineer consulted to do the ship inspection refused to participate on the project. One can speculate that racism intervened, but the record suggests that several engineers that were approached questioned the transaction.[16]

Secondly, there were only three black ship captains licensed in the industrialized world.[17] So although Garvey was willing to request advice from ship captains, there weren't very many viewpoints to choose from, and the leadership was willing to discount the advice they heard. We have seen the contention between Garvey and Cockbourne and how BSL vice president Thompson rebuffed Mulzac's efforts. Perhaps this response was justified to some degree. All the captains attempted to influence the building of BSL not only in the interests of black political amelioration but in the interests of their own employment opportunities, which evaporated after the war. One could argue that Cockbourne was dishonest, further compromising the BSL directors' only direct link to understanding the shipping industry. However, discounting their expertise probably led to unwise ship purchases that ultimately consumed the BSL's capital.

The resource put to the most prudent use was their legal team's expertise. The role of black lawyers in the ascendancy of the UNIA and BSL has been ignored. Not only did they successfully contend with court challenges, but they circumvented Kilroe's investigation. Their expertise probably went into the writing of the constitution, bylaws, and incorporation documents. The lawyers were also quiet links to black Republican politicians, facilitating Garvey's reentry into the country. They might have been able to reduce the fraud charges, but Garvey refused their intervention. However, they too were unfamiliar with the intricacies of ship contracting, and as a consequence did not protect the BSL's interests in shipping agreements. For instance, no demurrage clauses were negotiated to limit the costs incurred during port layovers, including unbudgeted payroll, ship maintenance, and supplies. These costs were extensive, particularly in the transport of the whiskey cargo.

Assimilative Effects

In addition to overt discrimination in access to education and employment opportunities, a hidden obstacle, which I will call inhibited assimilation, would have distorted their best efforts. The confluence of racism, miseducation, and inhibited assimilation clearly influenced the political goals and performance of the UNIA's shipping program. However, this impediment was amorphous and therefore any evaluation of its precise impact is difficult. The derogation of things African by white Americans prevented black people from being wholly assimilated into American culture and social life. They were marginalized and, as importantly, did not share the common European history from which most American social mores evolved. Throughout the slavery era, education was proscribed for the overwhelming majority of black people. Racism and Eurocentrism permeated political, social, and economic institutions; those of Western European descent controlled power and wealth. Both white and black populations in the United States and the rest of the diaspora internalized these customs. While retention of African cultural traditions throughout the diaspora has been documented, it was suppressed; because the enslaved population came from various ethnic groups, there was no one set of African cultural mores to which they could cling. Racism precluded the introduction or proliferation of mores and customs outside the Western European culture framework, and successive generations, both citizens and slaves, inherited these institutions.[18] However, the enslaved did not have access to all institutions and were forced to absorb those that insured their enslavement.

When educational programs finally were accessible, they were inevitably Eurocentric, whether deliberately or inadvertently. Yet black consanguinity and racial dignity generated historical writings, literature, and speeches that glorified black origins, that is to say, their African past. Such writings were used to resist negative manifestations of racism and stereotypical beliefs surrounding African civilization and capabilities. Robin Kelley cogently expresses this tenet when writing about African American historians of the nineteenth and twentieth centuries:

> By linking American Negroes to the ancient world, those authors were essentially making a claim for black people's humanity. Woodson makes his intentions quite explicit in the preface to *The African Background Outlined:* "The facts herein presented will show that the Negro has achieved much in various spheres, and to know the possibilities of the race a scientific appraisal of its past is necessary. The author considers the Negro as human—responding very much as others do to the same stimuli, advancing when free to go forward and lagging behind when hindered by obstacles not encountered by others."[19]

Africa was romanticized and its cultures jealously defended, even though diaspora descendents could not have known these cultures in depth. So with cultural memory impaired and Western institutions modified to attempt to meet their needs, the UNIA implemented the BSL and Liberian settlement programs. However, the intangible impact of inhibited assimilation contaminated their understanding of African political and economic realities, and led them to depreciate contemporary African capabilities while they simultaneously romanticized historic achievements. For example, the UNIA constitution contains this condescending statement: "The objects of the Universal Negro Improvement Association and African Communities League shall be: to establish a Universal Confraternity among the race; to promote the spirit of pride and love; to reclaim the fallen; to administer to and assist the needy; *to assist in civilizing the backward tribes of Africa . . . to promote a conscientious Spiritual worship among the native tribes of Africa.*"[20] They had internalized the very racism that they sought to eliminate or at least transcend. It must be noted that the UNIA was not the only black political organization that unconsciously was hindered by assimilative effects. They inherited these notions from noted nineteenth-century black historians and activists who were also drenched in religious activism.

This flaw marked Du Bois, one of the foremost scholars of the era. On several occasions, Du Bois made distinctions between "educated" or "civilized" Africans and the "natives."[21] Even within U.S. black politics, he often was accused of being elitist, not only by UNIA members but socialists such as Randolph and Owen.

The result of this retarding assimilation was an unavoidable obstacle between diaspora and West African activists. Imagine a Cambridge-educated West African reading the UNIA constitution or receiving the news that Garvey was the "provisional president of Africa." Such language complicated any contemplated alliance between West Africa and its diaspora. This is evident even after one factors in the similar deforming effect of European assimilation upon the West African comprador class, who disparaged their peasant brethren. Thus, West Africans approached the Black Star Line cautiously, with only some agreeing to an economic alliance. Others preferred to ally with Du Bois's pan-African movement. Continental Africans continually attempted to correct the erroneous cultural and political views of contemporary Africa held by its diaspora. Kobena Sekyi, a West African activist, suggested that the diaspora accept that they had suffered acculturation that had to be corrected before entering the African political arena. Sekyi suggested that African Americans send their children to Africa during the summer so they could adapt to their own cultural institutions and that African Americans help West Africa adapt Western industrial technology to African society.[22] The subtle negative impact of inhibited assimilation created complicated barriers that prevented effective unified action in their best interests. It is because of well-rooted historical ties and the political struggles of highly respected nationalists and other liaisons between diasporans and West Africans that they were able to get through this barrier at all. And while UNIA branches were formed in Africa, the BSL had failed by the time that they could effectively organize on the continent. Of course one cannot dismiss the pressure applied to West Africans by England and France, which will be addressed later in the chapter.

Pernicious assimilation may have had another subtle but corroding effect in the decline of the BSL and ultimately the UNIA itself. The West Indian members, who had a substantial presence in the leadership, suffered from the assimilative impact of British colonialism, while U.S. members were influenced by putatively more democratic political institutions. As we have seen, the UNIA constitution embraced both British and American political institutions, but the authoritarian leadership clearly displeased many U.S. American members. (This is not to say that all West Indian members accepted authoritarianism; in particular, West Indian socialists were vocal in their opposition.) Emonei Carter, a UNIA member, described in a letter the American thrusts to intervene in the closed administration of the BSL project and reorganize the financial and political structure: "We [U.S. Americans] will place the affairs of the organization on a solid financial basis, or else withdraw our influence from the body. Any such movement as this on the part of Americans now identified with the body, would mean its collapse."[23] As an aside, his letter verifies that Americans were an integral part of the BSL, contrary to what was suggested in articles in the *Crisis* and the *Chicago Defender*. They were present and influential not only in the leadership (Bruce,

Davis, Eason, and Ferris, for example), but also in the general membership, and most certainly purchased substantial stock in BSL. Carter's letter also indicates, however, the commitment that Americans had to the organization despite its authoritarianism and the overzealous nature of a Garveyite cadre:

> I find many foolish persons here as followers, who do not understand Mr. Garvey nor his movement, and they are constantly issuing wild silly statements, believing firmly that the movement is a provisional government already and that the Executive Council are in a position to carry out the prerogatives of a government within a government. My conclusion of the whole matter to date is that the whole movement is calculated to accomplish a real good in organizing the colored folks of the world to do something in a commercial way, because when ships are purchased and put on the high seas, they will find much trade in Africa and the colonies abroad. There is nothing revolutionary in the movement nor any secret affiliation with any foreign powers.

Mobilization Strategies

As we have seen, economic development was a principal goal of the UNIA, and the BSL was an integral program to reach this goal. It was theorized that the extraction of black workers and business from the grips of western exploitation was the key to achieving independence and equality. Independent programming was in keeping with that ideological position, and they used the capabilities and established productive institutions embedded in black society to create the Black Star Line.

Consequently, independent administration was an important strategy. The UNIA was an independent organization with minimal connections to white liberal, socialist, or conservative forces. This is not to say that members did not embrace these ideologies; rather, it is to point out that the organization was exclusively black in terms of leadership and membership and relied upon constituent funding. As a result, the goals and direction were not substantively influenced by outside forces whose goals may have been quite different, as had been the case during the Washington era. This independence was important because external funding and direction has been thought to constrain black political advancement. A British military intelligence officer explains this political tactic: "These new leaders, although better educated than their predecessors, are nevertheless more incapable of giving voice to any real radical opinions because of the economic necessities of their existence. Most of them, Booker Washington, Moton, DuBois, Pickins, Kelly Miller, etc. are connected with make their living from institutions which largely exist as a result of the philanthropy of industrial magnates who endow the majority with more important negro schools."[24] Imperialist powers understood that to contribute significantly to an organization is to purchase influence in its programming. And while British and American governments were concerned about black "radical" organizations affiliated with the socialist and communist parties becoming politically effective, research shows that such associations also may have hampered black activists' programs and strategies.[25]

The UNIA's independence provided flexibility and the opportunity for black activists and professionals to employ their own solutions on a scale and at an intensity of their own choosing. An assemblage of talented, experienced political activists and professionals developed programming and were able to interact with the black world using their own cultural norms and understanding of the political and economic issues. They quickly were able to attract attendance by using black institutional structures, particularly the arts and religious infrastructure, to connect with large segments of the population and deliver cogent messages that resonated with black people throughout the diaspora who were interested in political and economic improvements and, as a consequence, expanded UNIA's international membership.

The decision to centralize facilitated their ability to function independently. The constitution, laying out a structure that could expand and maintain communication with other members and headquarters, was crucial to establishing a market for the BSL and assuring the infrastructure for proselytizing, of both the political message and investment possibilities. This resourceful network was possible because of the participation of highly respected, internationally known independent and nationalist activists, who over the years had constructed strong alliances with their counterparts throughout the diaspora and Africa. Their certification of the UNIA's integrity and goals facilitated international interest in the organization's possibilities.

The strategy of relying on small contributions provided a way to raise sufficient capital for the enterprise. But these strategies were only the structure within which the shipping venture could operate. The strategy to operate a profit-making business within the structure was complex and novel. I use the term novel because, although in many respects the UNIA chose to function as a germinal state or provisional government, it decided to develop a profit-making venture to achieve its political goals. Promotional speeches often meshed these components together, calling upon constituents and supporters to invest for political amelioration and for profit. This merger of government and business is problematic for at least three reasons. First, the fact that it considered itself a provisional government or embryonic state tells us that the UNIA was not fully developed or funded. Therefore sufficient and stable revenue to fund government operations and the BSL until it became self-supporting was not available. Secondly, political institutions normally provide support for business and businesses influence politics; however, both do not operate from the same institutional base. Third, governments usually offer public goods that may involve a self-funding mechanism—that is to say one that relies on revenue to cover operating costs.

Despite the rhetoric designed to attract revenue, the primary purpose of the BSL was to link diaspora communities in an effort to enhance political and economic interaction between them and move black people closer to liberation. It was an integral step in the establishment of independent political institutions and ultimately a nation. BSL was intended to be a public service because its main goal was not profit per se but to provide a component of the infrastructure necessary for UNIA nation building and overall black economic development.[26] Again, the UNIA grafted together components of American financial and governmental institutions to create its own instruments for development, such as "tax" revenue to fund that development. This is not to say that the UNIA leaders did not want profitability from projects such as the Black Star Line. Indeed, with the perceived captive black shipping market, they expected to achieve this goal ultimately. And by stimulating trade and industrial development, even more streams of revenue were expected, so investors would earn some return, much like city bondholders.

The economic infrastructure, including trading partners, had to be built in order for the shipping line to succeed. Thus precedence was given to the linkage of diaspora communities. Two programs were to be funded—the shipping network and the manufacturing program, which was to provide exports—but only the BSL was fully implemented. The membership and investors did not show comparable interest in the Negro Factories Corporation. Transportation was the preference according to where investors risked their funds and what letter writers to the *Negro World* and participants to conventions focused on. Once the ship purchase contract was made, the UNIA had to repay the substantial loan or face the possible repossession of the ship, displeasure of its membership, and criticism from opponents.

This putting the cart before the horse was the downfall of the plan. If the UNIA had developed its manufacturing plan prior to the shipping venture, perhaps trade of less critical goods and services could have been viable. (Here I am referring to the fact that Europe would have prevented trade in those products essential to its rebuilding effort.) For instance, Jamaica could have sold bananas, and the United States and Canada could have produced manufactured commodities that were marketable in the Caribbean. The 1920–21 *Negro World* suggested that manufacturing was planned for parts of Central America as well. Another compatible exchange might have been residual West African palm oil to African Americans for the processing of nonperishable soap products.[27] Fine African timber had already proven profitable in small trade deals between an African American company and a West African producer: this market might have been expanded, perhaps into furniture manufacturing. And while the enclave economy development was key, speeches suggest that the UNIA would not have restricted trade to only African diaspora markets, where income levels were relatively small. This strategy would have ensured that ample markets were available to absorb black exports.

The membership did not support the National Factories Corporation, perhaps because it was not advertised. The *UNIA Papers* show little discussion about it. *Negro World* carried some advertisement, but not nearly as much as for BSL. As such, black Americans had nothing to export; what could be traded? Africa and its diaspora provide similar products to the international economy. Agrarian, colonized Africa and its diaspora supply raw materials to industrialized and richer countries. In some instances, they trade the same produce, such as bananas or cotton. Black farmers in colonized Africa and American sharecroppers did not control enough product to keep an adequate supply on the market; it is not known what plans, if any, the UNIA had to change this circumstance. Once they had goods to market, the relatively few independent black farmers in the hostile American South would have experienced great difficulty interfacing with the BSL. Its incorporation language included servicing the Mississippi River and the gulf, but it would have been difficult for such a service to be established in the region. Urban black businesses that had access to the BSL did not support it.

Because of colonization and past enslavement, the income of blacks in the Caribbean was infinitesimal. Thus import capability was minimal even if manufactured goods and foodstuffs were available. Stable wages were confined to the United States, Canada, and the Canal Zone. Canada's black population was arguably too small to consume ample manufactured goods to assure reasonable profits for a manufacturing venture. West Indian population in Europe also was small, and employment opportunities were limited after the war.

The reader must keep in mind, however, that the federal government confiscated the UNIA and BSL records: as a result, we cannot know how they planned to stimulate business activity and trade. The relationship between African American farmers and BSL is not clear; the meeting minutes presented as evidence during the trial did not speak to plans to motivate African American businesses to use the BSL or develop potential black exporters in the Caribbean and Africa. BSL supporters included experienced sailors who knew a great deal about shipping needs around the Atlantic, so there may have been viable plans to insure the BSL's marketability. Black farmers in the Caribbean and North America already had defied the odds to survive, albeit on a comparatively small scale. For that matter, the economic and political logic of the era argued against the capital accumulation that was achieved by the BSL. We know from African correspondence that there was some interest on the West Coast;[28] but strategies to get around colonial opposition as well as measures to identify specific producers and products to be traded remain unknown. The fact that Jamaica's banana farmers were able to survive in the shadow of the United Fruit Company's dominance suggests that there were viable mechanisms to protect and increase black international trade on some level.

Channels of Influence

The UNIA/BSL's access to power was limited. The obvious reasons are racism and the stigma of slavery. The Wilson administration had reinstituted segregation in the federal government bureaucracy. Further, Wilson headed the Democratic Party, and most of the UNIA's contacts (as for most blacks) in the federal government were with the Republican Party; partisanship would have minimized access as well. Scarce resources precluded buying political or electoral influence. However, as its membership grew as the result of the *Negro World*'s popularity and its inroads into the black church congregations, the UNIA began to gain the attention of some urban political machines, Tammany Hall in particular.[29] Twice, New York mayoral candidates addressed large mass meetings, and they might have made a mutually useful political compact that would have minimized at least municipal judicial intervention. However, during the BSL era, the UNIA did not pursue such an alliance.

When the Republicans regained the presidency, the UNIA leadership used its connections to the black Republican patronage system to gain access to services and time extensions for legal matters. These contacts included UNIA attorneys William Matthews and Wilford Smith, both of whom had represented Booker T. Washington, and the leading black Republican, Henry Lincoln Johnson. Some evidence suggests that the attorneys had made political arrangements to reduce or possibly eliminate the fraud charges against BSL directors, particularly Garvey, but, as stated earlier, Garvey refused to plead to a lesser charge or pay a bribe. Another person with influential ties was a disillusioned former Republican, John E. Bruce. Better known as "Bruce Grit," he kept in touch with old political allies and many international journalistic contacts.

Outside the United States, the UNIA was associated with West Indian unions. Several strikes disrupted Caribbean economic relations and exploded into violence, but they also led to pay increases. The BSL effort was very important to black islanders, who accounted for substantial BSL investment. Black workers would leave sugar and fruit plantations to see the ships and purchase stock. Consequently, colonial officers were concerned about the influence of UNIA and its ability to disrupt work operations and increase labor costs.

Briefly, the UNIA and its BSL program held sway with Liberian government officials. Cut off during the war from its major trading partner, Germany, Liberia needed cash infusions. However, pressure from England and France as well as the UNIA's inability to provide the $5 million needed led Liberia to turn to the U.S. government for assistance. Liberian government officials and activists were divided between the two principle diaspora ideologies: Garveyism and Du Boisian pan-Africanism. Ultimately, Liberia chose economic necessity over ideological or existential concerns. Du Boisian pan-Africanist activists had stronger links to black and white Republicans and access to the lobbying wing of the NAACP, and effective lobbying was key to acquiring the American loan.[30]

Impact on International Politics

Sheffer concluded that in efforts to address their internal needs, retain connections with their homeland, and support the homeland when opportunities permit, diasporas will have influence on international relations to which there may be responses. In explaining what he means by *influence,* Sheffer cautions that it would be necessarily subtle and "usually takes place in the gray areas of the international systems or sub-systems of host countries." For instance, effective lobbying may convince host countries to modify their foreign policies in such a way that benefits the diaspora's homeland but inconveniences other international actors. Economic activities may positively or negatively impact the economic agendas of host countries and cause them to take corrective action through consuls or international organizations.

The UNIA's impact upon international politics fits well within Sheffer's observation. The UNIA did try to lobby the peace talks and the League of

Nations in the interests of Africa as did other African diaspora groups. While it did not change the measures taken regarding Africa, it did help to publicize the repression taking place in Africa and within the diaspora. But the BSL specifically bolstered black activism by presenting the possibilities for both political and economic organization and advancement. In his coverage of the arrival of the *Yarmouth* to Jamaica, a West Indian reporter said, "They look upon this ship as a symbol of the spirit of enterprise and self-help, and they draw a deduction that what has been done in this particular instance can also be accomplished in other and equally useful directions."[31] Thus the BSL effort energized the politics of the Black Atlantic because it demonstrated the capacity to unify and raise funds to address political and economic problems. It suggested a latent strength and an alternative to, or additional means to, liberation beyond traditional lobbying and petitions. The BSL effort attracted enough interest to augment the membership of the UNIA, which grew into a mass movement. The diaspora's small nationalist movement was reinvigorated.

This was most visible in Caribbean labor relations. The BSL exemplified the belief that black people need not be trapped in menial labor and abject poverty. Black self-improvement during this era was on an immense scale. Political activism particularly in the Caribbean region was invigorated. Laborers in Central America stopped production on United Fruit Company plantations to participate in celebratory activities upon the first BSL ship's arrival, which buoyed symbolic black politics. Independent black banana growers anticipated increased access to transportation.

This animated political organizing, fund-raising, and belligerence disrupted labor and vexed relations with the British colonial administration. Fearful of labor disruption and loss of colonial control, the British increased repressive measures. These actions included banning the *Negro World*, disempowering Garvey by proscribing his movements in the Caribbean, and sharing intelligence regarding UNIA/BSL with the U.S. government. Surveillance was increased also because of concern about an alliance between UNIA and Sinn Fein and the movement of weapons into Caribbean colonies.

The domestic concerns of the United States were somewhat different than Europe's. Neither the UNIA nor the BSL disrupted labor relations for three reasons. First, it was clear that the wages of black industrial labor financed the BSL effort (and therefore the UNIA treasury). Secondly, the white-controlled labor movement marginalized black labor activists. American concern included possible escalation in racial violence, which disrupted municipal governance and economic activity after the war.

American concerns about the Caribbean were similar to those of Britain. Unlike in the United States, the UNIA leadership supported labor activism in the Caribbean because the black population was much larger and in control of that movement. Well integrated into union leadership, the UNIA did influenced political and labor activity in the Caribbean. The domestication of Caribbean labor unrest was important to the U.S. goal of facilitating economic activity in the region. Two economic imperatives were key for American policymakers: one geopolitical in nature and the other commercial. First, three UNIA strongholds probably were of great concern to the United States. Jamaica and Cuba are situated between the U.S. eastern seaboard and the Panama Canal, and Costa Rica is on the northern border of Panama. Labor disruption in these countries could disrupt fueling station operations, camouflage British operations, and diminish economic returns of American investors. The commercial issue revolved around canal operations. The canal would facilitate trade between the United States and Southeast Asia. Commercial traffic needed to flow smoothly through the Caribbean area, so American producers would be confident and risk expanding markets. Thus there was a strong motivation to keep any hostile forces in the region subdued. One of the best-organized "hostile forces" was the UNIA, and its membership was emboldened by the Black Star Line. The *Negro World* was banned in Panama, and American consuls closely monitored activities in the region.

More than concern about independent action by the BSL or the UNIA, the two hegemonic powers were most concerned with it being manipulated by a state interested in economic advancement in the region. Each of these powers could neutralize the effort by administrative action or minimal force. Tracing a connection between the BSL/UNIA and one of the powers or the socialist movement highlighted the fears of the powers as much as action by the UNIA itself. The United States saw the BSL as a Trojan horse for the British, intended to undermine U.S. economic arrangements in the Caribbean but also to impede economic ties with South America. The Monroe Doctrine spelled out the United States' rationale for interceding in British colonial operations in the western hemisphere. The Unites States government moved to thwart the UNIA's programming, particularly its umbilical cord to black American money, the BSL. Therefore the BI urged the USSB to deny the UNIA access to ships and prosecuted on charges of fraud. Any concrete measures taken by the Military Intelligence Division remain unknown. For its part, Britain was cognizant of America's alternatives in the region, and they carefully renegotiated business relations in place before the war.[32] They also watched for ties to Irish Americans or direct ties to Sinn Fein, and monitored the UNIA/BSL and curtailed its activities in the region.

Thus as Sheffer suggests, the BSL had a subtle impact on international politics, changing the agendas of Western powers and aggravating the relationship between them.

Evaluation of the Black Star Line Project

THE RISE

The particular circumstances of the international political economy of the interwar era set the stage for the BSL. Capital redeployment and the growing American industrial economy drew more black people into the monetized economy than at any earlier period. Prior to this time, many were trapped in the sharecropping economy; others had invested all of their scarce resources in farming or moving west to establish black towns or to work in mining and railroad businesses. So a large pool of black labor with regularized pay was a new economic factor. There was also a multiplier effect in that the small black professional and service class had a larger market to which to sell their services; artists had larger paying audiences. Many people saw the opportunity to leverage their newfound income into programs that could further strengthen their economic status. I call this the proactive group. Without these developments, resources might not have been available to the BSL, no matter how well organized the effort was.

However, adjustments in the labor market caused by the return of soldiers to the civilian economy led to racial violence in urban industrial centers. African Americans resisted displacement and attempts to reinstitute segregation. Others, frustrated by white supremacy and constant struggle, opted for emigration to Africa or the Caribbean. They had concluded that an equitable and interracial United States was impossible. I call these the reactive group.

In the UNIA, emphasis was placed on economic programming because it would extract blacks from the control of whites. These programs and its independent bent made the UNIA able to attract membership and resources. The BSL, in particular, met the needs of not only the UNIA's nationalist core constituency, but also the proactive and reactive groups. Sensing revitalization of the nationalist solution, the UNIA drew together international "race" activists in support of the movement. The endorsement of these seasoned black American and diaspora activists lent authenticity to the movement. Those in the reactive category saw the BSL as a way to emigrate to the venerated African homeland—anywhere but racist America. The proactive group saw the opportunity to not only strengthen the black economic position but turn a profit in the process.

But offering unique programming was only part of the rise of the BSL. The way in which the UNIA was organized permitted it to set up the BSL quickly, while people were motivated to address their political and economic problems. The creative use of Western institutions undergirded the rise. The UNIA had a centralized administrative structure delineated by its constitution and bylaws. There was a bureaucratic structure to carry out policy and a well-organized communications system to inform and manage its membership, and these structures were used to set up the BSL.

UNIA leaders understood how best to solicit resources from the people. The UNIA used the cultural institutions already well established in black society to attract potential investors. Well-planned musical events and orations involving popular figures drew black people to UNIA functions where, after the entertainment, they were proselytized in the UNIA political program. Using the well-established collection method associated with church, they collected money to establish the BSL. Most importantly, they relied on small contributions from throughout the diaspora, understanding that individual resources were constrained. They made it simple and painless to invest. Ironically, their fund-raising was enhanced by the forced incorporation of the BSL. During the meetings and through the *Negro World,* they taught members and supporters how to buy stock by mail and if necessary by installment. This formula was employed internationally. The UNIA's centralization of field processing and standardization of meetings and social affairs assured the effectiveness of this system. Published division reports in the *Negro World* lauding their accomplishments reveal that competitiveness was at work as well. All branches collected and reported in the same way and sent their contributions to the New York headquarters. The capital intake was made even larger by mail-in purchases and collections from meetings. The UNIA went from being just another small nationalist organization to being inundated with attention and funds. Populism seemed to have worked for the benefit of black nationalists. But the UNIA's authoritarian structure did not permit—at least directly—the membership's voice as to capital outlay.

The UNIA's legal team was indispensable to the efforts to establish the BSL. The lawyers blocked earlier legal efforts to impede the line. They probably were also responsible for the construction of the constitution. In addition to Bruce, they were best connected to the Republican Party and therefore able to defuse some of the efforts to dismantle to the UNIA and BSL.

THE FALL

The argument behind the BSL may have been more idealistic than practical, however. This is not to suggest that the plan was an attempt to defraud the UNIA membership and supporters. Rather, it is to point out that the resources and skills necessary for implementation of the ambitious program were not readily available in the black world. Beyond the primary problem of operating a complex international service, one at a disadvantage at colonial barriers, the venture had to overcome two resource dilemmas. There is the question of what could have been traded between communities that produced similar products. Additionally, black workers were employed but underpaid; a major portion were still in peasantry or hindered under colonization, so the question arises as to how they could pay for the products made available in the enclave economy. And due to the UNIA's revolutionary rhetoric, there probably were not customers beyond the black consumer market. Any supposed allies and supporters were, for the most part, behind colonial walls.

Let us consider resource limitations in more detail. The revenue realized by the BSL effort may have been unprecedented in black political organizations, but the financial requirements of a shipping line far exceeded the amount realized from stock sales. In addition to ship purchase, the capital had to fund operations, including salaries, fuel, equipment, stores, and insurance. One round trip between New York and Cuba was well over two thousand miles and took approximately two weeks; the crew size of the *Yarmouth* was at least forty-five men.[33] A fleet of ships would have been expensive to operate and maintain. Expenses would have increased substantially if the Africa fleet had been launched.

The headquarters staff had to be paid as well, and UNIA attitudes toward revenues meant salaries came from the same pool of capital funds. Here again, income from UNIA dues could not have covered salaries of all functioning UNIA corporations, even with some personnel serving more than one program. The high salaries paid to UNIA/BSL officers exacerbated this.[34] BSL clearly did not have enough capital to operate both legs of the shipping plan—linking the diaspora commercially and taking passengers and supplies to Liberia—it was running a deficit running only one. But abandoning a leg of the plan meant that at least one pool of BSL investors was not satisfied and would be less likely to continue their financial support. We know that the nationalists stayed with the effort, but the reactive group of investors and the proactive group could not be satisfied simultaneously.

This basic flaw in the concept was masked by immobilizing financial mismanagement. The UNIA displayed a keen ability to attract funding but ineptitude in allotting funds efficiently. Here I am not criticizing comingling of various program funds but rather inadequate bookkeeping and undocumented and extravagant spending. Salespeople did not have to document associated costs; fund-raising junkets often were very expensive. The processing of money was inefficient. Investment funds were not secured: they were visible to many workers in the BSL office. This exposure led to embezzlement.

Embezzlement and other misappropriation probably would have been sufficient to initiate criminal investigation—especially since UNIA staff, investors, and well-connected black political actors requested such intervention. However, the incorporation of BSL assured such intervention. Incorporation turned out to be a double-edged sword. On the one hand, it enhanced the BSL's legitimacy and fund-raising capabilities. But on the other hand, it gave the government authority to investigate and prosecute board members without appearing to have ulterior motives.

Inadequate financial resources and mismanagement were exacerbated by authoritarianism, inexperience, and insufficient skills. Garvey and his close supporters retained control over the BSL, discounting the insights of those with useful knowledge in shipping. Processing of incoming revenue was obstructed because mail could not be opened in Garvey's frequent absences. Those entrusted with management were inexperienced not only in shipping administration but in corporate financial management. This was partially due to forced exclusion from mainstream economic activity due to racism, but this does not excuse the impetuous decisions to purchase uninspected ships. Even after being proven correct about the hazards of voyages on ships in poor repair, those with shipping operations experience were disregarded.

Another type of inexperience hindered the BSL project as well. Though the UNIA was well informed about geopolitics and international economic relationships, the leaders had no experience interacting with nation-states or industrial leaders, and they underestimated the impact that their rhetoric had on the United States, Britain, and the shipping industry. Along with the unavoidable racism from U.S. institutions, the UNIA's revolutionary rhetoric disinclined shipping brokers and owners to deal with the BSL. It is unrealistic to espouse revolution against a group and then expect members of that group to provide professional assistance.

Thus the UNIA's entry into shipping was proscribed by inadequate financial resources, lack of knowledge, and disinterest on the part of the shipping industry. Consequently, the BSL had difficulty finding affordable vessels and engaging the necessary professionals. Predators were free to exploit them. And by the time they approached the equally inexperienced USSB, their funding was inadequate to purchase the ships they needed.

Ideological differences among diaspora activists were also problematic. Opposing activists were able to convince some investors and supporters to question the possibilities of the BSL's future, and eventually they turned to the federal government to dismantle the effort. In addition to administrative and operations challenges, the UNIA had to mount a campaign, ultimately fought in the courts, to counter these well-respected critics. These opposing diaspora activists had transnational programming as well and competed for the same income from the public that the BSL did.

Finally, there were geopolitical issues that impeded success of the BSL project. The British obviously controlled economic production and distribution of product from its colonies. The colonial office would have had to approve or at least would have had the authority to stop all trade considered outside its interests. Geopolitical competition and suspicion between the hegemonic powers also affected the BSL's operations. Relatively speaking, it was a small but irritating problem for Britain. At any point, the colonial power could have crippled the line by an administrative act such as cutting it off from insurance coverage, therefore preventing it from sailing. The United States had no reason to limit export trade with the countries formerly dominated by the European powers, and in fact may have preferred this to the action it finally took, charging the company with fraud. Neither power would entertain labor or any other economic disruption nor would they have risked the BSL's manipulation by other forces. The two threats the United States was most concerned with were the infiltration of the BSL by communist activists and, more remotely, some connection with a state considered a potential enemy, like Japan. Neither possibility materialized. Cyril Briggs and other black communists tried to infiltrate the UNIA but were successful only in getting the indictment. There is no credible evidence of a Japan/UNIA alliance.

It must be said that the U.S. subversion tactics may have exacerbated the problems of the UNIA. From Agent 800's reports, for example, we know that mail was tampered with and rivalries were inflamed between the ideological opponents. I argue that the government contributed toward the confusion with BSL operations although it was not directly responsible for the authoritarian response or the lack of financial and management skills available for the effort. There is no evidence that ties the United States or Britain to the repair problems of the ships or to missing funds. However, such subterfuge would have matched their ideological positions. The Bureau of Investigation did try to stop the purchase of the Africa ship. That intercept probably expedited the demise of the BSL, killing its last hope of earning money and recapturing support of black capitalist investors. Even if the ship had gone into service, however, rising unemployment would have continued to impede the UNIA's efforts to build a shipping line.

Thus there were reasons for the fall before the BSL even began and more that appeared as soon as it was launched. The rise was meteoric and could have lasted longer with better management. But given the economic realities, the most that could have been accomplished was perhaps a small apolitical shipping company serving the Caribbean region and the U.S. eastern seaboard. Without a fiery political agenda, such a line might have survived and possibly grown over time. This consequence makes Bertelson's point that a nonstate concern has to choose between audibility and durability.[35]

But as a component of a political program, indeed a symbol of revolution, a business diverts resources and talent to the profit-making motive. Investment cannot be supported if profit or at least long-range profitability is not in evidence. Therefore the BSL's attempt to use investment funds to achieve a political public service could not have survived in the American political economy as long as the line did not generate any additional income, even if misappropriation problems had not surfaced. The fall was inevitable due to incompatibility of simultaneous entrepreneurship and political activism, and the terrain of the international political economy.

9

Clear Waters: Implications for the Study of Diasporas

What does the Black Star Line tell us about diasporas and their political possibilities? First, it demonstrates that there is and has been an African diaspora operating politically. Even as ephemeral as the BSL effort was, it impacted politics in the Caribbean region and gave colonial powers pause in West Africa. For the United States, it raised concern about the safety of the Canal Zone and exacerbated its relations with Great Britain.

The example of the Black Star Line suggests that inadequate resources do not necessarily preclude liminal diasporas from being effective actors in the international arena. It is this lack of resources that is the primary characteristic distinguishing liminal diasporas from the so-called classic diasporas. The goals of the two types of diasporas are the same, but the capabilities available make them seem like two different entities. The classic diaspora has access to two types of resources crucial to continually successful political activity. Emigrants in a classic diaspora have financial resources, which usually spring from their most valuable resource: the ability to provide services and expertise needed in developing nations or in short supply in industrialized states. Emigrants in a liminal diaspora are hindered in this regard. Though they may possess more than manual labor, as we saw from the UNIA experience, they do not have many marketable skills that are scarce in the economies they enter.

Studying the BSL case in the context of liminal diasporas complements Sheffer's work. In addition to meeting most of the criteria raised by Sheffer, the case study corroborates his main argument that diasporas impact international politics. Further, it supports Sheffer and his fellow researchers' implicit argument that diasporas have their own physical characteristics and idiosyncrasies but are examples of the same organism. While their cultural retention, skill level, and geopolitical issues may vary, they all have the basic ingredients of a diaspora. Their communities are related and share problems and goals, they try to be connected to their homelands politically and economically, and they influence politics in their host countries because diasporas are using the latter's economic infrastructure and its political institutions to ameliorate the status of themselves and homeland. Further, states interact with these ethnic networks to protect or expand their own interests, which are usually economic or security related.

The close look at the example of the BSL adds to Sheffer's model in two areas. First, the case study clarifies the reasoning behind the configuration of a diaspora. Second, centralization may be key to the liminal diaspora's effective implementation of political activism. Finally, it illuminates another characteristic distinguishing the liminal from the classic diaspora. Liminal diasporas are hindered because of issues of authority.

Political economists also can use the diaspora model to better understand activity occurring in the international political economy. When political economy analysis is limited to traditional actors, it is easy to underestimate the significance of events to which states are responding: nonstate actors may be the reason for development of a particular policy. The study of liminal diasporas improves our understanding of international politics and economic activity by including actors ignored by more traditional methods of investigation.

Making the Case for the African Diaspora Designation

The building of the BSL highlighted the many black communities distributed throughout the black Atlantic that demonstrated through their correspondence, politics, and arts a sense of consanguinity, a key ingredient in the bonding of the African diaspora. As Walters points out, they are sister communities. Embarking on this business venture also illuminated the black activists interested in pan-African political and economic development. The perusal of the political and economic history of the black communities involved in the Black Star Line shows that the pan-African ideal and activism was embedded in many at least a half century before the UNIA was established. Newspapers circulated throughout the areas focused their work on the elimination of racial derogation and ways to ameliorate their political and economic status, not only in their host countries but internationally. Unity seemed to hold as long as the political work was confined to joint lobbying efforts of both the U.S. and British governments.

The perceived need for a shipping service that connected diaspora communities demonstrates that blacks around the Atlantic identified with the African continent, particularly with sub-Saharan Africa. The institution of slavery pulled its victims from many African nations, and it is difficult to delineate the boundaries of those nations. Nevertheless, reconnection to various contemporary West African nations was seen as a viable way to reestablish independent political and economic institutions and extract blacks from exploitative economic relations with Western states. It was also seen as reconnecting with *home* and helping with the elimination of colonialism and forming healthy black nation-states. A close look at the UNIA and BSL did not show that diaspora activists were interested in studying their origins in order to incorporate them; rather, they seemed focused on ancient political feats to buoy their self-esteem. Ironically, assimilative effects led them to the supercilious conclusion that contemporary African society needed diasporan guidance.

The inherent difficulties that the UNIA/BSL efforts encountered in pursuit of its goals are valuable clues as to the problems encountered by other liminal diasporas. Direct political participation within Africa by the UNIA was compromised due to assimilative effects that had permeated the diaspora communities as well as the educated and comprador classes in Africa. Further, the resources that diasporans were able to assemble for their foray into African politics were insufficient to last for the extensive period it would take to establish their shipping program—let alone settlement communities—in Africa. Efforts to replenish funding for even a modest venture had to be in addition to continued financial nourishment of the political organization functioning within the diaspora itself. Funding was not available for both political responsibilities simultaneously.

The BSL case study also revealed that continental Africans identified with the diaspora, and, beyond consanguinity, the adhesive was the joint African and diasporan resolve to end the derogation of the black race and economic repression. Black newspapers, conferences, and speeches all show that they realized that they were exploited by Western nations for the same reasons. However, African political interaction with the diaspora seemed to be dominated by the comprador class. As a result, diaspora ties directly to African nations and traditional leaders were blocked by a group that had a different solution for the amelioration of economic problems. The compradors wanted to be elevated to equal partnership in the international economy and therefore disagreed with the more aggressive political agenda of the UNIA. And it bears repeating that the comprador and educated classes probably were offended by the UNIA's disrespectful categorization of contemporary African capabilities.

We, therefore, can make few reasonable assumptions about the African diaspora's influence on homeland politics. The UNIA did have fleeting influence on Liberia. But the realization that the UNIA could not raise the $5 million needed to rebuild the Liberian economy, coupled with Western European pressure, ended this association. Gold Coast activists were interested in BSL investment but were not persuaded by the UNIA's political arguments. At most, West Africans would have entertained an economic relationship with the UNIA but would not have supported political rebellion against Britain.

Thus Sheffer's assertion of subtle effects is reasonable given the complex issues surrounding the diaspora's relationship to its multinational colonized homeland. This history also validates Skinner's argument that diasporas usually know that their communities in host countries will take on a permanency because of attenuated resources and obstruction by some host states and political exigencies with the homeland.[1] Consanguinity and existential issues committed diasporan activists to the African continent, but their attenuated resources and strained relations with the comprador classes tempered their ability to assist in the homeland's redevelopment, beginning with Liberia.

Strong connections between sub-Saharan Africa and its diaspora were blocked by the colonial powers, as both Harris and Edmondson theorized.[2] We have seen how Great Britain and France were interested in the industrial rubber potential in Liberia and, given the UNIA's war rhetoric, were concerned about the export of revolutionary rhetoric into their colonies, which bordered Liberia. For these reasons, they made incursions into Liberia and pressured the Liberian state to break relations with the UNIA. In addition, Great Britain moved to block the growth of the UNIA programming in both Nigeria and the Gold Coast.

Thus we see that the basic definition of a diaspora is met. The "sister" communities are related politically and socially. There was evidence of numerous connections with Africa, both through organizations and individual interactions. There was lobbying within the host countries and efforts to link together for international political development. The "homeland," in this case Liberia, responded to the efforts of the UNIA and its BSL. The *UNIA Papers* clearly document that host countries concerned about their economic agenda disrupted these connections, and Liberia followed the political road in its best interests. The three actors were involved in political activity that had been initiated in the African diaspora.

Implications

The African diaspora helps us understand how liminal diasporas survive in their host countries and in the international arena—at least during the era under study. The experience of the BSL operating in the African diaspora gives us insight into the mechanics of diaspora organization, highlighting the institutions that facilitate how these resource-poor entities function. It provides a close look at how programs are put into operation, how resources are accumulated, and how individual communities coordinate their actions to impact international activities.

The BSL study shows us something about the reasoning behind locations of communities. After slavery, black diaspora communities were located where opportunities for economic improvement—or at least reduction of repression—had arisen. These locations were not far from hegemonic transportation systems. We might deduce that liminal diasporas retain cohesion on the backs of hegemonic transportation and communications institutions. Diaspora communities are established at nodes of production or protection but tied to the system of travel that links these points. Liminal diasporas do not have the choice to settle in areas where economic development opportunities are incipient as do more classic diasporas. They may not have the resources to exploit such opportunities or lack the skills to sell to a society working on modernization.

This is because a state in the early stages of modernization would likely have surplus manual labor of its own; it requires technical skills not additional manual labor. Liminal diasporas are at well-established locations in need of labor and with reasonably stable, inexpensive transportation to their homelands and diaspora networks. Though the transportation system is geared toward the interests of hegemonic powers and other stable states integrated into the international economic system, liminal diasporas would not survive without this infrastructure. Interaction with homeland and compatriots must be affordable, even if pricing is relatively unfair. Otherwise interaction would be impossible and cultural and political links could not be maintained. Often ignored by host country media, diasporas form their own, which often become entrepreneurial outlets adding to income while providing necessary updates of homeland and diaspora-wide politics. Again, we saw this in the black Atlantic. The African diaspora did not have a way to learn of political activities in their communities and homelands without the entrepreneurial efforts of black journalists; it was practically ignored in the mainstream. Access to western infrastructure such as communication and transportation systems also may be necessary for the establishment of a reliable enclave economy. Without such access, diasporas would not be operational, and the exploitation of individual communities could become more prevalent.

Another point is suggested here. Liminal diaspora communities atrophy once capital departs. During the BSL era, the economic activity of sugar production concentrated in Cuba, leaving Jamaica. Cotton production declined in the U.S. American South and terrorism drove peasants from the area. Atrophied communities may be less politically active because the members that leave first in search of employment may be its strongest members. The existence of atrophying communities suggests that not all diaspora communities will be involved in joint political efforts and that among those that are, there will be inequalities of resources at their disposal. As Joseph Harris suggested, diasporas are dynamic.[3] They have to be in order to survive.

The initial flight of financial resources would trigger other resource loss that results in a diaspora community being politically inactive. As communities move further and further from defunct economic sites, increasing distance requires more resources to cross. The newer communities may not be able to retain other than communication links if they are to maintain themselves as well as contribute to political activity and help the homeland. Hegemonic transportation links will adjust to reflect the new economic production realities, so this would hinder travel to dying communities. Older communities would have to concentrate their resources on subsistence and relocation issues, which become more complicated due to the withdrawal of transportation options.

Another barrier to political activity is language. In the case of the African diaspora, enslaved members from different language groups were forced to adopt one of several European languages. In the Caribbean, these were English, Spanish, and to a lesser extent, French. Because of interselling of captive labor and later migration patterns, many Afro-Caribbeans were at least bilingual. Language very well may be one of the reasons that Brazil, where the dominant language is Portuguese, was not involved in the BSL effort. We know through other scholastic studies that Afro-Brazilians had relations with Africa, particularly with Nigeria. However, there were not strong connections between Afro-Brazilian activists and UNIA or other black nationalist groups in the era. Other liminal diasporas may have similar language issues.

Another important attribute useful to diasporas raised by the BSL experience is the crucial role of centralization. Without coordination of its political activity, a liminal diaspora's ability to influence international politics and its homeland is attenuated. Without centralization there is no clear voice representing the diaspora's interests. It is reduced to providing remittances and/or conveying various political opinions, perhaps without the homeland population being cognizant of its contributions and concerns. Or there may be sporadic and disjointed lobbying on behalf of the homeland. Under such circumstances, the homeland might take advantage of the diaspora's resources with no accountability necessary to a strong political group. However, if diaspora activists combine resources and agree upon a political goal, it increases the ability to influence the homeland and as such empower the diaspora.

Centralization also facilitates economic empowerment. Centralization suggests ability and commitment to carry through; this in turn suggests empowerment. This was one of the most important intangible assets of the UNIA. Its international membership speaking with one voice implied power. Its ability to raise funds did the same. Other political actors take into consideration the possibility of an additional competitor in the international arena when such resources are visible. Such a diaspora political organization can become a serious lobbyist for the homeland in its host countries, or it can become the voice of a repressed homeland population. It can combine economic resources and provide a source of capital for its homeland. Since most liminal diasporas were formed due to homeland economic deprivation, financial contributions toward the homeland's economic development may be one of the most important the diaspora can make.

Issues of authority can also hinder liminal diasporas, however. There are two areas to be addressed here:

Diaspora organizations have no legal authority over activists and resource extraction and allocation.

Diaspora organizations may not evade their host states' legal authority.

Despite (or perhaps because of) its authoritarian structure, ultimately the UNIA could not control its membership. Disgruntled members routinely left the organization. The UNIA had to refer alleged embezzlement cases to the state criminal justice system, which was not amenable to the BSL effort. If the UNIA attempted to use force or punishment to control membership, then the state could intervene directly into its activities. Thus, there were few incentives, other than loyalty, ephemeral political satisfaction, and prestige, to bind activists to the UNIA/BSL effort, despite its designation of itself as a state.

Because of its lack of enforcement powers, dependable funding became a problem. Even with a committed core membership, stable funding is necessary to carry out programming. Unlike states, the UNIA could not force its membership or supporters to contribute funds (or pay taxes) to carry out its political agenda nor force investment in its corporations; BSL investors were persuaded to contribute. States can devise a tax code and then create law to legitimize the forced extraction of resources should the designated taxpayers refuse to cooperate. No higher authority can prevent such confiscation, and therefore the state has access to reliable funding. Then the state can develop programs based on projected revenue. It can factor in the cost of administration and carry out its agenda. Even a committed membership may not supply enough resources for a diaspora to be able to do this. A liminal diaspora may have a functioning middle class, but overall its economic resources are limited. Therefore its programming must be focused on a finite agenda, not unbounded goals such as those envisioned by the UNIA and BSL board of directors. A diaspora may be most productive by augmenting its homeland's ability to assemble wealth.

This differs from a classical diaspora in that emigrants of the latter may have influential links to the host countries' rulers because of their valuable skills and services to the state.[4] Such diaspora activists have close proximity to the bureaucracy and politicians of the host countries. In such cases, the state might disregard minor legal infractions by diaspora leaders to discipline its members, as long as no state interests are compromised. Classical diasporans may have a sophisticated understanding of the hosts' financial system and be able to manipulate it to maximum gain, or in a way to avoid prosecution for any financial anomalies. Classical diasporas can more effectively proceed with their political and economic agendas without close scrutiny by host state officials.

Issues of authority were even more readily apparent in terms of transnational administration of the BSL. National governments determine the rules for shipping in their territorial waters, including ports, so the consulates of the British government in the Caribbean islands had major influence over the BSL's ability to use ports and other ship-related services. They also intervened in disputes between BSL crew and UNIA leadership. Political operations within various states by liminal diaspora activists that interact with these government services can be monitored, manipulated, changed, or discontinued if the host government suspects criminality, political intrigue, or economic disruption: government legally controls public institutions that regulate transportation systems and commercial activity.

The government's responsibility for the public safety also gives it legitimate recourse to monitor political activity within its borders. If one diaspora site publishes materials for dissemination in other communities under another state's jurisdiction, such materials can be legally confiscated. A diaspora organization attempting to supervise members within another jurisdiction is problematic for the same reason.

The Utility of Diaspora Studies for Political Economists

This study suggests that diaspora political activity may help us to understand international politics better. Yet liminal diasporas, in particular, may seem too unstable to be taken seriously by political scientists as a phenomenon with international impact. But the phenomenon may be more durable than it looks for a reason that is not obvious. What seems at first to be a drawback, the amorphous homeland of the African diaspora, may point to the strength underlying all diasporas. Sheffer reasoned that diasporas wish to save their culture, including a particular language and perhaps religion. But the desire may be even more basic than that. Diaspora activists may cohere not just to save the accouterments of their besieged societies, such as the language and religion, but the very people and the society that had been built over centuries. Within a society, language and religion may evolve due to technological innovation or political disruption. But to suppress a people's innate inclination or capability to exist together as a group may be considered by them an existential issue, as it was with the African diaspora. And when preservation becomes the motivating issue, then a group might attempt what seems irrational to a more secure grouping. Diaspora activists will redirect scarce resources and take risks in efforts to survive. If their activism is adequately organized, it may interrupt highly integrated political and economic relationships. Or, as will be discussed in more detail later, the diaspora may serve as a bridge or liaison via agreements with host nations.

As such, diasporas become nonstate actors on the international stage. So in some instances, states may not be responding to another nation-state, but rather to a nonstate actor that has interfered with some goal. Considering diasporas in this way may shed light on heretofore inexplicable actions by states. Perhaps diasporas can show us why states deploy agents or resources in a way that sources of evidence indicate is ineffective. I do not suggest that the study of diasporas should replace more traditional approaches. Rather, considering diaspora activity may provide additional information or clarity regarding international political phenomena.

I agree with Kim Butler that diaspora study can be particularly helpful when investigating a developing state and even a political movement.[5] The status of a state's émigrés determines the resources available and the political possibilities for the homeland. First, the configuration of the diaspora should be determined. This determination must go beyond the identification of all communities; it must be refined to emphasize those that are politically active or economically contributing to the diaspora network and or the homeland. This exercise clarifies the diaspora network and will facilitate identification of the relevant activists and the workforces providing resources for the political activity as well as for the homeland.

Each community within a liminal diaspora may be acting independently, a group of communities might be working together, or a diaspora-wide coalition might be in force. In the BSL effort, the United States, Canada, the larger Caribbean islands, and Central America were most active. Other communities were peripheral to the effort, such as small black communities in England and the Caribbean islands in the Lesser Antilles. Once specific political and/or economic activity is identified, then the cumulative effect of their contributions must be measured. The researcher should access the political contribution of the individual communities, determining what homeland movements or parties receive the predominate support. At a minimum, political economists should look at the remittances that go to a homeland from each community.

After identifying a diaspora, perhaps the next important task for a researcher would be to identify the ideologies functioning within the diaspora. This helps determine not only their political condition but their strength. If there is serious ideological contention within the diaspora (as there was in the UNIA as well as between it and other black diaspora organizations), then its ability to support its homeland or influence international politics may be compromised. If one ideological contingent is decidedly stronger, that may indicate the type of political influence it will attempt in the international political economy. It may also help to determine the resources available to the diaspora's homeland government, as will be expanded in the discussion on remittances. If the homeland has the support of its diaspora, then it may have access to more resources than were indicated in more traditional studies. If the homeland government is opposed by the diaspora, then the strength of the diaspora may determine the stability of that government. That is to say, the diaspora may commit its resources to opposition groups, including militarized organizations. Examples of this would include financing opposition political parties; a militarized instance would be support in the Irish diaspora of the Irish Republican Army.

Diasporas are not ideologically monolithic. Although committed to the racial and cultural attributes of their societies, in most cases, their ideological position for change and economic modernization is probably Western. This is because diasporas are looking for ways to rebuild the economies and possibly the political systems of their societies. If a viable economy is the goal, then it is necessary to organize it in a way that links to the international economy or at least into some type of enclave economy. It is in the West and from academia that workable alternatives are located. In terms of economic models, the classical choices are capitalism and socialism, and ideologies reflect this. These two ideological positions were the principal reason for division in the UNIA.

The homeland encumbrances that impede African diaspora political activism do not operate in most liminal diasporas. And as a result, most liminal diasporas are able to send remittances to their families, social and political organizations, or directly to state operations. We learned from Sheffer that remittances might be the only currency available to relatives still living in the homeland. But we learned from the BSL experience that small contributions could be assembled into a large capital fund; in other words, remittances given to family groups and/or social institutions can total a large amount, enough to augment the efforts of international organizations such as the International Monetary Fund (IMF) attempting to stimulate economic growth in that developing nation. The study of India and more recently Mexico indicate that if remittances are diverted to capital and other economic development, entire villages may be transformed by the efforts of diaspora activists: modest infrastructure may be put in place facilitating significant economic development for a village without waiting for the assistance of the developing state. These developments increase the receiving state's economic position while supplementing its resources, making them reach further. Such substantial help might ingratiate the homeland government to those components of its diaspora that provide this capital investment. Yet these projects may be relatively small by the standards of outside researchers and international organizations, and may not be considered in evaluations of developing nation-states. But the assets of diasporas should be weighed, as should their political strength.

One method would be as follows.[6] First, the researcher should identify the best-established communities in the diaspora, those where workers are employed in large numbers on a continuous basis. A survey could be designed to determine the average salary of workers and from that an average remittance might be determined. This amount should be added to the average annual income of the developing country's workers. A more refined survey might determine how much is sent to community and other social organizations; this amount should be added to whatever investment income is made available to families through diaspora remittances. The resulting calculation represents the amount of capital outside of state and international organizations that is available for a particular country. An even more detailed survey might determine what amount is geared toward state use or for private community/regional capital projects. Such information would help construct a more realistic evaluation of a country's economic development possibilities.

All diaspora activity is not political, and most remittances may not be meant for political use but for the economic well-being of the families of diaspora residents. But when political work is intended, then unified action might prove expedient. Remember that the BSL experience suggests that centralization augments the power of a diaspora. The shipping line could not have been launched without the financial support from several communities within the same time span. Secondly, the skills of many experienced activists helped the effort to be accepted and to coordinate tasks. Because the resources of liminal diasporas are relatively sparse, concentrating resources either within the diaspora or in a specific cause, program, movement, or government in the homeland increases the ability to influence the political issue targeted. Centralization may also imply a large group of activists. At least in democratic states, a large following is useful in lobbying efforts and may produce local and regional political influence. Thus, the researcher needs to discover the resources that diaspora communities have been able to acquire from host countries and other allies.

A researcher studying an industrialized or modern state might also be interested in diaspora relations. States have several reasons to be involved in diaspora politics; chief among them are economic priorities, interstate competition, and alliances.

Economic priorities include the protection and expansion of markets. This goal can become particularly sensitive during economic downturns. As we saw for the BSL, the war depleted the financial resources of one hegemonic power and increased opportunities for the rising power. One result of those realities was increased sensitivity to economic obstacles. It was crucial that economic programs in place not be interrupted as the consequences were more immediately felt. For Britain, that would have hindered the rebuilding of its crumbled economy. For the United States, such interruption could have impeded efforts to open up new markets in South America, necessary to stop the contraction of American production.

For similar reasons, states are concerned about the accessibility to resources. Crucial transportation links had to be protected as well; this included sea-lanes and other routes to raw materials. Markets could not be served if materials were unavailable for processing into goods. For the United States, this meant the protection of its new Panama Canal, which cleared the way for unprecedented accessibility to Asian markets. If trade relations could be established in Asia, the U.S. economy would expand its markets and therefore halt the contraction of its economy, decreasing unemployment and racial/labor unrest. Because of its function in achieving these economic goals, the canal had to be protected at all costs. Another economic priority for states is to protect transportation links needed for military reasons; the Panama Canal was just as vital to military strategy. Americans assumed other powerful states and competitors wanted ownership of the canal and access to raw materials. Access to transportation networks has been sufficient cause for nations to go to war.

In addition to the competition issues, both Britain and the United States were concerned about communist incursion in the region. Wary of the plans of each other and the intentions of Russia, the British and Americans were not going to chance the UNIA or its BSL impeding economic relations or military preparedness in the region. Similar scenarios are plausible for other regions that have transportation advantages or supply important resources. In these locations, diasporas become a problem if they in any way obstruct transportation networks. Pressure for their removal will occur if they block accessibility to key resources.

A related concern is the control of labor. Liminal diasporas tend to form at points of raw resource excavation and industrial production. This is so because their populations are usually overwhelmingly composed of manual labor. Again, this is not to say that there are not professionals present in the diasporas but that this labor pool is much smaller and not the part that earns subsistence for the communities. If a dominant state has become reliant upon a pool of manual labor, it does not welcome disruption of production. It is here, in particular, that a state would be concerned about the political affiliations of diasporas. The European experience had shown that socialists and communists were effective operatives within labor organizations. With such evidence of how politicized labor can disorganize a capitalistic economy, a state may move to stop political activity seen as the cause of labor or production disruption.

These are reasons that the BSL was seen as a problem. It was not seen as a competitor or formidable foe, but an obstacle at worst; and at the very least, an irritant. For a state to stop such diaspora activity was a relatively easy task; but for the diaspora, it could be devastating. State intervention could destroy intricately built networks, which may explain why some diasporas remain in a liminal stage for extensive periods.

And it is not simply the diaspora's operation that concerns states. A diaspora can be manipulated or compromised to serve the interest of a stronger entity, especially competitors or political foes. To avoid such manipulation, a state may disrupt the diaspora's political or economic programming.

Finally, a host state may see diasporas as conduits to their homelands. A state may need to achieve a political alliance or economic agreement in a region where one of its diaspora's homelands is located. If the diaspora is reasonably situated with regard to the two countries, then the host state may request that the diaspora support its attempts to persuade the homeland to contribute to some goal or task. This intermediary is particularly important if there are geopolitical disturbances in the region and more direct communication between the host country and homeland would provoke disorder. By the same token, a host country might request that its diaspora settlement persuade a sister community to some particular action. A diaspora may improve its position with powerful states by providing assistance, and in the process improve its economic opportunities.

Conclusion

The diaspora concept has been used successfully in cultural and historical research. One purpose of this study has been to determine if the diaspora concept is applicable in political economy studies of transnational politics, particularly by African diaspora activists. Gabriel Sheffer et al., J. A. Armstrong, and Ron Walters have looked at its applicability to political science.[1] The study edited by Sheffer included a useful political science definition of a diaspora and structural inputs for the development of a workable paradigm. Diaspora networks, according to Sheffer and Walters, can influence international politics. Though many of the findings demonstrating the applicability of the concept to political science studies are instructive, it has not been incorporated into the approaches used in the political science discipline.

This rejection may be due in part to the variability in the characteristics and capabilities of these networks; diasporas can be categorized into at least two types. A *classic diaspora* is firmly established in most of its host countries. This type of network was created in ancient and medieval eras, and over centuries, émigrés honed skills and political acumen useful to keeping their diasporas alive. These émigrés had saleable skills wanted in the host countries that were developing into modern states; they created institutions that connected them to government officials and to the economy. These amenable ties helped the classic diaspora to acquire some wealth and form mutually beneficial relationships with host governments. In such an atmosphere, the diaspora can nourish its own community and culture, and it can divert resources and time to the homeland and to sister diaspora communities.

The émigrés of *liminal diasporas*, on the other hand, were formed in modern times, usually during the colonial era. These émigrés may have skills beyond manual labor but not ones in demand in industrialized countries. Or they may be culturally or racially incompatible with the ethnic groups of the host countries. Under these conditions, they do not acquire sufficient wealth or form mutually beneficial relations with the host countries. They are therefore marginalized in economic and political relations.

Another concern with the liminal diaspora concept may be that the fragile links and activities in these networks are so subtle that political scientists dismiss the triad network of diaspora, host, and homeland as irrelevant to international political economy issues. For instance, the intricate connections of black activists across countries seem to remain beyond the detection of students of international political economy and other political scientists. Sheffer's doubt about the actuality of an African diaspora makes this point. One reason may be the ephemeral character of liminal diasporas' political activity, possibly due to scarce resources that temper their ability to sustain political activity. It also has been suggested that the lack of direct cultural linkages limit the African diaspora's possibilities. Yet through Edmondson's work, we know that members of the African diaspora have served as effective lobbyists for Africa and were involved in the liberation movements of African states.

Many of Sheffer's conclusions are persuasive, however, and they proved useful in helping me build a model for empirical study of transnational politics of black activists distributed throughout the black Atlantic. To minimize the obstacles to discerning diaspora political activity, I modified the model by conjoining it with an institutionalist political economy approach. This modification allowed me to probe all institutions used in activism looking for the political and economic strategies and resources employed. As such, it becomes a model that strengthens Sheffer's, magnifying what might seem to be peripheral political and economic activity for examination.

The political economy approach as demonstrated by Woo-Cumings helped me identify the motivations behind the choices and reactions of the actors.[2] This is because the political economy itself formed the circumstances that the actors had to consider in pursuit of their goals. The Black Star Line was possible because of the transformation of the American economy from agrarian to industrial. Black people from the American South and the Caribbean earned considerably more than had been possible in earlier economic eras. Some had cash income for the first time. A significant number among them chose to use some of their newfound income to invest in a better economic future for the race. This goal underscores a key motivating factor for activism within the diaspora: its concerns with survival of the race.

I decided that a case study could be used to test the robustness of my model applied to the African diaspora (which must be characterized as liminal). The case study looked at the efforts of the UNIA to launch the Black Star Line as an instance of African diaspora political (and economic) activity. The diaspora theory component of my model helped to identify all the relevant actors. It also enveloped the émigré communities constituent to the diaspora. Framed in that way, I learned that each community offers different contributions—if any. Participation was determined by the economy in which each community was based. If it was an old or fading economic node, then the community would be most occupied with relocation to an economically viable region. The communities of liminal diasporas are dependent upon economic production that can at least assure subsistence: Harris's thesis on dynamism within the diaspora network is supported.[3] That is to say, in addition to leaving a troubled homeland, émigrés change diaspora community locations when economic or political problems become overwhelming. In a thriving economy, émigrés are more likely to contribute more than remittances to the homeland. In these communities, more definitive political activity takes place. As Walters has argued, not every community is involved in diaspora politics, and participant communities contribute in varying degrees. This proved true for the BSL effort. Investors in the United States could buy several shares, while those in rural Costa Rica had to share the cost of one share.

The ideological difference observed among black activists proves that the African diaspora is not politically monolithic. While this may suggest that democratic politics prevails in African American politics, ideological contention also attenuates scarce resources available for transnational political projects. Walters coined the phrase "two-line struggle" for the negative impact that political contention has on efforts to establish a strong political presence not only to implement transnational political programming but to support African politics and economic development.[4]

The presence of different programs illuminated another point. Centralized activity, while concentrating the strength and capabilities of a diaspora, may be difficult to achieve under competitive political circumstances. The two-line struggle tempers the possibility of strong centralized programming by one group as organizations contend for personnel, financial resources, and the attention of the people who can participate in international politics. In circumstances of limited resources such as the African diaspora, centralized movements like the UNIA are atypical. Yet centralization was important to the brief success of the BSL. The UNIA's strategies to attract and organize its membership and programming made centralization possible. A discussion of the most significant of these strategies provides insight into how the UNIA managed its transnational network as well as on the ways by which activism occurs in the African diaspora.

The UNIA used artistic and cultural institutions to gain access to both members and investors. By including popular and religious music in its programs along with familiar "soapbox" political speakers and professional orators, the UNIA attracted ordinary working people along with those that were already politically inclined. Using the familiar proselytizing methods of the black church, the UNIA educated its audiences on contemporary political issues and economic development. Also using church mores and social club methods, it collected small contributions from attendees. Funds accumulated in this manner enabled the organization to build institutions that augmented its strength and political organizing potential.

Secondly, the UNIA used the resources that had been collected for business start-ups and additional institution building. UNIA leadership used western institutions to organize its membership and programming. They developed a written constitution, which insured a uniform understanding by members of the organization's doctrine, structure, and regulations. Administrative policies were employed, including a clearly defined leadership hierarchy and standardized procedures and regulations.

Their news organ, the *Negro World,* supplemented the UNIA's ability to control its membership by communicating the administrative policies of the various programs; the newspaper also facilitated the organization's ability to counter criticism and update its followers. Thus administrative centralization was achieved, which enabled effective program implementation and management but also provided the political infrastructure for authoritarian rule. The application of these methods was especially useful to organize collection of funds nationally and internationally, leading to the accumulation of sufficient revenues in the New York headquarters to apply to programming.[5] Government intervention ironically created circumstances that led the UNIA to apply more formal financial procedures to the Black Star Line, namely converting simple fund-raising into corporate stock sales. Adopting the structure of American financial institutions improved collection procedures, providing better supervisory regulations for field agents and bringing professional financial language to fund-raising presentations. Prudently relying upon many small contributions from throughout the diaspora was fundamental to the UNIA's success in assembling start-up funds for the BSL. By keeping the unit share price affordable, its predominately low-income constituency could risk contributing toward a program that could improve their economic plight and transportation options.

Acting as entrepreneurs rather than political activists, the UNIA assembled approximately $800,000 in capital to provide a service for which there seemed to be a substantial market. The UNIA addressed a problem that no nationalist organization had been able to solve before: it assembled financial resources to implement a program that addressed paralyzing economic repression of black communities. The UNIA focused on economic deprivation, which it saw as one of the most critical concerns of the diaspora and the homeland. Theoretically, a shipping line would enable economic growth and linkage of the diaspora to Africa, creating a sustainable enclave economy. This program would offer services, be self-funding, and ultimately provide profits to the parent organization and investors.

Perhaps the fundamental mistake was trying to incorporate this entrepreneurial goal into the UNIA's state-building goal. BSL directors departed from the legal restrictions of incorporation and used investment funds as tax revenue to finance other programs in addition to the Black Star Line. Had the UNIA chosen a less complicated venture than shipping, it may have been able to lay the groundwork of its proposed enclave economy in a way that did not invite federal prosecution. Shipping had seemed a viable option because it would lay a foundation for the enclave economy, it had strong support among potential investors and contributors throughout the diaspora, and it had income-producing potential.

But the shipping industry was (and is) complex and expensive, and trying to launch such a project led to mismanagement and deficit spending. It proved to be the Achilles heel of the popular UNIA, one of the few nationalist organizations to gain widespread support and authenticity. The inexperience of UNIA/BSL managers points to the inchoate political and economic characteristics of the African diaspora. Segregated educational institutions and discriminatory hiring practices in the international economy had not allowed African Americans in the black Atlantic to gain skill and experience that would have facilitated the management of a shipping line or any other complex industrial enterprise.

Continual mismanagement logically led to decreased stock sales until only committed nationalist support remained. Unemployment, brought about by contraction in the economy, eventually led to flat stock sales and contributed toward the demise of the BSL. Following the lifespan of the BSL helps us to see the variables that contribute to the ephemeral nature of liminal diaspora projects. Resources, human and financial, are fragile so that the capability to withstand obstacles is tenuous. Yet consanguinity and other strong motivational forces lead diaspora activists to continue to attempt linkage to the homeland/region and activism in the international political economy to ameliorate derogation and economic deprivation of the black race.

Assimilative effects also impaired their political performance. Living so intimately inside other nations, émigrés internalize some mores and beliefs of the hosts whether intentionally or not. These social influences permeate their interactions with the homeland and with sister communities who face the same circumstances: socialization cannot be avoided. And while overall political goals may have been the same, diaspora communities' economic positions, along with assimilation into different host countries, made their specific reasons for participating in the BSL different because each was trying to address the different needs and opportunities faced in their respective economies and political structures.

There is a deeper political irony. Although struggling against the oppression imposed by the United States and Great Britain, African diaspora activists are imbued with the political philosophies of these states. It could not be otherwise, since it was through these nation-states that their introduction to and study of formal political activism occurred. Consanguinity may have undergirded their focus on Africa, but the political philosophies of Africa, particularly in the era under study, were not available to diaspora activists for study and reproduction. Rather, the political goals of diaspora activists were realized through Western political philosophy and organizational modes.

And while the United States and Great Britain's political evolution were similar, the former became more democratic than the latter. This divergence in political growth of the oppressive states was reflected in the political relations between the sister communities of the diaspora. African Americans resisted authoritarianism embedded in the BSL administration and openly attempted to change its leadership.[6] This political disagreement aggravated the internecine struggles facing the UNIA/BSL. In addition to concerns about financial management and operations, there was withdrawal from the organization due to differentiation in political belief systems, one being more populist than the other. Changes in the BSL program affected members and investors differently and influenced their continued support and investment. Contrary to claims in some earlier studies, all BSL supporters were not nationalists; some investors privileged other goals including profitability and equitable, efficient transportation.

The host countries reacted to the BSL effort because it could disrupt intricately developed and indispensable conditions such as labor relations and transportation-related activities of the Panama Canal. Labor unrest and disruption along the eastern seaboard and at Caribbean fueling stations and around the canal itself would negatively impact the profitability of American business. The federal government had prioritized market expansion in Asia, and efficient transportation through the isthmus was integral to achieving this goal. Colonial powers were also concerned that the BSL effort would incite upheaval in West Africa and disturb plans to exploit the resources of Liberia. International competition for the control of rubber—necessary to the nascent automobile industry—was intense during this era. Nationalist pronouncements alerted colonial powers to the possibility that their African territories might be inspired to revolt or join the UNIA's network, which would jeopardize the efficient extraction of raw materials, especially gold and palm oil, from West Africa, needed to rebuild Western economies. Already faced with proletarian uprisings in their metropoles, they did not want to further strain their military resources.

As importantly, the United States and Britain were concerned that the diaspora effort could be manipulated by an enemy and used against hegemonic interests. Their intense competition also made them wary of each other manipulating the BSL to derail the other's economic expansion goals. These concerns may explain, in part, why both governments conducted surveillance and fomented contention and confusion within the UNIA organization.

The United States and Britain were also concerned about the UNIA's "designated" homeland base, Liberia, enough so that the colonial powers put Liberia under pressure to break relations with the UNIA. Liberia had its own reasons to cut its ties: Liberian officials were concerned that the UNIA would displace them as the government. For these reasons, Liberia aligned itself with more moderate diaspora activists, many of whom were associated with the NAACP, including Du Bois.

The BSL's example shows that host countries have reason to become involved in diaspora political networks. On some occasions, host country interest may extend to cooperative political activities as well. Host countries may have a political goal in a region that one of its diaspora communities' homeland is located. The host country might seek an alliance with the diaspora to serve as a conduit to the homeland government. The same is true for the homeland; it might need the diaspora to lobby a particular host country on a crucial issue. And, of course, diaspora remittances often provide a significant contribution to the homeland's national income.

The case study sheds light on a conundrum that may be a primary reason that liminal diasporas maintain that status sometimes for generations. Diasporans must learn the rules and mores of the host societies whose economies provide their economic livelihood; they constantly have to negotiate their positions. They often have no choice but to learn and use the political and economic institutions of these societies. However, they cannot use these institutions in the same way as do natives of host countries because they do not have the standing, political sovereignty, or military or financial institutions to engage in their strategies. Instead they find creative ways to redesign the institutions to meet their needs. The UNIA was briefly successful by doing this, but the UNIA did not implement these methods beyond setting up the business offices and the Black Star Line. For example, it did not redesign domestic political institutions to augment the inchoate power that the BSL brought to the UNIA. It moved defensively toward ship leasing because of New York district attorney Kilroe's pressure to purchase a ship or return member contributions. Scarce financial resources precluded returning contributions, so the UNIA entered the shipping business prematurely. This may be the key difference between liminal and classic diasporas: the latter have learned and institutionalized systems that underscore amenable political relations simultaneous with effective transnational activism.

The case study also suggests that the diaspora model captures the political relationship of the actors—the nonstate activists in an ethnic network, the host countries, and the homeland—and what issues motivate each actor. The diaspora model improves our understanding of the political purposes and mechanics operative in the African diaspora by illuminating how particular black communities or organizations may assemble resources and decide to link with like communities for the purposes of political and/or economic amelioration.

The experience of the BSL shows that diaspora activity, including that of liminal diasporas, can influence international politics (albeit subtly and ephemerally), disrupting the dynamics of the international political economy, and in turn determining the political and economic fortunes of diasporas. The study of other liminal diasporas would be enhanced by viewing them through this model. Sheffer's model could be integrated with other political science approaches, tailored to fit the needs of researchers. For example, the study of immigration and guest workers might be enhanced by looking beyond the domestic interests of the host country to the analysis of the transnational political goals and projects of the immigrant groups. By doing so, an enhanced understanding of nonstate transnational politics may be achieved.

Notes

Chapter 1: A New Take on an Old Term

1. Please note that in this study the term *African American* is used to refer to black populations throughout the Americas and the Caribbean.

2. The term *international political economy* refers to the political and economic agreements worked out among nation-states to ensure smooth resource extraction and trade relations. One of the first political studies that focused on this political attribute of the diaspora concept was Gabriel Sheffer, ed., *Modern Diasporas in International Politics* (New York: St. Martin's, 1986), arguing that a diaspora has three political actors: the homeland, the host countries, and the émigrés that settle in those host countries.

3. Elliot P. Skinner, "The Dialectic between Diasporas and Homelands," in *Global Dimensions of the African Diaspora,* ed. Joseph Harris (Washington, D.C.: Howard University Press, 1982), 11–40. A refugee community often evolves into a diaspora when resolutions of the homeland's problems turn out to be intractable.

4. See, for instance, Stuart Hall, "Cultural Identity and Diaspora," in *Colonial Discourse and Post Colonial Theory: A Reader,* ed. P. Williams and L. Chrisman (New York: Columbia University Press, 1994), 392–403; James Clifford, "Diasporas," *Cultural Anthropology* 9, no. 3 (1994): 302–38; Paul Gilroy, *Black Atlantic: Modernity and Double Consciousness* (Cambridge, Mass.: Harvard University Press, 1993).

5. St. Clair Drake, "Diaspora Studies and Pan-Africanism," in *Global Dimensions of the African Diaspora,* ed. Joseph Harris (Washington, D.C.: Howard University Press, 1982), 451–514.

6. See for example, Robin Kelley, "Black History's Global Vision: 1883–1950," *Journal of American History* 86 (Dec. 1999): 1045–77.

7. See Robert Andersen, "Why Adoptees Search," *Child Welfare* 67, no. 1 (1988):

15–19. Andersen is a psychiatrist and adoptee. Also look at J. Triseliotis, *In Search of Origins: The Experiences of Adopted People* (London: Routlege and Kegan Paul, 1973).

8. This is not to say that all African-descended people are active in diaspora activities or that they hold affinity for Africa. There are those who are appalled by African participation in slavery and disavow kinship and those who are ashamed by African genealogy. However, both of these positions suggest passion around their origins and therefore impact on their identity.

9. Sheffer, ed., *Modern Diasporas.*

10. My view on the institutionalist school of political economy is greatly influenced by the works of Douglass North, *Institutions, Institutional Change, and Economic Performance* (Cambridge: Cambridge University Press, 1993); and John Zysman, *Governments, Markets, and Growth* (New York: Cornell University Press, 1994). The development of the institutionalist school is attributed to Thornstein Veblen in his classic, *Theory of the Leisure Class* (New York: MacMillan, 1899).

11. Aldon Morris, *The Origins of the Civil Rights Movement: Black Communities Organizing for Change* (New York: Free Press, 1984).

12. One exception is the work of Sidney Tarrow. He looked at protests in Eastern Europe following the disintegration of the Soviet Union. Tarrow noted how social movements developed within each state to reform government and institute democratic government. See Tarrow, *Power in Movement: Social Movements, Collective Action, and Politics* (Cambridge: Cambridge University Press, 1994).

13. Ronald Walters, *Pan-Africanism in the African Diaspora: An Analysis of Modern Afro-Centric Political Movements* (Detroit: Wayne University Press, 1997).

14. Here the term *resources* refers to more than financial resources such as money and other assets. I also include education—particularly skill levels, including knowledge of the mechanics of the international economy and expertise in key fields such as finance, business, general administration, shipping, and infrastructure management—fields beyond general labor.

15. See Joseph Rothschild, *Ethnopolitics: A Conceptual Framework* (New York: Columbia University Press, 1981).

16. I have chosen the word *liminal* to distinguish the more fragile, inexperienced diasporas from the classic, well-established diasporas, such as those of the Jews and Armenians. A complete discussion is in chapter 2.

Chapter 2: An Exploration of the Relevant Literature

1. There are many well-received cultural studies on the African diaspora; these include Paul Gilroy, "It Ain't Where You're From, It's Where You're At," in *Small Acts: Thoughts on the Politics of Black Cultures* (London: Serpent's Tail, 1993), 120–45; also see Gilroy's *The Black Atlantic.* Also see Hall, "Cultural Identity and Diaspora"; Clifford, "Diasporas."

2. See Kim Butler, "Defining Diaspora, Refining a Discourse," *Diaspora* 10, no. 2 (2001): 189–219.

3. See J.A. Armstrong, "Mobilized and Proletarian Diasporas," *American Political Science Review* 70, no. 2 (1976): 393–403. Also see Sheffer, *Modern Diasporas.*

4. Rothschild, *Ethnopolitics.*

5. Abdul Said and Luis Simmons, *Ethnicity in an International Context* (New Brunswick, N.J.: Transaction Books, 1976).

6. Judy S. Bertelsen, *Non-State Nations in International Politics: Comparative System* (New York: Praeger, 1977).

7. See Sheffer, ed., *Modern Diasporas.*

8. See Walker Conner, "The Impact of Homelands upon Diasporas," in Sheffer, ed., *Modern Diasporas,* 16–46.

9. See Iliya Harik, "The Palestinians in the Diaspora," in Sheffer, ed., *Modern Diasporas,* 315–52.

10. See Locksley Edmondson, "Black America as a Mobilizing Diaspora: Some International Implications," in Sheffer, ed., *Modern Diasporas.* In discussing pan-Africanism, Edmondson goes back to the early twentieth century, specifically looking at the Pan-African Congresses. But overall his study concentrates on the 1960s and forward.

11. Clarence Contee, "DuBois, the NAACP, and the Pan-African Congress of 1919," *Journal of Negro History* 57, no. 1 (1972): 13–28. Contee did an interesting comparison of the Du Boisian Pan-African Congresses with the UNIA's International Negro Conventions, which were held throughout the 1920s. This excellent work was his dissertation, "W. E. B. DuBois and African Nationalism" (American University, 1969); it will be discussed in chapter 5.

12. See Shepperson, "Pan-Africanism and 'pan-africanism.'"

13. Vincent Bakpetu Thompson, *The Making of the African Diaspora in the Americas, 1441–1900* (New York: Longman Group, 1987).

14. See Julius S. Scott, "The Common Wind: Currents of Afro-American Communication in the Era of the Haitian Revolution" (Ph.D. dissertation, Duke University, 1986).

15. Joseph Harris, *Global Dimensions of the African Diaspora* (Washington, D.C.: Howard University Press, 1982), 8–9.

16. See J. Ayodele Langley, *Pan-Africanism and Nationalism in West Africa, 1900–1945* (Oxford: Clarendon, 1973), and "Garveyism and African Nationalism," *Race* 11 (Oct. 1969): 157–72.

17. See Walters, *Pan-Africanism in the African Diaspora.*

18. Michael G. Hanchard, "Afro-Modernity: Temporality, Politics, and the African Diaspora," *Public Culture* 11, no. 1 (1999): 272–97.

19. *Global Mappings of the African Diaspora,* a Web site developed at Northwestern University in 2000. A description of the project may be found at http://www

.diaspora.northwestern.edu, last accessed July 17, 2007; the atlas itself is no longer available online. I served as one of the research assistants on this project and learned significantly more about the extent to which English- and Spanish-speaking African diaspora communities relate politically.

20. See Jean Blackwell Hutson, "An Interview with Aubrey H. DeSouza," SC Visual VRB 1692–1696, and Judith Stein, "An Interview with F. Levi Lord," Imprint 1983–05–12, MIRS SC Visual VRA-43, both housed at the Schomburg Center for Research in Black Culture, New York Public Library, New York.

21. See, for example, Judith Stein, *The World of Marcus Garvey: Race and Class in Modern Society* (Baton Rouge: Louisiana State University Press, 1986); Emory Tolbert, *The UNIA and Black Los Angeles: Ideology and Community in the American Garvey Movement* (Los Angeles: Center for African-American Studies, University of California, 1980); and Theodore Vincent, *Black Power and the Garvey Movement* (Berkeley: Ramparts Press, 1971).

22. See Tolbert, *The UNIA and Black Los Angeles,* for more information on the special collection.

23. From *Negro World* editorial by William Ferris, Jan. 6, 1923. Such editorials by Ferris and Bruce appear throughout the zenith of the BSL; see, for instance, the editorial of July 2, 1921, p. 2.

24. The letter is from Mrs. Iris B. McDonald, Monte Livio, P.O. The name seems to be Spanish and suggests a Central American or Spanish Caribbean address, but I was unable to discern if "P.O." in this case was the abbreviation for "post office." See *Negro World,* Apr. 9, Correspondence Section.

25. It is unclear if Briggs was officially a member of the Communist Party during the years of BSL. Most researchers conclude that he and colleagues probably joined in 1921. See Cedric Robinson, *Black Marxism: The Making of the Black Radical Tradition* (London: Zed, 1983), for a fascinating discussion on black radicals and their struggles within the Communist Party in the twentieth century. Also see Robert Hill, ed., *The Marcus Garvey and Universal Negro Improvement Association Papers,* 3; hereinafter referred to as *UNIA Papers.*

26. W. A. Domingo, "Figures Don't Lie, But Liars Do Figure," *Crusader,* Oct. 1921.

27. Floyd J. Calvin, "The NAACP vs. the UNIA," *New York Amsterdam News,* Feb. 21, 1923.

28. Hill, ed., *UNIA Papers.*

29. The African Legion had been accused of violent attacks against critics and wayward UNIA membership. The most serious accusation was that they had assassinated Rev. James Eason, who was accused of treason. Eason, the UNIA's U.S. leader, was rumored to have written an exposé in a rival newspaper, and some believed that he could dismantle U.S. African American support. Eason was killed after delivering a speech critical of the UNIA in Louisiana. Also see Stein, *The World of Marcus Garvey.*

30. John Henrik Clarke, *Marcus Garvey and the Vision of Africa* (New York: First Vintage Books, 1974).

31. See Julius Scott, "The Common Wind," as well as W. Jeffrey Bolster, *Black Jacks: African-American Seamen in the Age of Sail* (Cambridge, Mass.: Harvard University Press, 1997).

32. See Ula Taylor, *The Veiled Garvey: The Life and Times of Amy Jacques Garvey* (Chapel Hill: University of North Carolina Press, 2002). Note Jacques Garvey was the second wife of Marcus Garvey. His first wife, also named Amy, was involved in the founding of BSL, while the second wife was instrumental from 1920 forward.

33. Amy Jacques Garvey, *Garvey and Garveyism,* 3rd ed. (New York: Macmillan, 1970). She also edited the *Philosophy and Opinions of Marcus Garvey,* 3rd ed. (New York: Majority, 1986). This volume was assembled after the effort and speaks to his ideological positions, values, and evaluations of other political viewpoints, social mores, and political organization. It also has excerpts from the trial.

34. See Hugh Mulzac, *A Star to Steer By* (New York: International Publishers, 1963). Also see "Account of BSL by Capt. Hugh Mulzac in Cleveland Gazette," in Hill, ed., *UNIA Papers,* 5.

35. See, for instance, Derek H. Aldcroft, *The Inter-War Economy: Britain, 1919–1939* (New York: Columbia University Press, 1970), and W. Arthur Lewis, *Economic Survey, 1919–1939,* 7th ed. (London: Unwin University Books, 1970).

36. Mulzac, *A Star to Steer By,* 84.

37. E. David Cronon, *Black Moses: The Story of Marcus Garvey,* 2nd ed. (Madison: University of Wisconsin Press, 1974); Tony Martin, *Race First: The Ideological and Organizational Struggles of Marcus Garvey and the Universal Negro Improvement Association* (Westport, CT: Greenwood, 1976); and Stein, *World of Marcus Garvey.*

38. Other works include Vincent, *Black Power;* Rupert Lewis and Patrick Bryan, eds., *Garvey: His Work and Impact* (Trenton: Africa World Press, 1991); Elton Fax, *Garvey: The Story of a Pioneer Black Nationalist* (New York: Dodd Mead, 1972); and Tolbert, *The UNIA and Black Los Angeles.*

39. Len S. Nembhard, *Trials and Triumphs of Marcus Garvey* (Kingston: Gleaner, 1940; reprint Millwood: Kraus Reprint, 1978).

40. See Lewis and Bryan, eds., *Garvey.*

41. James C. Boyd, "Primitives on the Move: Some Historical Articulations of Garvey and Garveyism, 1887–1927" (Ph.D. dissertation, University of California, Los Angeles, 1982).

42. Tolbert, *The UNIA and Black Los Angeles.*

43. Joe Trotter, "African Americans in the City: The Industrial Era, 1900–1950," in Kenneth Goings and Raymond Mohl, eds. *New African American Urban History* (Thousand Oaks, Calif.: Sage, 1996), 299–319.

44. Ramla Bandele, "The Underdevelopment of Black Towns" (master's thesis, University of Illinois, 1984).

45. See Sundiata K. Cha-Jua, "A Warlike Demonstration: Legalism, Violent Self Help, and Electoral Politics in Decatur Illinois, 1894–1898," *Journal of Urban History* 26, no. 5 (2000): 591–629.

46. Arthur Kaskow, *From Race Riot to Sit-In: 1919 and the 1960s* (New York: Anchor Books, 1966).

47. Goings and Mohl, *New African American Urban History.*

Chapter 3: Still Waters

1. The term *international political economy* is defined here as the political arrangements, treaties, and trade agreements reached between major states to facilitate international trade and the orderly exploitation of raw materials.

2. See Eric Hobsbawm, *The Age of Empire, 1875–1914* (New York: Pantheon, 1987); N. Gordon Levin, *Woodrow Wilson and World Politics: America's Response to War and Revolution* (New York: Oxford University Press, 1968); and Arthur S. Link, *American Epoch: A History of the United States Since the 1890s,* 3rd ed. (New York: Alfred A. Knopf, 1967).

3. Karl Polanyi, *The Great Transformation* (Boston: Beacon Press, 1944).

4. The discussion of the Versailles Treaty and African attempts to influence it relies upon the following works: George L. Beer, *African Questions at the Paris Peace Conference,* ed. Louis H. Gray (New York: Macmillan, 1923; reprint, New York: Negro Universities Press, 1969); Hill, ed., *UNIA Papers;* Langley, *Pan-Africanism and Nationalism.*

5. The United States floated bonds (Liberty Bonds), raised taxes, and resorted to deficit financing to equip itself for the war effort and underwrite the agricultural expansion necessary to meet the market created by the war. However, over $10 billion of this went to Europe: $6.7 billion to the war effort of Britain, France, and Belgium and $3.3 billion for reconstruction of Europe. See D. H. Aldcroft, *From Versailles to Wall Street* (London: Penguin, 1977); W. Arthur Lewis, *Economic Survey*; and George Soule, *Prosperity Decade: From War to Depression, 1917–1929* (New York: Rinehart, 1947).

6. Link, *American Epoch.*

7. See Anne Orde, *The Eclipse of Great Britain* (New York: St. Martin's, 1996), for insight into the symbiotic but competitive relationship between Britain and the United States during this period. See 1919 and 1920 issues of the *Economist* for coverage of Britain's struggle to rebuild its economy and retain its international prestige during this volatile political era.

8. See Aldcroft, *From Versailles.*

9. Paul Kennedy, *The Rise and Fall of the Great Powers: Economic Change and Military Conflict from 1500–2000* (New York: Random House, 1987); John M. Keynes, *Economic Consequences of Peace* (London: Macmillan, 1919); Orde, *The Eclipse of Great Britain;* Robert Service, *Lenin: A Political Life* (Bloomington: Indiana University Press, 1995).

10. See Gregory Freeze, ed., *Russia: A History* (Oxford: Oxford University Press, 1997); and David McFadden, "After the Colby Note: The Wilson Administration and the Bolsheviks, 1920–21," *Presidential Studies Quarterly* 25, no. 4 (1995): 741–50.

11. This section is informed by the research of M.C. Morgan, *Lenin* (London: Edward Arnold, 1971); and Service, *Lenin,* who studied recently released documents on Lenin and the era; and Aldcroft, *From Versailles,* which is an excellent study of the economics of the era.

12. Service notes that Marx had written about peasant-based revolution, suggesting that Russian peasants might be able to "inaugurate a socialist society based on the peasant land communes." See Service, *Lenin,* 3:128.

13. Susan Campbell, "Black Bolsheviks and Recognition of African-America's Right to Self-Determination," *Science and Society* 58, no. 4 (1994): 440–70; Philip Foner and James Allen, eds., *American Communism and Black Americans: A Documentary History, 1919–1929* (Philadelphia: Temple University Press, 1987).

14. The role of the American Negro was included in Lenin's *Theses on the National and Colonial Question* and was the basis of the discussion according to Foner and Allen, eds., *American Communism and Black Americans.* Also see Theodore Draper, *American Communism and Soviet Russia* (New York: Viking, 1960); Wilson Record, *The Negro and the Communist Party* (Chapel Hill: University of North Carolina Press, 1951); and Robinson, *Black Marxism.*

15. McKay, *Long Way From Home* (New York: L. Furman, 1937); Martin, *Race First;* Robinson, *Black Marxism.*

16. See Winston James, *Holding Aloft the Banner of Ethiopia: Caribbean Radicalism in Early Twentieth-Century America* (London: Verso, 1998), as well as Vincent, *Black Power.*

17. Oscar Berland, "The Emergence of the Communist Perspective on the Negro Question in America, 1919–1931," *Science and Society* 63, no. 4 (1999): 412.

18. See Alfred F. Havighurst, *Twentieth Century Britain* (New York: Harper and Row, 1962), and Charles L. Mowat, *Britain between the Wars, 1918–1940* (Chicago: University of Chicago Press, 1958).

19. In a report on wartime finance, the *Economist* put total indebtedness at $7.4 billion, which represented approximately 8 percent of the British GDP for 1918. See *Economist* (London), Jan. 18, 1919, 66–67. The 1918 GDP for Britain was $95.9 billion according to *One Hundred Years of Economic Statistics* (New York: Facts on File, 1989). The foreign debt figure of $1.2 billion comes from Keynes, *Economic Consequences of Peace,* 258.

20. For more detail on the Conliffe Committee report, see Barry Eichengreen, ed., *The Gold Standard in Theory and History* (New York: Methuen, 1985); and the *Economist* (London), Jan. 4 and July 26, 1919.

21. The principal British colonies producing gold were South Africa, India, and the Gold Coast, West Africa. Within the white dominions, there were gold mines in Australia and Canada.

22. Havighurst, *Twentieth Century Britain.*

23. D. H. Aldcroft, "Port Congestion and the Shipping Boom of 1919–1920," *Business History* 3 (1961): 97–106.

24. Palm kernel oil also was used by government to manufacture nitroglycerin, a key ingredient in explosives. Other West African raw materials crucial to Britain's economy were the cocoa plant and the rubber plant, instrumental in the automobile industry.

25. See Keynes, *Economic Consequences of Peace;* Havighurst, *Twentieth Century Britain;* W. Arthur Lewis, *Economic Survey,* 74–90.

26. Aldcroft, "Port Congestion."

27. See Keynes, *Economic Consequences of Peace;* also Aldcroft, *From Versailles.*

28. Orde, *Eclipse of Britain.*

29. See Paul Kennedy, *The Rise and Fall of the Great Powers.*

30. Langley, *Pan-Africanism and Nationalism.*

31. Daniel Baku, "Intellectual in Nationalist Politics: The Contribution of Kobina Sekyi to the Evolution of Ghanaian National Consciousness" (Ph.D. dissertation, University of Sussex, 1987).

32. Only three black states were considered free and therefore able to interact with European and American delegates. These were Liberia, Ethiopia, and Haiti. Diaspora organizations often conveyed their issues through these states to Europeans.

33. Africans participated in the Du Boisian Pan-African Congresses and also the UNIA's International Negro conventions.

34. Beer, *African Questions,* and Contee, "W. E. B. DuBois," point out that colonial political activists were not included in substantive discussions or consulted on agreements or colonial policies.

35. See Ralph L. Crowder, *John Edward Bruce: Politician, Journalist, and Self-Trained Historian of the African Diaspora, 1856–1924* (New York: New York University Press, 2004). Also see W. F. Elkins, *Black Power in the Caribbean* (New York: Revisionist Press, 1977).

Chapter 4: Home Dock

1. David Goldfield, *The American Journey: A History of the United States* (Upper Saddle River, N.J.: Prentice Hall, 2001).

2. In the late 1920s, these countries worked through the Inter-America Conference to prevent any one nation from intervening with another nation in the region. Of course, the United States spurned such policy proposals. See Goldfield, *The American Journey.*

3. Ibid.

4. See Levin, *Woodrow Wilson;* Mark Gilderhus, *Pan-American Visions: Woodrow Wilson in the Western Hemisphere* (Tucson: University of Arizona Press, 1986); and Jeffrey Safford, *Wilsonian Maritime Diplomacy, 1913–1921* (New Brunswick: State University Press of New Jersey, 1978).

5. The Monroe Doctrine effectively halted any additional European colonization in the Western hemisphere. President Roosevelt added a policing function to the doctrine when he arranged to intervene (on Europe's behalf) in any political or economic dispute between Europe and countries in the region. The goal was to keep European military power out of the region by insuring that the smaller states complied with any financial or political agreements. Wilson moved toward outright regional hegemony. See Link, *American Epoch.*

6. Gilderhus, *Pan-American Visions,* 35.

7. Goldfield, *The American Journey.*

8. Ibid., and also Safford, *Wilsonian Maritime Diplomacy.*

9. See K. Jack Bauer, *A Maritime History of the U.S.: The Role of America's Seas and Waterways* (Columbia: University of South Carolina Press, 1988).

10. See Paul Zeis, *American Shipping Policy* (Princeton: Princeton University Press, 1938).

11. Zeis provides an in-depth analysis of the questionable management decisions made by the Wilson administration and the shipping board. For an instructive discussion about the economic complexities facing the shipping industry in the postwar era economy, see Aldcroft, "Port Congestion."

12. Safford, *Wilsonian Maritime Diplomacy,* 246.

13. Levin, *Woodrow Wilson.*

14. These acts included the Espionage Act of 1917, the Sedition Act, and the Alien Act. See David Kennedy, *Over Here: The First World War and American Society* (New York: Oxford University Press, 1980); Link, *American Epoch,* and Kaskow, *From Race Riot to Sit-In.*

15. Link, *American Epoch.*

16. See Joe Trotter and Earl Lewis et al., *The African American Experience* (New York: Palgrave McMillan, 2004), and Goldfield, *The American Journey.*

17. See Veblen, *The Theory of the Leisure Class.*

18. White Americans used everything from biblical creationist theory to evolutionist theory to derogate black Americans; African Americans not only repudiated these theories, they empowered themselves with their history and by building viable social institutions; see Ivan Hannaford, *Race: The History of an Idea in the West* (Washington, D.C.: Woodrow Wilson Center, 1996).

19. See Trotter and Lewis, *African American Experience;* also Goings and Mohl, eds., *New African American Urban History.*

20. Alan W. Cafruny, *Ruling the Waves: The Political Economy of International Shipping* (Berkeley: University of California Press, 1987).

21. Soule, *Prosperity Decade.*

22. W. Arthur Lewis, *Economic Survey,* and Aldcroft, "From Versailles." Note that the BSL's existence, 1919–1921, straddled both the boom and the slump. It had to have been impacted by these forces in the economy; the cost of the first ship, for example, was influenced by the shortage of ships and freight space, more than likely inflating the price.

23. See Service, *Lenin.*

24. Aldcroft, "Port Congestion," 100.

25. Although Cafruny deals primarily with the period after World War II, his argument applies to the earlier era just as well.

26. See Elkins, *Black Power in the Caribbean,* for a discussion of riots and black attempts to seek political redress.

27. Link, *American Epoch;* Goldfield, *The American Journey;* David Kennedy, *Over Here.*

28. Liesl Orenic and Joe Trotter, "African Americans in the U.S. Economy," in *Historical Roots of the Urban Crisis: African Americans in the Industrial City, 1900–1950,* edited by Henry L. Taylor and Walter Hill (New York: Garland, 2000), 177–208.

29. See Waskow, *From Race Riot to Sit-In.*

30. See Waskow's discussion on the Urban League's take on the Chicago riot, ibid.

Chapter 5: Charting the Black Atlantic

1. Cha-Jua, "A Warlike Demonstration." *Terrorism* is the appropriate term for the physical attacks, lynchings, and firebombing of homes and black businesses in the South. Less violent forms of discrimination included voting restrictions, the curtailment of legal protections, and inequitable distribution of government resources such as education, roads, and housing.

2. Quintard Taylor, "Urban Black Labor in the West, 1849–1940," in *African American Experience,* edited by Joe Trotter and Earl Lewis, et al. (New York: Palgrave Macmillan, 2004), 99–120.

3. See Michael C. Dawson, *Black Visions: The Roots of Contemporary African American Political Ideologies* (Chicago: University of Chicago Press, 2001).

4. The introduction of the sugar beet in Europe reduced the cost to process sugar, and as this alternative to cane sugar made its way into the economy, cane sugar became less profitable. For an informative discussion on the role of sugar production in the Caribbean economy during the era, see Ralph Thompson, "The Role of Capitalism in Jamaica's Development," *Caribbean Quarterly* 12, no. 2 (1966): 22–28; and Eric Williams, "The Historical Background of British Guiana's Problems," *Journal of Negro History* 30, no. 4 (1945): 357–81.

5. See, for example, W. F. Elkins, "Hercules and the Society of Peoples of African Origin," *Caribbean Quarterly* 11, no. 4 (Oct. 1971); Martin, *Race First;* Shepperson, *Pan-Africanism;* and Ralph L. Crowder, "John Edward Bruce and the Value of Knowing the Past: Politician, Journalist, and Self-Trained Historian of the African Diaspora, 1856–1924" (Ph.D. dissertation, University of Kansas, 1994).

6. Eric Williams, *The Negro in the Caribbean* (New York: Haskell House, 1971), 16.

7. Ibid., 62.

8. See Elkins, "Hercules and the Society," and Martin, *Race First.*

9. See Aubrey Bonnett and G. Llewellyn Watson, eds., *Emerging Perspectives on the Black Diaspora* (Lanham, MD: University Press of America, 1990).

10. Dawson, *Black Visions,* passim.

11. See Michael Goldstein's excellent work on African American politics in this era: "Race Politics in New York City, 1890–1930: Independent Political Behavior" (Ph.D. dissertation, Columbia University, 1973).

12. The latter goal was pursued by monetary contributions to black newspapers in large urban centers, enabling them to compete with other papers. The machine was also known to withdraw patronage jobs from uncooperative politicians or rebels. Nevertheless, criticism of Washington and aggressive activism among black journalists prevailed.

13. See Ira Katznelson, *Black Men, White Cities: Race, Politics, and Migration in the United States, 1900–1930, and Britain 1948–1968* (London: Oxford University Press, 1973), 46–52.

14. See Kenneth Goings and Raymond Mohl, "Urban Black Labor in the West," in *New African American Urban History,* ed. Goings and Mohl.

15. The Niagara Movement was the forerunner of the NAACP.

16. Details of the case can be found in David Levering Lewis's excellent biography *W. E. B. Du Bois: The Fight for Equality and the American Century, 1919–1963* (New York: Henry Holt, 2000); see volume 2.

17. See Roderick Bush, *We Are Not What We Seem: Black Nationalism and Class Struggle in the American Century* (New York: New York University Press, 1999), and Robin D. G. Kelley and Earl Lewis, *To Make Our World Anew: A History of African Americans from 1880,* vol. 2.

18. See, for instance, Kelley and Lewis, *To Make Our World Anew;* and Philip Foner, *American Socialism and Black Americans* (Westport, CT: Greenwood, 1977).

19. During the 1918 election, socialists captured up to 15 percent of the black vote in New York City and elected socialist candidates, but this electoral surge proved temporary. See Foner, *American Socialism.*

20. In later years, socialism would permeate African American politics. For example, A. Philip Randolph would go on to organize the railroad industry's sleeping car porters and vindicate the usefulness of unionism in African American politics.

21. Jervis Anderson, *A. Philip Randolph: A Biographical Portrait* (New York: Harcourt Brace Jovanovich, 1972), provides an interesting comparative analysis between the politics and personalities of Randolph, Du Bois, Garvey, and other activists with whom Randolph interacted.

22. Anderson, *A. Philip Randolph,* 92.

23. Several researchers debate the Comintern's understanding of black America and the wisdom of its programming for this population. See, for instance, Bush, *We Are Not What We Seem;* Jeffrey B. Perry, ed., *A Hubert Harrison Reader* (Middletown: Wesleyan University Press, 2001); James, *Holding Up the Banner of Ethiopia.* The UNIA Papers have extensive coverage of Briggs and the ABB.

24. See Hill, ed., *UNIA Papers,* vols. 2 and 3.

25. Lowell W. Barrington, "'Nation' and 'Nationalism': The Misuse of Key Concepts in Political Science," *PS: Political Science and Politics* 30, no. 4 (1997): 712–16.

26. See Clarke, *Marcus Garvey;* Vincent, *Black Power.*

27. See Langley, *Pan-Africanism and Nationalism,* and the John Edward Bruce Papers.

28. William Seraile, *Bruce Grit: The Black Nationalist Writings of John Edward Bruce* (Knoxville: University of Tennessee Press, 2003), 170.

29. See J. R. Casimir Papers, Box 1 and 2, Sc MG 110, Archives and Rare Books, Schomburg Center for Research in Black Culture, New York Public Library, New York, N.Y. Casimir's correspondence includes his requests for different papers and discussions between him and correspondents about political events.

30. The UNIA's goals did include two political elements: providing representation to all black communities in every nation and supporting the development of independent African states. However, these components were not implemented in Jamaica.

31. Marcus Garvey was well traveled, having lived and worked as a journalist and payroll clerk in Central America and Britain, and having visited other West European states.

32. See Hill, ed., *UNIA Papers,* 1–3.

33. Ibid. I do not mean to imply that he did not respect these speakers in their own right. Garvey admired these activists. In fact, many of his programs included representatives of other revolutionary organizations. For example, the Irish revolutionary movement Sinn Fein had a great impact on Garvey's political programming.

34. See "Editorial Letter by Marcus Garvey," in Hill, ed., *UNIA Papers,* 1:352–53.

35. Robert Hill and Barbara Bair, ed., *Marcus Garvey: Life and Lessons. A Centennial Companion to the Marcus Garvey and UNIA Papers* (Berkeley: University of California Press, 1987), 356.

36. See "The Constitution and Book of Laws—Made for the Universal Negro Improvement Association, Inc. and African Communities League, Inc. of the World," in Hill, ed., *UNIA Papers,* 1:256–77.

37. Perhaps the most famous ICU leader was Clements Kadalie, one of the key activists in strikes and other political activities in Southern Africa. See Hill, ed., *UNIA Papers,* 3:233.

38. For example, the *Black Man* in South Africa carried UNIA information, and the *Negro World* carried the *Black Man*'s news as well; see Hill, ed., *UNIA Papers,* 3.

39. See, for example, "Bureau of Investigation Report," by Agent Davidson, Hill, ed., *UNIA Papers,* 1:326.

40. See "Launching of the 'Liberty League of Negro Americans,'" in Hill, ed., *UNIA Papers* 1:209–11.

41. "Editorial Letter by Marcus Garvey," in Hill, ed., *UNIA Papers,* 1:352; *Negro World,* Feb. 1, 1919.

42. This depreciatory terminology for African people lends credence to my argument that the UNIA may have preferred to establish a Western state under black control rather than the reestablishment (or the refurbishment) of original African state systems, which their speeches extol.

43. From "Constitution and Book of Laws," in Hill, ed., *UNIA Papers,* 1:257.

44. This is an excerpt from a speech given by Garvey in Newport News, Virginia, a week before the planned launch of the first BSL vessel, Oct. 25, 1919 (Hill, ed., *UNIA Papers,* 2:118).

45. See "British Military Intelligence Report," in Hill, ed., *UNIA Papers* 2:84; both British and American intelligence report on possible interchange with Japan.

46. Hill, ed., *UNIA Papers,* 3; Vincent, *Black Power;* Edwin S. Redkey, "The Flowering of Black Nationalism: Henry McNeal Turner and Marcus Garvey," in *Key Issues in the Afro-American Experience,* ed. Nathan I. Huggins, Martin Kilson and Daniel Fox (New York: Harcourt Brace Jovanovich, 1971).

47. "Report of UNIA Meeting" (*Negro World,* Mar. 13, 1920), in Hill, ed., *UNIA Papers* 2: 241–59, excerpt from 254–55. For further examples of this sentiment, see Hill, ed., *UNIA Papers,* 4:921.

48. Langley, *Pan-Africanism and Nationalism;* Contee, "W. E. B. DuBois."

49. Du Bois wrote an interesting two-part analytical article on Garvey in *Crisis,* Dec. 1919 and Jan. 1920.

50. Crowder, *John Edward Bruce;* also see Bruce Papers.

51. See *Negro World,* 1923, passim.

Chapter 6: Shipping Politics

1. Amy Jacques Garvey, *Garvey and Garveyism.*

2. Vincent, *Black Power,* 101–5.

3. The letter was from Cadet to H. Dorsinville, Jan. 13, 1919. It was included in correspondence of W. E. Allen, acting chief, Bureau of Investigation, to William M. Offley, New York division superintendent, Washington, D.C., Feb. 10, 1919 (Hill, ed., *UNIA Papers,* 1:357–59). This strategy is confirmed in a Garvey speech nine months later in "Report of UNIA Meeting, Newport News, VA Oct. 25, 1919," in Hill, ed., *UNIA Papers,* 2:112–20, especially 119.

4. Hill, ed., *UNIA Papers* 1:413. Garvey maps out this strategy in the June 4, 1919, issue of the *Negro World* in an editorial letter.

5. See "Bureau of Investigation Report, New York City, May 28, 1919," in Hill, ed., *UNIA Papers,* 1:411–15. A Bureau of Investigation agent, Mortimer Davis, reported that after the meeting, in a private conversation, Garvey discussed a shipping charter plan in more detail and the planned pursuit of "financial backing" from the Japanese. Davis was one of the more professional agents of the BI in that his reports are veritable; the facts presented in most instances can be corroborated by other sources, and he refrained from using racist, condescending commentary. In addition to BI agents, British military intelligence reported on possible association (particularly commercial) between Japan and the UNIA.

6. Ibid.

7. These were businesses managed by the UNIA's commercial wing, the African Communities League (Hill, ed., *UNIA Papers,* 1:411). An interesting account of the

dispute appears in "Memorandum" by Edward O'Toole of the *World* [newspaper] New York, June 30, 1919 in Hill, ed., *UNIA Papers,* 1:451–52. Also see the testimony for Edgar Grey, p. 1:62–66, and Richard Warner, p. 1:147, in U.S. Circuit Court of Appeals, for the Second Circuit, *Marcus Garvey v. United States of America,* appellate case trial number 30924, 4 vols. (hereafter cited as *Garvey v. U.S.*). The full transcript is housed in the National Archives, Record Group 267, in two locations: in the Supreme Court archives, no. 959, for Oct. 1924 term (although the Supreme Court refused to hear the case) and in the National Archives in New York, where the case was tried originally in U.S. District Court for the Southern District of New York, 1923.

8. To place this occurrence in context, Hill notes that the audit committee's action may have grown out of an internal UNIA dispute discussed later in this chapter.

9. See cross-examination of Kilroe in *Garvey v. U.S.,* 132–41.

10. See *Garvey v. U.S.,* testimonies of Edgar Grey, Henrietta Vinton Davis, Joshua Cockburn, Leo H. Healy, and Marcus Garvey. There is confusion regarding the financial organization and fund-raising institutions in place. Although Kilroe continuously referred to the BSL selling stock before incorporation, the fact is that prior to the June 1919 incorporation, BSL was funded through contributions and member loans to the effort.

11. See Hill, ed., *UNIA Papers,* 1: 444, n. 1.

12. For example, see "African Speaker Thrills New York Audience" (*Negro World,* June 14, 1919), in Hill, ed., *UNIA Papers,* 1:420–22.

13. See *Garvey v. U.S.,* Edgar Grey testimony, 69–70; Henrietta V. Davis, 1091–92; and Hill, ed., *UNIA Papers,* 1:420–21; idem, appendix 4, 560.

14. Edgar Grey reported the missing stock book to the Delaware secretary of state and spoke with Kilroe. He testified that as secretary of the BSL, he did not want to be responsible for financial mismanagement. Garvey countercharged that Edgar Grey was trying to distract attention from UNIA suspicion of his embezzlement of UNIA funds and BSL contributions. The point is lack of structured financial reporting impeded the development of BSL. See Jeremiah Certain's testimony, *Garvey v. U.S.,* 1290–96, Garvey's testimony, 2199–2206; also Hill, ed., *UNIA Papers,* 1: 420–21.

15. Also, see Amy Jacques Garvey, *Garvey and Garveyism,* 39–41. She discusses in detail Garvey's request that she develop procedures to facilitate the processing of stock purchases, contributions, and reliable reporting procedures. Amy J. Garvey became Garvey's second wife in 1923.

16. See Amy Jacques Garvey, *Garvey and Garveyism,* 39–40. Garvey's account is similar to those of other BSL administrators and demonstrated that attempts were made to organize and professionally manage the Black Star Line. However, standard accounting procedures were not implemented until professional accountant O. M. Thompson joined the staff in 1921.

17. The following discussion relies heavily upon the testimony of the chief salesperson, Harry R. Watkis, 783–831, another salesman, Arden Bryan, 1379–86, and of Eli Garcia, in *Garvey v. U. S.*

18. See Watkis testimony, 791, *Garvey v. U.S.*

19. Fragmentary copies of the 1920 *Negro World* document the coordinated writings of these columnists and their success in presenting not only the need for the shipping line but in placing the effort in the context of the overall economic development priorities that the UNIA espoused.

20. See testimony of Henrietta Vinton Davis, DeBourg, and Richardson in *Garvey v. U.S.* Two very interesting letters from Davis about her tours are included in the John E. Bruce Papers, which are housed in the Schomburg Collection, New York Public Library. Also see Irma Watkins-Owens, *Blood Relations: Caribbean Immigrants and the Harlem Community, 1900–1930* (Bloomington: Indiana University Press, 1996).

21. BSL Daily Transaction Report, New York, Jan. 7, 1920, in Hill, ed., *UNIA Papers,* 2:176.

22. See Rene De La Pedraja, *A Historical Dictionary of the U.S. Merchant Marine and Shipping Industry* (Westport, CT: Greenwood, 1994).

23. W. V. Packard, *Sale and Purchase,* 2nd ed. (London: Fairplay, 1988).

24. See Cockbourne's testimony, 339, and that of UNIA member and BSL supervising engineer, Edwin T. Wright, 2009, in *Garvey v. U.S.*

25. According to trial testimony, Estrada may have been working for Harriss and Magill.

26. The contract agreement contains the codicil, which added $3,500 to the purchase price in order to extend the time BSL needed to sell enough stock to make the down payment for the *Yarmouth.* See Memorandum of Agreement, New York City, Oct. 20, 1919, in Hill, ed., *UNIA Papers,* 2: 80–82.

27. Ibid., 269, n. 1; the bill of sale was not transferred until 1920. See Leo Healy's testimony in *Garvey v. U.S.*

28. Hill, ed., *UNIA Papers,* 2:166.

29. Many researchers of the UNIA have suggested that purchase prices of BSL vessels were exorbitant. While I agree that the prices were high, I would argue that the price—particularly for the *Yarmouth*—must be considered in light of the tight supply of ships and shipping space immediately following the war. The purchase of the other ships occurred as the prices were dropping in the spring of 1920. Vincent, *Black Power,* draws a similar conclusion. Also see Aldcroft, "Port Congestion."

30. See the testimony of Harriss's attorney, Leo Healy, in *Garvey v. U.S.*

31. My research has not uncovered the actual classification of the *Yarmouth.* Lloyd's Registry (letter received July 5, 2000) states the ship was not classified by its agency; the American Bureau of Shipping (Aug. 9, 2000) reports the same and also notes there are no inspection records for the *Yarmouth.* ABS pointed out that classification was voluntary, particularly during the era. However, it would seem that since the *Yarmouth* was insured, classification must have occurred at some juncture.

32. This practice is similar to the classification process. Classification is for insurance purposes, but the government inspection is for safety and to make sure that ships meet the criteria of the nation under which they are registered. Yet these related institutions failed to guard against inadequate ships sailing.

33. See Department of Commerce Steamboat Inspection Service, *General Rules and Regulations Prescribed by the Board of Supervising Inspectors, as amended at Board Meeting of January 1918* (Washington, D.C.: Government Printing Office). Note these rules were in place during 1919. American shipping protocol is based on British procedures.

34. This was a highly contentious point during the trial. Cockbourne testified that he told Garvey, "It is customary to have a ship docked and examine her hull. It is also customary to have a marine engineer to examine her boilers and engine." But he says Garvey replied, "You just want to run the corporation into unnecessary expense." Garvey testified that Cockbourne "recommended to us that the boat was in good condition, and worth the price, and the directors voted the purchase of the boat." Garvey also testified about the board's concern about the age of the boat, to which Cockbourne replied "that it didn't matter because older boats than the Yarmouth were afloat and were able to go on sailing." Garvey implies that Cockbourne's explanation for wanting the ship was reasonable politically. Again, Garvey's testimony on Cockbourne's rationale for purchasing the *Yarmouth:* "this is the best boat you could have because I can get a British crew and with a British captain, there is no colored American captain, and, therefore, we must have this boat" (*Garvey v. U.S.*, 295–96 and 2212–15). The BSL minutes for Sept. 11, 1919, indicate that Cockbourne did recommend the purchase of the *Yarmouth.* However, being a captain did not qualify Cockbourne to inspect the vessel. Further, he indicated in his testimony that he had no broker's license. The attorney for Harriss, Magill and Company commented during his cross-examination by Garvey regarding Cockbourne's role in the Yarmouth purchase, "I think he got a little commission for bringing you to Harriss." *Garvey v. U.S.*, 252–53.

35. Captain Mulzac served as first officer aboard the *Yarmouth* on two voyages; he had been promised the captaincy of the *Phyllis Wheatley.* Mulzac was on the second and most controversial voyage of the *Yarmouth.* Mulzac ultimately left the BSL effort, citing mismanagement and the BSL board's dismissal of the opinions and knowledge of its ship captains and crews. However, his description of BSL's impact upon a heretofore relatively powerless population (regardless of class) is telling, and may help to explain what has been termed uncritical support among ordinary black people for the goals of the Black Star Line. Both excerpts are from Hugh Mulzac, *Memoirs of a Captain of the Black Star Line,* in Clarke, ed., *Marcus Garvey,* 132–33. Also see Mulzac's autobiography, *A Star to Steer By.*

36. *Ballast* means that there is insufficient (or no) cargo to keep the ship properly afloat and heavy material must be placed in the hold in the ship to insure stability.

37. For a detailed description of the vessels' voyages under BSL management, see Cronon, *Black Moses,* Martin, *Race First,* and Stein, *World of Marcus Garvey.*

38. The ship did not have the appropriate containment features, and Cockbourne was concerned that the cargo would slide about, causing the ship to be imbalanced.

39. Hill, ed., *UNIA Papers,* 2:211, n. 5, and 241, n. 1.

40. The *Shadyside* was insured by Frank B. Hall and Co. (report by Special Agent Mortimer J. Davis, New York, Mar. 8, 1922, in Hill, ed., *UNIA Papers,* 4:544–45).

41. Testimony of Jacob Wise, a captain and pilot of the *Shadyside, Garvey v. U.S.,* 423.

42. Martin, *Race First,* 157; Capt. Leon R. Swift's testimony in *Garvey v. U.S.,* 1712–13. No source discussed the reasons why the ship was stored rather than taken to the Caribbean to work as a passenger vessel and deliver cargo throughout the archipelago. It is reasonable to assume that by this time, funds were not available to fuel the vessel for the thousand-mile trip.

43. See "Monthly Summary of Shares," Hill, ed., *UNIA Papers,* 3:775–76. These figures must be used cautiously because the Bureau of Investigation confiscated all BSL books and presented this data in its case against the BSL. Therefore, one can argue reasonably that the data are tainted, skewed to make the federal government's case.

44. From testimony of Capt. Adrian Richardson, *Garvey v. U.S.,* 433–35.

45. Ibid., see Henrietta Vinton Davis' testimony, 1206, Thompson's testimony, 1905–1906, Richardson's testimony. Also see telegrams from Captain Adrian Richardson to the BSL, New York Office, Havana, Apr. 25, 1921, and O. M. Thompson to Marcus Garvey, New York, Apr. 25, 1921, in Hill, ed., *UNIA Papers,* 3:365 as examples.

46. See memorandum from O. M. Thompson to Louis LaMothe in Hill, ed., *UNIA Papers,* 3:38. Also see *Garvey v. U.S.* transcript for letters from Thompson to Captain Mulzac in government's exhibits 53 and 54, 2554–55.

47. Both the *Messenger* and the *Crusader* continually ran analytical but vituperative articles on the BSL problems and the UNIA's ideology. Initially, more balanced analysis of the BSL were written by Du Bois in the *Crisis,* Dec. 1919 and Jan. 1920. However, as acrimony increased between the NAACP and UNIA, Du Bois's scholastic objectivity was replaced by vitriol. Also see E. Ethelred Brown analysis of the BSL; he presents a plausible financial analysis in "Garveyism, a Dispassionate, Unprejudiced Appraisement" (*Jamaica Times,* May 20, 1922), in Hill, ed., *UNIA Papers,* 4:635–39; and excerpts from the *Emancipator* in Hill, ed., *UNIA Papers,* 2:271–79.

48. *Garvey v. U.S.,* 2135.

49. See telegrams from O. M. Thompson to the BSL, Havana, Apr. 26, 1921, and O. M. Thompson to Captain Adrian Richardson, Apr. 26, 1921, in Hill, ed., *UNIA Papers,* 3:362–66.

50. See Mattuck's cross-examination of Henrietta Vinton Davis in *Garvey v. U.S.,* 1199–1200, for an example of the expenses accumulated on stock-selling campaigns.

51. Langley, *Pan-Africanism and Nationalism,* 91.

52. Ibid.

53. Ibid., 99; also see Baku, "An Intellectual in National Politics."

54. This is substantiated by 1920–22 issues of the *Negro World* as well as in the works of Hill, ed., *UNIA Papers,* passim, and Martin, *Race First.*

55. The John E. Bruce papers contain correspondence from two descendants of a

deceased colleague and fellow activist; see Document No. MS 267 3. One warned that his cousin was irresponsible and other more qualified people could better represent the BSL in Nigeria. Also see Martin, *Race First,* 164.

56. See Hill, ed., *UNIA Papers,* 3:365, n. 1 for detail on the contractual agreement between the Black Star Line and A. Rudolph Silverston, the proprietor of the New York Shipping Exchange. While Hill spells the name without an "e," the trial transcript spells it "Silverstone." Interestingly, Silverston did not appear at the trial.

57. At the trial, BSL board member Fred Toote disclosed that the shipping broker, Silverston, convinced the board that it was racism that prevented the BSL efforts in the shipping industry: "we were informed by Mr. Silverstone being a white man and we being colored that if we represented ourselves it would prejudice men against us; so we got Mr. Silverstone to act as our agent" (*Garvey v. U.S.,* 1587).

58. *Garvey v. U.S.,* 1778. See p. 1773 for similar statements by Thompson.

59. "Reports of the 1921 Convention," Hill, ed., *UNIA Papers,* 4: 668–93. Also see article in *California Eagle,* ibid., 170.

60. The auditor general's report, as well as the high chancellor's presentation of the annual financial report, is in Hill, ed., *UNIA Papers,* 4:620–29.

61. After Noah Thompson reported on the financial quagmire, the Los Angeles branch of the UNIA revolted and formed an organization called the Pacific Coast Negro Improvement Association. See Tolbert, *UNIA and Black Los Angeles.*

62. Although it seems plausible that sales would have leveled off further, the stock books were recalled because Thompson no longer authorized his signature on them. Thompson cancelled the negotiations with the USSB; some researchers suggest that he did so to obtain the $22,500 deposit in the USSB's possession. Several participants tried to obtain this money, including Nolan, Silverston, and Garvey (Hill, ed., *UNIA Papers,* 4, passim; and Martin, *Race First*).

63. Speech by Marcus Garvey, "Only Secondary to the Larger Plan," New York City, Feb. 13, 1922, in Hill, ed., *UNIA Papers,* 4:509.

64. From 1922 convention reports, in Hill, ed., *UNIA Papers,* 4: 870.

65. Ibid., 874–75.

66. See Martin, *Race First,* 163–65; also Hill, ed., *UNIA Papers,* 5, passim.

Chapter 7: Stormy Seas

1. By January 1922, Congress roundly criticized the USSB; calls were made to disband it or have the Commerce Department assume its responsibilities. During hearings, the USSB was severely criticized for mismanagement. See *New York Times,* Mar. 4, Mar. 31, and Apr. 5, 1922. Also see De La Pedraja, *A Historical Dictionary of the U.S. Merchant Marine,* 563–66.

2. The bureau's new chief, William Burns, wrote this memo to Frank Burke, head of the USSB's Investigation Department. Burns capitalized Garvey's name in the memo. See William J. Burns to Frank Burke, Washington, D.C., Aug. 31, 1921, in Hill, ed., *UNIA Papers,* 3:730. This was not the first time a government institution had tried

to influence a ship purchase by BSL; New York state prosecutor Kilroe had tried to stop the *Yarmouth* sale (British military intelligence report, New York, Dec. 10, 1919, in Hill, ed., *UNIA Papers,* 2:166).

3. The first mention of government surveillance is "Report by the American Protective League to the Bureau of Investigation, New York, June 3, 1918," in Hill, ed., *UNIA Papers,* 1:244. The American Protective League informed the BI that an informant had reported the UNIA "preached against whites." Also see a BI memorandum regarding the "Negro Question." It discussed hiring Negroes nationally as informants (Capt. Henry G. Sebastian to Col. Alexander B. Coxe, Washington, D.C. Aug. 9, 1919, in Hill, ed., *UNIA Papers,* 1:477).

4. Much of the information reported by these moles can be verified. Hill points out that P-138 may have been among a group of Jamaicans who sent a letter to the government denouncing Garvey.

5. See "Reports by Special Agent 800, New York City, July 14, 1920" in Hill, ed., *UNIA Papers,* 2:424. Another example appears on page 202 of the same text, "Report by Special Agent Jones, Norfolk, Va, Feb. 9, 1920." Other reports indicate that he searched Garvey's files in search of information. See "Confidential Informant 800 to George F. Ruch," New York, Sept 23, 1921, in Hill, ed., *UNIA Papers,* 4:73. Like many black BI agents, Agent 800 (James Wormley Jones) was a veteran. He had served as an army captain in World War I.

6. See Hill, ed., *UNIA Papers,* vol. 3 and 4.

7. Confidential Informant 800 to George F. Ruch, New York City, Oct. 6, 1921, in Hill, ed., *UNIA Papers,* 4:105. Jones also gave Briggs a confidential memo that included information about the UNIA's project to develop a settlement within Liberia that was highly critical of the government there. Publication was very damaging to the UNIA.

8. Hill, ed., *UNIA Papers,* as well as Martin, *Race First,* and others document the dissension in the UNIA/BSL management. The trial transcript, *Garvey v. U.S.,* also captures the distrust and hostility between former administrators.

9. Biographical material on Boulin appears in Hill, ed., *UNIA Papers* 2:541, n. 3, and 3:730. Again, a discount is in order since Garvey may have known about Boulin's clandestine activities. However, this nugget (Garvey discovering that Boulin was a spy) comes from Agent 800!

10. "Reports by Special Agent P-138, New York City, Nov. 6, 1920," in Hill, ed., *UNIA Papers,* 3:71.

11. Exceeded in notoriety only by the IWW and the U.S. Communist Party.

12. This memo was written to Lewis J. Baley, chief of the bureau near the time of Garvey's Caribbean tour. See Hill, ed., *UNIA Papers* 3:177. For information on Caribbean monitoring, see ibid., 249–77.

13. This happened in 1921, during the Harding administration, which is still known as one of the most corrupt administrations of American history. Several agents reported the purported bribe. Garvey's highly regarded attorneys did have connec-

tions to the Republican Party. His principal attorneys were black men educated in Ivy League schools; Matthews had served as an assistant attorney general in Massachusetts. See Hill, ed., *Marcus Garvey: Life and Lessons,* 408. For information on the bribe, see, for example, J. Edgar Hoover to William J. Burns, Washington, D.C., Jan. 16, 1922, and Confidential Informant 800 to George F. Ruch, New York, Jan. 17, 1922, in Hill, ed., *UNIA Papers,* 4:372–74.

14. Maj. E. J. Ely, acting chief, Negative Branch, Military Intelligence Division of the War Department, sent this directive. The Negative Branch was the unit that investigated and contained "subversive" activities within U.S. borders. The Positive Branch was assigned intelligence matters related to foreign countries. See Hill, ed., *UNIA Papers,* 1:293–95.

15. British military intelligence report, New York, in Hill, ed., *UNIA Papers,* 2:166. The report was dated Dec. 10, 1919, and a copy was sent to the U.S. Department of War. Note Magill's first name was not used in the report, or in relation to the Harriss, Magill and Company. The West European branch of MID also suggested that the department monitor the UNIA in Liberia. There was concern about the growth of the UNIA, and indirectly the Black Star Line since it would provide the transportation link, for two reasons. First there was the immediate economic concern about the control of Liberian rubber trees. And secondly, Liberia had been one of Germany's key trading partners prior to the war. That relationship was rekindled in 1920. See Draft Memorandum by John Cooper Wiley, Division of European Affairs, Washington, D.C., Aug. 1921, in Hill, ed., *UNIA Papers,* 3:740–43, and ibid., 4:47.

Monroe Trotter was an African American political activist and journalist who, after being denied a passport to attend the peace conference, went as an employee on a steamer. There was no connection between Trotter, an independent activist, and the nationalist UNIA.

16. The indictees included Marcus Garvey, George Tobias, treasurer, Orlando Thompson, vice president, and Elie Garcia, BSL secretary.

17. One report of funds transferred from Canada to the Caribbean was shown to be for the *Kanawha;* the prosecution did not refute this explanation. See *Garvey v. U.S.*

18. William Burns to W. B. Matthews, Bureau of Investigation, Washington, D.C., Sept. 1, 1921, in Hill, ed., *UNIA Papers,* 4:4. Also look at "Report by Special Agent Mortimer J. Davis, New York, Dec. 12, 1921," in ibid., 306, and Complaint Against Marcus Garvey, New York, Jan. 12, 1922, U.S. v. Marcus Garvey, Complaint, violation 215 USCC, in ibid., 340–41, for the reasoning behind as well as the text of the formal complaint.

19. Eason was highly respected and had been elected to the UNIA position "leader of American Negroes" during the 1920 convention when the constitution outlined several leadership positions. In addition there was a leader of the West Indies, a potentate, but the political power stayed with Garvey. See *UNIA Papers* and Hill, ed., *Marcus Garvey: Life and Lessons.*

Chapter 8: Marooned

1. The black communist movement is not included here because it was concentrating on building a base in the United States, thus its focus was more domestic at that time. It must be noted, however, that Briggs's political vision included an Africa-based movement. See Vincent, *Black Power,* and Martin, *Race First.*

2. See Hill, ed., *UNIA Papers,* vol. 4.

3. Bureau of Investigation summary of the minutes of BSL board of directors' meetings, in Hill, ed., *UNIA Papers,* 2:684. These goals were also given in UNIA speeches and editorials. Similar goals were articulated in the trial transcript; also see Amy Jacques Garvey, *Philosophy and Opinions.*

4. Vincent, *Black Power,* discusses the importance of the Declaration of Rights to our understanding of the UNIA's political goals. The declaration is presented in its entirety in Hill, ed., *UNIA Papers,* 2:571–580.

5. They were well versed in the ancient history of many African nations and familiar with some cultural institutions, but this knowledge does not seem to have extended into the ways in which Africans handled political activities prior to colonization. At this stage, most continental Africans involved in UNIA leadership were from Liberia and Sierra Leone. Both of these states had been established by the West and therefore used Western political institutions. UNIA potentate Gabriel Johnson was a descendant of "freedmen"—meaning freed from American slavery. His grandfather immigrated to Liberia in the nineteenth century. See Robert Hill and Barbara Bair, eds., *Marcus Garvey: Life and Lessons* (Berkeley: University of California Press, 1987). Across West Africa, most activists were educated in either British or French educational systems, and many of them embraced Western political institutions. See Langley, *Pan-Africanism and Nationalism.*

6. Martin, *Race First,* 42.

7. My thinking on authoritarianism is most influenced by Mark E. Warren, "Deliberative Democracy and Authority," *APSA* 90, no. 1 (1996); and Paul Brooker, *Non-Democratic Regimes: Theory, Government, and Politics* (London: Macmillan, 2000). *Political authority* is distinguished from *authoritarianism* in political science, although the definitions of both are still contested. Here *authoritarianism* is the abuse or misuse of political authority and the distortion of a system to protect and perpetuate the agenda and managers of the regime. This is usually achieved through the co-optation (and, if necessary, neutralization) of democratic participation, including electoral institutions, protests, and the usurping of the authority assigned to key administrative positions. O'Donnell's populist-authoritarianism found in regimes with modest modernization levels comes closest to capturing the UNIA's modus operandi. In such regimes, community activism is often co-opted to achieve an inflexible economic program.

8. See Vincent, *Black Power,* 196, for a discussion of dissension in the UNIA nationalist ranks.

9. See *Negro World,* Sat., July 2, 1921, p. 2 in UCLA collection, 1920–1926.

10. For an example of the promotional utility of the financial terms, see Fax, *Garvey,* 114–18; also see Hill, ed., *UNIA Papers,* passim.

11. While there is documentation of limited West African investment, primarily from Sierra Leone, Liberia, and possibly Nigeria, the majority of investors were U.S. American, Caribbean, Central American, and Canadian.

12. Fellow researcher Wautella Graham must be credited for the insight.

13. This discussion is informed by the work of Mark Casson, *The Entrepreneur: An Economic Theory* (Totowa, N.J.: Barnes and Noble, 1982).

14. See Ian Duffield, "Pan-Africanism and the Idea of an Independent Black State in Africa, 1911–1923," in *Constitutions and National Identity,* ed. Thomas J. Barron, Owen Dudley Edwards, and Patricia Storey (Edinburgh: Quadriga, 1993), 218–37.

15. Although he was an elected representative to the convention, Ferris did not sign the Declaration of Rights. He may have judged it imprudent not only for the organization but for himself. See "Reports by Special Agent P-138, New York, Aug. 17, 1920," in Hill, ed., *UNIA Papers,* 2:598. Bruce was not a convention representative and seemed to have served in the capacity of adviser, editorialist, and middleman in UNIA international affairs and also to black Republican Party activists. His correspondence suggests that he disagreed with some rhetoric also. Both men remained close to Garvey and other UNIA leaders throughout the era of BSL. After a lingering illness, Bruce died in 1924; during the tumultuous end of BSL, Bruce was incapacitated. See Ralph L. Crowder, *John Edward Bruce.*

16. Cockbourne's testimony, *Garvey v. U.S.* Although Cockbourne's motivation is in question, Garvey's cross-examination of him discusses trying to consult with an engineer. Garvey did not contradict this point, nor did the lawyers for the other defendants.

17. All three were in the British merchant marine; U.S. segregation ended black captaincy in the nineteenth century. Mulzac relocated to United States and became the first black captain licensed in the American fleet, but once the economy contracted he did not command a ship until World War II. See Mulzac, *A Star to Steer By.*

18. See Veblen, *Theory of the Leisure Class.*

19. See Kelley, "Black History's Global Vision."

20. Hill, ed., *UNIA Papers,* 1:257; my emphasis.

21. Contee, "DuBois, the NAACP," addresses this as does Du Bois himself, in editorials in the journal *Crisis,* passim.

22. See Baku, "Intellectual in National Politics." Baku includes an interesting discussion on an essay Sekyi wrote on this topic, "Our Brothers Abroad." This essay is in Sekyi's papers housed in the Ghanaian Archives.

23. Hill, ed., *UNIA Papers,* 3:656–57. G. Emonei Carter wrote the letter to BI agent Howe. He was discussing the UNIA convention of 1921, that is, the year it became clear that the three BSL ships were disabled. It is unclear if Carter realized that Howe

was an agent, because, like Agent 800, he may have been posing as a loyal member. Carter seemed loyal to the organization and moved up in rank over time.

24. Memorandum written by Capt. John B. Trevor to Brig. General Marlborough Churchill, Apr. 5, 1919, in Hill, ed., *UNIA Papers,* 1:401.

25. Contee, "W. E. B. DuBois," documents the struggles of W. E. B. Du Bois under NAACP control; he eventually left the organization. Foner, *American Socialism and Black Americans,* and Robinson, *Black Marxism,* document the struggle of activists such as A. Philip Randolph and Chandler Owen with the radical parties. Many eventually left to pursue more independent application of their political strategies.

26. I distinguish the term *public service* from a *public* or *collective good,* as defined by Mancur Olson, *The Logic of Collective Action: Public Goods and the Theory of Groups* (Cambridge, Mass.: Harvard University Press, 1971). A collective good provides a necessary service and does not restrict use. A public service can restrict free riders by imposing a fee to offset costs, but may not pursue profit. The public service itself is considered profitable in that it facilitates some important public activity or interaction like the enhancement of the quality of life available to citizens or improves the business environment and thus ultimately increases community wealth.

27. However, expatriate colonial companies, such as Lever Brothers, may have disrupted this option as well. Since African American capacity to create products would have been comparatively small, Lever Brothers' production or markets probably would not have been impacted.

28. The John E. Bruce Papers include letters from Nigeria indicating interest; also Langley, *Pan-Africanism and Nationalism,* documents NCBWA interest in the BSL. At the annual UNIA conventions, many West Indians and several continental Africans discuss the business potential of the BSL; see Hill, ed., *UNIA Papers.* Duse Mohamed Ali and Bruce believed business could be facilitated, but their complete reasoning has not been discovered.

29. See Goldstein, "Race Politics," for discussion on the UNIA and Tammany Hall.

30. Esman, "Diasporas in International Relations," in Sheffer, ed., *Modern Diasporas,* observed that "states [or perceived homelands] will not risk important security or economic interests for the sake of diaspora communities." Both Martin, *Race First,* and Stein, *World of Marcus Garvey,* discuss the loan. Also see I. K. Sundiata, *Black Scandal: America and the Liberian Labor Crisis, 1929–1936* (Philadelphia: Institute for the Study of Human Issues, 1980).

31. *Daily Gleaner,* Kingston, Jamaica, Dec. 12, 1919, 3.

32. Safford, *Wilsonian Maritime Diplomacy.*

33. Hill, ed., *UNIA Papers,* 2:183–85.

34. The BSL may have come to see this problem because steps were taken to miti-

gate salary expenses. Some officers received only partial payment of salaries; they were required to "loan" or invest their salaries into the UNIA businesses.

35. Bertelsen, *Non-State Nations in International Politics.*

Chapter 9: Clear Waters

1. Skinner, "The Dialectic between Diasporas and Homelands."

2. Joseph Harris, *Global Dimensions;* and Edmondson, "Black America as a Mobilizing Diaspora," in Sheffer, ed., *Modern Diasporas.*

3. See Joseph Harris, *Global Dimensions.*

4. See Armstrong, "Mobilized and Proletarian Diasporas."

5. Kim Butler, "Defining Diaspora, Refining a Discourse," *Diaspora* 10, no. 2 (2001): 189–219.

6. The UN produces general reports on remittances. However, the political scientist would want to nuance these estimates by considering the characteristics of each diasporic sister community and its place in the international political economy. For example, the researcher would look at the diversity in job skills and income levels as well as the stability of the host country's economy.

Conclusion

1. Armstrong, "Mobilized and Proletarian Diasporas"; Sheffer, ed., *Modern Diasporas;* Walters, *Pan-Africanism in the African Diaspora.*

2. Meredith Woo-Cumings, *Race to the Swift: State and Finance in Korean Industrialization* (New York: Columbia University Press, 1991).

3. Joseph Harris, *Global Dimensions.*

4. Walters, *Pan-Africanism in the African Diaspora.*

5. Money collected included membership dues, death tax, and eventually an annual head tax. Stock purchases were a different program, but once at headquarters these funds were folded into general revenues.

6. As discussed in chapter 6, not all West Indians rallied around the leadership. Most West Indians who were populist or socialist left the organization earlier in 1919–20. Many primary materials show that it was ardent nationalists and the West Indian members who voted with Garvey and the board in the tumultuous 1921 convention when UNIA/BSL leadership was vigorously opposed.

Bibliography

Aldcroft, D. H. *From Versailles to Wall Street.* London: Penguin Books, 1977.

———. *The Inter-War Economy: Britain, 1919–1939.* New York: Columbia University Press, 1970.

———. "Port Congestion and the Shipping Boom of 1919–20." *Business History* 3 (1961): 97–106.

Anderson, Jervis. *A. Phillip Randolph: A Biographical Portrait.* New York: Harcourt Brace Jovanovich, 1972.

Andersen, Robert. "Why Adoptees Search." *Child Welfare* 67, no. 1 (1988): 15–19.

Armstrong, J. A. "Mobilized and Proletarian Diasporas." *American Political Science Review* 70, no. 2 (1976): 393–403.

Baker, Ray S. "The Versailles Treaty and After." *Current History* 88 (January 1989): 20–23.

Baku, Daniel. "Intellectual in Nationalist Politics: The Contribution of Kobina Sekyi to the Evolution of Ghanaian National Consciousness." Ph.D. dissertation, University of Sussex, 1987.

Baltimore *Afro-American,* 1919–1925.

Bandele, Ramla. "The Underdevelopment of Black Towns." Master's thesis, University of Illinois, 1984.

Barrington, Lowell W. "Nation and Nationalism: The Misuse of Key Concepts in Political Science." *P.S. Political Science and Politics* 30, no. 4 (1997): 712–16.

Bauer, K. Jack. *A Maritime History of the U.S.: The Role of America's Seas and Waterways.* Columbia: University of South Carolina Press, 1988.

Baughman, Judith S. *American Decades, 1920–1929.* New York: Gale Research, 1996.

Beer, George Louis. *African Questions at the Paris Peace Conference,* ed. Louis H. Gray. New York: Macmillan, 1923; reprint, New York: Negro Universities Press, 1969.

Berland, Oscar. "The Emergence of the Communist Perspective on the 'Negro Question in America: 1919–1931.' *Science and Society* 63, no. 4 (1999): 411–32.

Bertelsen, Judy S. *Non-State Nations in International Politics: Comparative System.* New York: Praeger, 1977.

Blake, George. *Lloyd's Register of Shipping 1760–1960.* Sussex: Lloyd's Register of Shipping at Garrett House, 1960.

Bolster, W. Jeffrey. *Black Jacks: African-American Seaman in the Age of Sail.* Cambridge, Mass.: Harvard University Press, 1997.

Bonnett, Aubrey, and G. Llewellyn Watson, eds. *Emerging Perspectives on the Black Diaspora.* Lanham, M.D.: University Press of America, 1990.

Bose, Arun. "Modern Marxian Political Economy." In *What Is Political Economy?* ed. David Whynes. Oxford: Basil Blackwell, 1984, 90–115.

Boyd, James C. "Primitives on the Move: Some Historical Articulations of Garvey and Garveyism, 1887–1927." PhD. dissertation, Los Angeles: University of California, 1982.

Brisbane, Robert H. *The Black Vanguard.* Valley Forge, P.A.: Judson, 1970.

Brooker, Paul. *Non-Democratic Regimes: Theory, Government, and Politics.* London: Macmillan, 2000.

Bruce, John Edward. Papers, 1872–1927. Archives and Rare Books, Schomburg Center for Research in Black Culture, New York Public Library, New York.

Bush, Roderick D. *We Are Not What We Seem: Black Nationalism and Class Struggle in the American Century.* New York: New York University Press, 1999.

Butler, Kim. "Defining Diaspora, Refining a Discourse." *Diaspora* 10, no. 2 (2001): 189–219.

Cafruny, Alan W. *Ruling the Waves: The Political Economy of International Shipping.* Berkeley: University of California Press, 1987.

California *Eagle,* 1919–1925.

Campbell, Susan. "Black Bolsheviks and Recognition of African-America's Right to Self-Determination." *Science and Society* 58, no. 4 (1994): 440–70.

Casimir, J. R. Ralph. J. R. Casimir Papers, 1919–1981. Archives and Rare Books, Schomburg Center for Research in Black Culture, New York Public Library, New York.

Casson, Mark. *The Entrepreneur: An Economic Theory.* Totowa, N.J.: Barnes and Noble, 1982.

Cha-Jua, Sundiata Keita. "'A Warlike Demonstration': Legalism, Violent Self Help, and Electoral Politics in Decatur Illinois, 1894–1898." *Journal of Urban History* 26, no. 5 (2000): 591–629.

Chicago *Defender,* 1919–1925.

Clarke, John Henrik. *Marcus Garvey and the Vision of Africa.* New York: First Vintage Books, 1974.

Clifford, James. "Diasporas." *Cultural Anthropology* 9, no. 3 (1994): 302–38.

Cohn, Michael, and Platzer, Michael. *Black Men of the Sea.* New York: Dodd, Mead, 1978.

Contee, Clarence G. "DuBois, the NAACP, and the Pan-African Congress of 1919." *Journal of Negro History* 57, no. 1 (1972): 13–28.

———. "W. E. B. DuBois and African Nationalism." Ph.D. dissertation, American University, 1969.

Crisis, 1919–1925.

Cronon, E. David. *Black Moses: The Story of Marcus Garvey,* 2nd ed. Madison: University of Wisconsin Press, 1974.

Crowder, Ralph L. "John Edward Bruce and the Value of Knowing the Past: Politician, Journalist, and Self-Trained Historian of the African Diaspora, 1856–1924." Ph.D. dissertation, University of Kansas, 1994.

———. *John Edward Bruce: Politician, Journalist, and Self-trained Historian of the African Diaspora, 1856–1924.* New York: New York University Press, 2004.

Crusader, 1919–1925.

Dawson, Michael D. *Black Visions: The Roots of Contemporary African American Political Ideologies.* Chicago: University of Chicago Press, 2001.

Delany, Martin R. *Official Report of the Niger Valley Exploring Party.* New York: T. Hamilton, 1861; reprint, Philadelphia: Rhistoric, 1969.

De La Pedraja, Rene. *A Historical Dictionary of the U.S. Merchant Marine and Shipping Industry.* Westport, Conn.: Greenwood, 1994.

Department of Commerce Steamboat Inspection Service, *General Rules and Regulations Prescribed by the Board of Supervising Inspectors, as amended at Board Meeting of January 1918* (Washington, D.C.: Government Printing Office).

Drachler, Jacob. *Black Homeland, Black Diaspora: Cross Currents of the Relationship.* New York: Kennikat Press, 1975.

Drake, St. Clair. *Black Folk Here and There: An Essay in History and Anthropology.* Los Angeles: Center for Afro-American Studies, University of California, 1987.

———. "Diaspora Studies and Pan-Africanism," in *Global Dimensions of the African Diaspora,* ed. Joseph Harris. Washington, D.C.: Howard University Press, 1982, 451–514.

Draper, Theodore. *American Communism and Soviet Russia.* New York: Viking, 1960.

Du Bois, W. E. B. "Back to Africa." *Century* 105, no. 4 (1923): 539–48.

Duffield, Ian. "Pan-Africanism and the Idea of an Independent Black State in Africa, 1911–1923." In *Constitutions and National Identity,* ed. Thomas J. Barron, Owen Dudley Edwards, and Patricia J. Storey. Edinburgh: Quadriga, 1993, 218–37.

Economist. (London) 1919–21.

Eichengreen, Barry, ed. *The Gold Standard in Theory and History.* New York: Methuen, 1985.

Elkins, W. F. *Black Power in the Caribbean.* New York: Revisionist Press, 1977.

———. "Hercules and the Society of Peoples of African Origin." *Caribbean Quarterly* 11, no. 4 (1971): 47–59.

Elliott, John E. "The Institutionalist School of Political Economy." In *What Is Political Economy?* ed. David Whynes. Oxford: Basil Blackwell Publisher, 1984, 59–89.

Essien-Udom, Essien Udosen. *Black Nationalism: A Search for an Identity in America.* Chicago: University of Chicago Press, 1962.

Fax, Elton. *Garvey: The Story of a Pioneer Black Nationalist.* New York: Dodd Mead, 1972.

Foley, Barbara. *Spectres of 1919: Class and Nation in the Making of the New Negro.* Urbana: University of Illinois Press, 2003.

Foner, Philip. *American Socialism and Black Americans.* Westport, Conn.: Greenwood, 1977.

Foner, Philip, and James Allen, eds. *American Communism and Black Americans: A Documentary History, 1919–1929.* Philadelphia: Temple University Press, 1987.

Freeze, Gregory, ed. *Russia: A History.* Oxford: Oxford University Press, 1997.

Fyfe, Christopher. "Using Race as an Instrument of Policy: A Historical View." *Race and Class* 36, no. 2 (1994): 69–77.

Garrett, Romeo B. *The Presidents and the Negro.* Peoria: Associated Publishers, 1982.

Garvey, Amy Jacques. *Garvey and Garveyism,* 3rd ed. New York: Macmillan, 1970.

———. *The Philosophy and Opinions of Marcus Garvey,* 3rd ed. Dover, Mass.: Majority Press, 1986.

Gatewood, Willard. *Aristocrats of Color: The Black Elite, 1880–1920.* First Midland Book edition. Bloomington: Indiana University Press, 1993.

Geiss, Imanuel. *The Pan-African Movement: A History of Pan-Africanism in America, Europe and Africa.* New York: Africana, 1974.

Gilderhus, Mark T. *Pan-American Visions: Woodrow Wilson in the Western Hemisphere.* Tucson: University of Arizona Press, 1986.

Gilroy, Paul. *The Black Atlantic: Modernity and Double Consciousness.* Cambridge, Mass.: Harvard University Press, 1993.

———. "It Ain't Where You're From, It's Where You're At." In *Small Acts: Thoughts on the Politics of Black Cultures.* London: Serpent's Tail, 1993, 120–45.

Gittens, Uriah. UNIA Letters, 1925–1929. Archives and Rare Books, Schomburg Center for Research in Black Culture, New York Public Library, New York.

Goldfield, David. *The American Journey: A History of the United States,* 2nd ed. Upper Saddle River, N.J.: Prentice Hall, 2001.

Goldstein, Michael L. "Race Politics in New York City, 1890–1930: Independent Political Behavior." Ph.D. dissertation Columbia University, 1973.

Goings, Kenneth, and Raymond Mohl, eds. *New African American Urban History.* Thousand Oaks, Calif.: Sage, 1996.

Guzman, Jessie Parkhurst, ed. *Negro Year Book: A Review of Events Affecting Negro Life.* New York: Wise, 1952.

Hall, Stuart. "Cultural Identity and Diaspora." In *Colonial Discourse and Post Colonial Theory: A Reader,* ed. P. Williams and L. Chrisman. New York: Columbia University Press, 1994, 392–403.

Hanchard, Michael G. "Afro-Modernity: Temporality, Politics, and the African Diaspora." *Public Culture* 11, no. 1 (1999): 272–97.

Hannaford, Ivan. *Race: The History of an Idea in the West.* Washington, D.C.: Woodrow Wilson Center Press, 1996.

Hargreaves-Heap, Shaun, and Marlin Hollis. "Bread and Circumstances: The Need for Political-Economy." In *What Is Political Economy?* ed. David Whynes. Oxford: Basil Blackwell Publisher, 1984, 7–30.

Harris, Abram L. "Negro Labor's Quarrel with White Workingmen." *Current History* 24 (Sept. 1926): 903–8.

Harris, Joseph. *Global Dimensions of the African Diaspora.* Washington, D.C.: Howard University Press, 1982.

Havighurst, Alfred F. *Twentieth Century Britain.* New York: Harper and Row, 1962.

Haywood, Harry. *Black Bolshevik: Autobiography of an Afro-American Communist.* Chicago: Lake View Press, 1978.

Hill, Robert, ed. *The Marcus Garvey and Universal Negro Improvement Association Papers.* 10 vols. Berkeley: University of California Press, 1983–.

Hill, Robert, and Barbara Bair, eds. *Marcus Garvey: Life and Lessons. A Centennial Companion to the Marcus Garvey and UNIA Papers.* Berkeley: University of California Press, 1987.

Hine, Darlene Clark, William C. Hine, and Stanley Harrold. *African Americans: A Concise History,* 2nd ed. Upper Saddle River, N.J.: Pearson Education, 2006.

Historical Statistics of the United States, Colonial Times to 1970. Washington, D.C.: U.S. Department of Commerce, Bureau of the Census.

Hobsbawm, Eric J. *The Age of Empire, 1875–1914.* New York: Pantheon, 1987.

Holland, R. F. *European Decolonization, 1918–1981.* New York: St. Martin's, 1985.

Hopkins, A. G. "Economic Aspects of Political Movements in Nigeria and the Gold Coast, 1918–1939." *Journal of African History* 7, no. 1 (1966): 133–52.

Hughes, Jonathan. *Industrialization and Economic History.* New York: McGraw-Hill, 1970.

Hutchinson, Earl Ofari. *Blacks and Reds: Race and Class Conflict, 1919–1990.* East Lansing: Michigan State University Press, 1995.

Hutson, Jean Blackwell. *An Interview with Aubrey H. DeSouza.* SC Service Copy Video. VRB 1692–1696. Original of SC Visual VRA 43, SC Visual VRB 1341–1343. MIRS, Schomburg Center for Research in Black Culture, New York Public Library, New York.

James, Winston. *Holding Aloft the Banner of Ethiopia: Caribbean Radicalism in Early Twentieth-Century America.* London: Verso, 1998.

Jastram, Roy W. *The Golden Constant: The English and American Experience, 1560–1976.* New York: John Wiley and Sons, 1977.

Johnson, James Weldon. *Black Manhattan.* New York: Knopf, 1930.

Katznelson, Ira. *Black Men, White Cities: Race, Politics and Migration in the United States, 1900–1930, and Britain, 1948–68.* London: Oxford University Press, 1973.

Kelley, Robin. "Black History's Global Vision, 1883–1950." *Journal of American History* 86 (December 1999): 1045–77.

Kelley, Robin D. G., and Earl Lewis. *To Make Our World Anew: A History of African Americans from 1880.* Oxford: Oxford University Press, 2000.

Kennedy, David M. *Over Here: The First World War and American Society.* New York: Oxford University Press, 1980.

Kennedy, Paul. *The Rise and Fall of the Great Powers: Economic Change and Military Conflict from 1500–2000.* New York: Random House, 1987.

Keynes, John Maynard. *Economic Consequences of Peace.* London: Macmillan, 1919.

Langley, J. Ayodele. "Garveyism and African Nationalism." *Race* 11 (Oct. 1969): 157–72.

———. *Pan-Africanism and Nationalism in West Africa, 1900–1945.* Oxford: Clarendon, 1973.

Levin, N. Gordon. *Woodrow Wilson and World Politics: America's Response to War and Revolution.* New York: Oxford University Press, 1968.

Lewis, David Levering. *W. E. B. Du Bois: The Fight for Equality and the American Century, 1919–1963.* New York: Henry Holt, 2000.

Lewis, Rupert. *Marcus Garvey: Anti-Colonial Champion.* Trenton: Africa World Press, 1988.

Lewis, Rupert, and Patrick Bryan, eds. *Garvey: His Work and Impact.* Trenton: Africa World Press, 1991.

Lewis, W. Arthur. *Economic Survey, 1919–1939,* 7th ed. London: Unwin University Books, 1970.

Lewison, Edwin R. *Black Politics in New York City.* New York: Twayne Publishers, 1974.

Link, Arthur S. *American Epoch: A History of the United States since the 1890s,* 3rd ed. New York: Alfred A. Knopf, 1967.

Makonnen, Ras. *Pan-Africanism from Within.* Nairobi: Oxford University Press, 1973.

Marcus Garvey vs. United States of America, Transcript of Record, Error to the United States District Court for the Southern District of New York, United States Circuit Court of Appeals, for the Second Circuit, 4 Volumes. Records of the U.S. Supreme Court, Record Group 267, file no. 30924, National Archives and Records Administration, Washington, DC.

Martin, Tony. *Race First: The Ideological and Organizational Struggles of Marcus Garvey and the Universal Negro Improvement Association.* Westport, Conn.: Greenwood, 1976.

McFadden, David W. "After the Colby Note: The Wilson Administration and the Bolsheviks, 1920–1921." *Presidential Studies Quarterly* 25, no. 4 (1995): 741–50.

McKay, Claude. *Long Way from Home.* New York: L. Furman, 1937.

Meredith, David. "The British Government and Colonial Economic Policy, 1919–1939." *Economic History Review* 28 (1975): 484–99.

Messenger, 1919–1925.

Morgan, M. C. *Lenin.* London: Edward Arnold, 1971.

Morris, Aldon D. *The Origins of the Civil Rights Movement: Black Communities Organizing for Change.* New York: Free Press, 1984.

Mowat, Charles L. *Britain between the Wars, 1918–1940,* 2nd ed. Chicago: University of Chicago Press, 1958.

Mulzac, Hugh. *A Star to Steer By.* New York: International Publishers, 1963.

Negro World, 1919–1925.

Nembhard, Len. *Trials and Triumphs of Marcus Garvey.* Kingston: Gleaner, 1940; reprint Millwood: Kraus Reprint, 1978.

New York *Amsterdam News,* 1919–1925.

New York Times, 1919–1925.

North, Douglass C. *Institutions, Institutional Change, and Economic Performance.* Cambridge: Cambridge University Press, 1993.

Olson, Mancur. *The Logic of Collective Action: Public Goods and the Theory of Groups.* Cambridge, Mass.: Harvard University Press, 1971.

Olusanya, G. O. "Notes on the Lagos Branch of the Universal Negro Improvement Association." *Journal of Business and Social Studies* 1, no. 3 (1969): 133–43.

One Hundred Years of Economic Statistics. New York: Facts on File, 1989.

Orde, Anne. *The Eclipse of Great Britain.* New York: St. Martin's, 1996.

Orenic, Liesl, and Joe Trotter, "African Americans in the U.S. Economy." In *Historical Roots of the Urban Crisis: African Americans in the Industrial City, 1900–1950,* ed. Henry L. Taylor and Walter Hill. New York: Garland, 2000, 177–208.

Osofsky, Gilbert. *Harlem: The Making of a Ghetto, Negro New York, 1890–1930,* 2nd ed. New York: Harper and Row, 1971.

Packard, W. V. *Sale and Purchase,* 2nd ed. London: Fairplay, 1988.

Padmore, George. *Pan-Africanism or Communism.* London: D. Dobson, 1956.

Patterson, Tiffany R., and Robin D. G. Kelley. "Unfinished Migrations: Reflections on the African Diaspora and the Making of the Modern World." *African Studies Review* 43, no. 1 (2000): 11–45.

Perry, Jeffrey B., ed. *A Hubert Harrison Reader.* Middletown: Wesleyan University Press, 2001.

Pinkney, Alphonso. *Red, Black and Green: Black Nationalism in the United States.* London: Cambridge University Press, 1976.

Polanyi, Karl. *The Great Transformation.* Boston: Beacon Press, 1944.

Record, Wilson. *The Negro and the Communist Party.* Chapel Hill: University of North Carolina Press, 1951.

Redkey, Edwin S. "The Flowering of Black Nationalism: Henry McNeal Turner and Marcus Garvey." In *Key Issues in the Afro-American Experience,* ed. Nathan I. Huggins, Martin Kilson, and Daniel Fox. New York: Harcourt Brace Jovanovich, 1971, 107–22.

Robinson, Cedric J. *Black Marxism: The Making of the Black Radical Tradition.* London: Zed, 1983.

———. *Black Movements in America.* New York: Routledge, 1997.

Rothschild, Joseph. *Ethnopolitics: A Conceptual Framework.* New York: Columbia University Press, 1981.

Safford, Jeffrey S. *Wilsonian Maritime Diplomacy, 1913–1921.* New Brunswick, N.J.: Rutgers University Press, 1978.

Said, Abdul, and Luis Simmons. *Ethnicity in an International Context.* New Brunswick, N.J.: Transaction Books, 1976.

Scott, Julius S. "The Common Wind: Currents of Afro-American Communication in the Era of the Haitian Revolution." Ph.D. dissertation, Duke University, 1986.

Seraile, William. *Bruce Grit: The Black Nationalist Writings of John Edward Bruce.* Knoxville: University of Tennessee Press, 2003.

Service, Robert. *Lenin: A Political Life.* 3 vols. Bloomington: Indiana University Press, 1995.

Sheffer, Gabriel. *Diaspora Politics: At Home Abroad.* Cambridge: Cambridge University Press, 2003.

Sheffer, Gabriel, ed. *Modern Diasporas in International Politics.* New York: St. Martin's, 1986.

Shepperson, George. "Pan-Africanism and 'pan-Africanism': Some Historical Notes." *Phylon* 22, no. 3 (1961): 346–58.

Skinner, Elliot P. "The Dialectic between Diasporas and Homelands." In *Global Dimensions of the African Diaspora,* ed. Joseph Harris. Washington, D.C.: Howard University Press, 1982, 11–40.

Soule, George. *Prosperity Decade: From War to Depression, 1917–1929, The Economic History of the U.S.,* vol 8. New York: Rinehart, 1947.

Staniland, Martin. *What Is Political Economy: A Study of Social Theory and Underdevelopment.* New Haven: Yale University Press, 1985.

Starr, Frederick. "Liberia After the World War." *Journal of Negro History* 10, no. 2 (1925): 113–30.

Stein, Judith. *An Interview with F. Levi Lord.* Imprint 1983-05-12, MIRS SC Visual VRB 1692–1696, 5 video cassettes. Schomburg Center for Research in Black Culture, New York Public Library, New York.

———. *The World of Marcus Garvey: Race and Class in Modern Society.* Baton Rouge: Louisiana State University Press, 1986.

Sundiata, I. K. *Black Scandal: America and the Liberian Labor Crisis, 1929–1936.* Philadelphia: Institute for the Study of Human Issues, 1980.

———. *Brothers and Strangers: Black Zion, Black Slavery, 1914–1940.* Durham: Duke University Press, 2003.

Tarrow, Sidney. *Power in Movement: Social Movements, Collective Action, and Politics.* Cambridge: Cambridge University Press, 1994.

Taylor, Quintard. "Urban Black Labor in the West, 1849–1940." In *African American Experience,* ed. Joe Trotter and Earl Lewis et al. New York: Palgrave Macmillan, 2004, 99–120.

Taylor, Ula. *The Veiled Garvey: The Life and Times of Amy Jacques Garvey.* Chapel Hill: University of North Carolina Press, 2002.

Thompson, Ralph. "The Role of Capitalism in Jamaica's Development." *Caribbean Quarterly* 12, no. 2 (1966): 22–28.

Thompson, Vincent Bakpetu. *Africa and Unity: The Evolution of Pan-Africanism.* New York: Longman, Green, 1969.

———. *The Making of the African Diaspora in the Americas, 1441–1900.* New York: Longman Group, 1987.

Thornton, John. *Africa and Africans in the Making of the Atlantic World, 1400–1680.* Cambridge: Cambridge University Press, 1992.

Thoumin, Richard. *The First World War,* ed. and trans. Martin Kieffer. London: Secker and Warburg, 1963.

Tolbert, Emory J. *The UNIA and Black Los Angeles: Ideology and Community in the American Garvey Movement.* Los Angeles: Center for African-American Studies, University of California, 1980.

Tompkins, Vincent. *American Decades: 1910–1919.* Detroit: Gale Research, 1996.

Triseliotis, J. *In Search of Origins: The Experiences of Adopted People.* London: Routledge and Kegan Paul, 1973.

Trotter, Joe, and Earl Lewis et al. *The African American Experience.* New York: Palgrave McMillan, 2004.

Trotter, Joe W. "African Americans in the City: The Industrial Era, 1900–1950." In *New African American Urban History,* ed. Kenneth W. Goings and Raymond Mohl. Thousand Oaks, Calif.: Sage, 1996, 299–319.

Usher, Roland G. *The Story of the Great War.* New York: MacMillan, 1919.

Veblen, Thornstein. "The Socialist Economics of Karl Marx and His Followers." *Quarterly Journal of Economics* 20 and 21 (1906): 575–95 and 299–322.

———. *The Theory of the Leisure Class.* New York: MacMillan, 1899.

Vincent, Theodore G. *Black Power and the Garvey Movement.* Berkeley: Ramparts Press, 1971.

Von Eschen, Penny Marie. *Race against Empire: Black Americans and Anticolonialism, 1937–1957.* Ithaca: Cornell University Press, 1997.

Walters, Ronald W. *Pan-Africanism in the African Diaspora: An Analysis of Modern Afro-Centric Political Movements.* Detroit: Wayne University Press, 1997.

Warren, Mark E. "Deliberative Democracy and Authority." *APSA* 90, no. 1 (1996): 46–60.

Waskow, Arthur I. *From Race Riot to Sit-In: 1919 and the 1960s.* New York: Anchor Books, Doubleday, 1966.

Watkins-Owens, Irma. *Blood Relations: Caribbean Immigrants and the Harlem Community, 1900–1930.* Bloomington: Indiana University Press, 1996.

Williams, Eric. "The Historical Background of British Guiana's Problems," *Journal of Negro History* 30, no. 4 (1945): 357–81.

———. *The Negro in the Caribbean.* 2nd ed. New York: Haskell House, 1971.

Woo-Cumings, Meredith (Jung En). *Race to the Swift: State and Finance in Korean Industrialization.* New York: Columbia University Press, 1991.

Zeis, Paul. *American Shipping Policy.* Princeton: Princeton University Press, 1938.

Zysman, John. *Governments, Markets, and Growth.* New York: Cornell University Press, 1994.

Index

RAMLA M. BANDELE is an assistant professor of political science at Indiana University–Purdue University at Indianapolis, where she teaches American, African American, and urban politics and American political development.

The University of Illinois Press
is a founding member of the
Association of American University Presses.

Composed in 10.5/13 Adobe Minion Pro
with Meta display
by Celia Shapland
at the University of Illinois Press
Manufactured by Thomson-Shore, Inc.

University of Illinois Press
1325 South Oak Street
Champaign, IL 61820-6903
www.press.uillinois.edu